ND## FROM DAKOTA TO DIXIE

A Nation Divided: Studies in the Civil War Era
Orville Vernon Burton and Elizabeth R. Varon, *Editors*

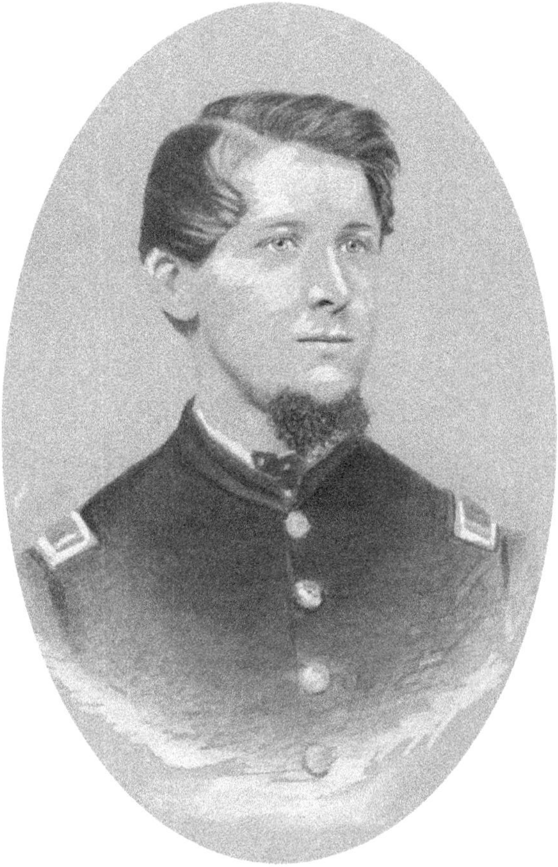

From Dakota to Dixie

George Buswell's Civil War

EDITED BY

Jonathan W. White and Reagan Connelly

UNIVERSITY OF VIRGINIA PRESS
CHARLOTTESVILLE AND LONDON

The University of Virginia Press is situated on the traditional lands of the Monacan Nation, and the Commonwealth of Virginia was and is home to many other Indigenous people. We pay our respect to all of them, past and present. We also honor the enslaved African and African American people who built the University of Virginia, and we recognize their descendants. We commit to fostering voices from these communities through our publications and to deepening our collective understanding of their histories and contributions.

University of Virginia Press
© 2025 by the Rector and Visitors of the University of Virginia
All rights reserved
Printed in the United States of America on acid-free paper

First published 2025

1 3 5 7 9 8 6 4 2

LIBRARY OF CONGRESS CATALOGING-IN-PUBLICATION DATA

Names: Buswell, George W., 1841–1921, author. | White, Jonathan W., editor. | Connelly, Reagan, editor.
Title: From Dakota to Dixie : George Buswell's Civil War / [diaries by] George W. Buswell ; edited by Jonathan W. White and Reagan Connelly. Other titles: George Buswell's Civil War
Description: Charlottesville : University of Virginia Press, 2025. | Series: A nation divided : studies in the Civil War era | Includes bibliographical references and index.
Identifiers: LCCN 2024047417 (print) | LCCN 2024047418 (ebook) | ISBN 9780813952772 (hardcover) | ISBN 9780813952789 (paperback) | ISBN 9780813952796 (ebook)
Subjects: LCSH: Buswell, George W., 1841–1921—Diaries. | United States. Army—Officers—Diaries. | United States. Army. Colored Infantry Regiment, 68th (1864–1866). Company K—Biography. | West (U.S.)—History—Civil War, 1861–1865—Personal narratives. | Dakota Indians—Wars, 1862–1865—Personal narratives. | United States. Army. Minnesota Infantry Regiment, 7th (1862–1865)—Biography. | United States. Army—Military life—History—19th century. | Minnesota—Biography.
Classification: LCC E492.94 68th .B87 2025 (print) | LCC E492.94 68th (ebook) | DDC 973.7/415092—dc23/eng/20241231
LC record available at https://lccn.loc.gov/2024047417
LC ebook record available at https://lccn.loc.gov/2024047418

Frontispiece: George W. Buswell. (George W. Buswell Papers, The Huntington Library, San Marino, California)

Cover art: Carte de visite of George W. Buswell. (George W. Buswell Papers [HM 46332], The Huntington Library, San Marino, California)
Cover design: Cecilia Sorochin

For the presidents of Christopher Newport University—
Paul S. Trible, who built Christopher Newport
University into what it is today;
Adelia Thompson, who provided leadership
during turbulent times;
and William G. Kelly, who has taken the helm

CONTENTS

List of Illustrations — xi

Foreword by Gary W. Gallagher — xiii

Introduction — xvii

Note on Method — xxix

Abbreviations and Short Titles — xxxi

Part I. The Dakota War

1. "They Were All Brave and Fearless": From Enlistment to Execution, August 13–December 26, 1862 — 3

2. "On Guard Again": Furlough and Winter Quarters, December 27, 1862–May 12, 1863 — 48

3. "An Attack Expected Tonight": The Sibley Expedition, May 13–September 20, 1863 — 69

Part II. The Civil War

4. "Away To Dixie": Travels in Missouri, Illinois, and Tennessee, September 21–December 21, 1863 — 105

5. "Had a Talk with Some Prisoners": Guard Duty and Promotion in St. Louis, December 22, 1863–June 1, 1864 — 126

6. "A Close Shave": Duty in Memphis and the Battle of Tupelo, June 2–July 23, 1864 — 166

7. "Remained Out in the Wet": From Memphis to the Tallahatchie Swamps, July 24–August 29, 1864 — 193

8. "A Change Is What the Soldiers Like": Memphis and Fort Pickering, August 30–December 31, 1864 — 207

Epilogue	241
Acknowledgments	247
Index	249

ILLUSTRATIONS

Col. Henry H. Sibley	18
Col. Stephen Miller	20
Lt. Col. William R. Marshall	22
Col. William Crooks	24
"Sioux Squaw and Pappoose"	25
Gusa Godfrey	31
Little Crow	58
Laura Duley and her children	65
Sibley Expedition	85
Thomas Wakeman	95
Col. J. Blackburn Jones	161
Maj. Gen. Andrew J. Smith	181
Jackson's Monument at Memphis, Tennessee, Defaced by the Rebels	197
Forrest's Raid into Memphis—Rebel Attack on the Irving Prison	208

Maps

1. Locations of important sites in Minnesota during the US–Dakota War	4
2. Routes of the expeditions of Brig. Gen. Henry H. Sibley and Brig. Gen. Alfred Sully, June–September 1863	71
3. Battles and cities mentioned by George W. Buswell in 1864	168

FOREWORD

George W. Buswell's diary adds a distinctive and revealing voice to the vast trove of published testimony from Union soldiers during the Civil War. His entries extend from the autumn of 1862 through the end of 1864, transporting readers across a spacious landscape extending from Minnesota and Dakota Territory to West Tennessee and the Tallahatchie swamps. Observant, perceptive, and sometimes opinionated, this Massachusetts-born resident of Minnesota helps twenty-first-century readers understand the people and events of his tumultuous world.

Buswell was typical of most Union soldiers in two important ways and atypical in two others. His motivation for enlisting placed him among the overwhelming majority of volunteers. Twenty-one years old, he donned a uniform to help save "this glorious old union" by suppressing "one of the most formidable rebellions ever on the face of the known earth." He signed up for three years' service following Abraham Lincoln's call on July 1, 1862, for three hundred thousand volunteers—a summons to the loyal citizenry that also inspired George Frederick Root to compose "The Battle Cry of Freedom." The chorus of Root's famous marching song delivered a clear message:

> The Union forever, Hurrah, boys, Hurrah!
> Down with the traitor, Up with the star; while we rally round the flag boys,
> Rally once again, Shouting the battle-cry of Freedom.

The chorus echoed Daniel Webster's stirring evocation of "Liberty and Union, now and forever," as did Buswell's affirmation that mustering in had united him and his comrades in the 7th Minnesota Infantry "with the U.S. Army, in the great cause 'Liberty, Union one & inseparable.'" He meant to fight "for liberty and our glorious old stars & stripes, emblematical of the best country that ever existed."

Buswell also reflected a strong wartime consensus that the massive military effort against the Confederacy and the fighting with Native peoples in Minnesota and Dakota Territory represented two separate conflicts. He enlisted to put down the Confederate rebellion, an upheaval that threatened the fundamental fabric of the nation bequeathed by the founding generation. He resented being deployed against Indigenous people, whose actions in Minnesota affected only a tiny portion of the nation's population. On August 14, 1863, while campaigning near Mount Bottineau in modern North Dakota, he betrayed frustration at being posted in what he considered a backwater far removed from great events: "Just one year ago I signed the papers that made me a soldier, have seen some hard service, and have not accomplished much either." A few days earlier, he had indicated plainly where he wished to be serving. Newspaper accounts reported "no great victories for our forces since Vicksburgh & Gett[y]sburg," he commented, adding hopefully, "I expect we will before long be down in Dixie to help to fight it out." Pronouncing the Dakotas "too far on the frontier to soldier it," he observed, "I prefer going South." By mid-October 1863, Buswell's regiment had shifted southward to St. Louis, and the fifteenth of that month brought long-anticipated orders. The 7th Minnesota would "take 3 days rations in knapsacks, to go West on some expedition, and all was excitement over our first initiatory expedition in rebeldom." For Buswell, after more than a year of operations involving Native opponents, the real war finally had begun.

Unlike most white Union soldiers, Buswell became an advocate of emancipation as a moral imperative. He had been too young to vote in the 1860 presidential election but would have cast his vote for Democrat Stephen A. Douglas rather than for Abraham Lincoln. The war caused him to consider more carefully the issues that had fomented sectional discord, and he pronounced slavery an evil that should be ended. During the election of 1864, Confederates attacked Abraham Lincoln and the Republicans as abolitionists—which helped persuade Buswell, "with some considerable degree of pride," to cast his ballot for "Father Abe." The large majority of Union soldiers would have shunned association with abolitionists—though a majority supported Lincoln as a war leader who would push through to victory.

Buswell's decision to accept a commission in the 68th United States Colored Infantry (USCT) also set him apart. He left the 7th Minnesota in early February 1864 and praised his new regiment's commander as "a staunch Union man, and a great friend of the black race." Exposure to the rank-and-file of the 68th stoked his sense of outrage at "that curse of an Institution, slavery, more than at any other time in my life." Serving with men who only recently had escaped from slavery permitted Buswell to see "the evil as near as I can ever see it." Noting that Democrats in Washington opposed raising USCT units, he affirmed that African American soldiers should "assist in carrying on the war, not only to save the Union, but because the war has been the means of striking off their shackles." On election day in November 1864, Buswell identified Union and emancipation as equivalent war aims: "[T]he votes of the people will decide many great questions—Slavery or Freedom to 5 millions of human beings, honorable war or a dishonorable peace, Union or Disunion possibly."

Buswell's diary ends on December 31, 1864. The entry closes with an assessment of his part in the war and a hope for peace in a restored Union. "The last day of the year," he recorded, "and I am fully discharging my duty not only to my country, but to myself, how many more years of such toil and excitement and suspense. May the time be speedy when this service shall terminate and peace once more shall reign upon and over a united Country."

Although his service included none of the conflict's great battles, he had experienced a range of activities in widely disparate theaters. His diary helps us recover valuable information and insights about the war and the citizen-soldiers who waged it.

Gary W. Gallagher
August 9, 2024

INTRODUCTION

George W. Buswell was working as a carpenter on the new county courthouse in Winona, Minnesota, when he "slid from the roof" on August 13, 1862, and "enrolled my name for liberty and our glorious old stars & stripes."[1] In the wake of Union general George B. McClellan's failed Peninsula Campaign, Abraham Lincoln had issued calls for three hundred thousand volunteers in July and three hundred thousand nine-month men in August. The twenty-one-year-old farmer from Whitewater Township, Winona County, enthusiastically mustered in as a private in the 7th Minnesota Infantry at Fort Snelling in St. Paul on August 17. Buswell hoped he would be placed in a regiment in the Western Theater where he would fight against the Southern Rebels. Instead, he spent the next year fighting Indians in Minnesota and the Dakota Territory, witnessing some of the most important moments and events of "Minnesota's other civil war," for as he was receiving his physical examination, war was erupting elsewhere in his home state on that very same day. One veteran recalled that "events more startling than defeats or victories on the Potomac or in the Western army, because nearer to the homes of the citizens of Minnesota, were then occurring which gave a sudden impulse to the filling up of the great call.... At once the cry rang out all over the state for the immediate filling up and putting into the field of defense the regiments then forming." White Minnesotans filled up five regiments.[2]

Buswell had been born on May 15, 1841, in the mill town of Lowell, Massachusetts. His father, Michael W. Buswell (1810–1899), appears in the 1850 US census as a carpenter in Lynn, Massachusetts. Michael had married Martha Cheever Skinner (1818–1903) in 1836 in Lynn, and over the ensuing years the couple had five children—George in 1841, Lucy in 1844, Andrew in 1847, Flora in 1853, and Frank in 1857.[3] At some point

---

1. Diary entry for August 13, 1862. While the US census for 1860 lists Buswell as a farmer, his pension record states that he was a carpenter at the time of his enlistment.

2. *Minnesota in Wars, 1861–1865*, 300–304, 347.

3. US census and genealogical records on ancestry.com/ and findagrave.com/.

about 1854 or 1855, the Buswells moved to Minnesota, but they never lost touch with friends and family back in the Bay State.[4] Throughout his Civil War diary, Buswell mentions receiving newspapers and letters from Lynn.

Migrants from New England, New York, and elsewhere flooded into the Minnesota Territory throughout the 1850s. Two 1851 treaties between the federal government and the Dakotas had opened nearly 24 million acres of rich farmland to white settlement.[5] Promoters quickly touted the opportunities the new territory would afford migrants from the east. The *New York Independent* announced that the soil of Minnesota was a sure "foundation for permanent prosperity." *The Minnesota Handbook, for 1856-7* similarly promised that migrants would "find hard-wood timber land and beautiful rolling prairies, waiting to be claimed and settled," and that "the soil can be brought into cultivation" with "ease ... in comparison with the amount of labor expended."[6] These sorts of appeals led men like Michael W. Buswell to move westward, and he appears to have adopted an agricultural life once he reached Minnesota. While the 1857 Minnesota state census lists his occupation as a carpenter, the 1860 and 1870 US censuses identify him as a farmer.[7]

The Buswells were one of thousands of families to make the trek from the East to Minnesota. Indeed, the white population of Minnesota exploded between 1850 and 1860, from 6,038 to 169,395 (41,296 of whom

---

4. Michael W. Buswell is listed in George Adams, *The Lynn Directory, Embracing the City Record, the Names of the Citizens, and a Business Directory, with an Almanac for the Year 1854* (Lynn, Mass.: Thomas Herbert, 1853), 57; however, he is not listed in George Adams, *The Lynn Directory, Containing the City Record, the Names of the Citizens, and a Business Directory, with an Almanac for the Year 1856* (Lynn, Mass.: T. Herbert, 1855), 66.

5. *Dakota War*, 2–3. For full accounts of the treaties, see Mary Lether Wingerd, *North Country: The Making of Minnesota* (Minneapolis: University of Minnesota Press, 2010); William E. Lass, *The Treaty of Traverse Des Sioux* (Saint Peter, Minn.: Nicollet County Historical Society Press, 2011). Henry H. Sibley, a trader who would go on to lead the expedition against the Dakotas in 1862–63, urged higher prices be paid to the Indians for their land so that the Indians would have money to pay debts to traders (like Sibley). When matters seemed to be at an impasse, Sibley helped persuade Chief Little Crow to agree to the treaty. See *Massacre in Minnesota*, 22–23, 26–28.

6. Nathan H. Parker, *The Minnesota Handbook, for 1856-7* (Boston: John P. Jewett, 1857), iii–iv, 94, 99, 109–10, 130.

7. US censuses for 1860 and 1870; Minnesota State Census for 1857.

were military-age men, ages eighteen to forty-five). Immigrants made up a large portion of this migration. The foreign-born population of the state in 1860 was 58,728, an increase of 56,680 over the 1850 population. (Minnesota's population was 33.78 percent foreign-born in 1860, compared with 13.15 percent nationwide.)[8] Meanwhile, the Dakota population of Minnesota stood at about 6,000—and following the treaties of 1851 and another in 1858, they were pinched onto two reservations along the Minnesota River.[9]

To white migrants, Minnesota was a land of opportunity. To the Dakotas, white migration brought disruption to Indigenous ways of life. Historian Scott W. Berg captures the contrasting perspective of the various residents of the new state: "What was frontier to whites, the expanding edge of possibility, was to the Dakota just the opposite: the center of their world, growing smaller. Farms that signaled civilization to settlers were to many Dakotas, even to some who kept small acreages, a tool designed to fence them in, the symbol of a permanent halt to centuries of seasonal migration."[10] Dakota leader Wamditanka, or Big Eagle, later remarked, "There was great dissatisfaction among the Indians over many things the whites did. . . . Then the whites were always trying to make the Indians give up their life and live like white men—go to farming, work hard and do as they did—and the Indians did not know how to do that, and did not want to anyway. It seemed too sudden to make such a change. If the Indians had tried to make the whites live like them, the whites would have resisted, and it was the same way with many Indians."[11]

Throughout the 1850s and into the 1860s, the Dakota peoples suffered from starvation and mistreatment at the hands of corrupt white traders and Indian agents.[12] In March 1862—five months before the outbreak of fighting—Episcopal Bishop of Minnesota Henry B. Whipple warned President Abraham Lincoln, "The sad condition of the Indians of this state who are my heathen wards compels me to address you on their

---

8. J. D. B. DeBow, *The Seventh Census of the United States: 1850* (Washington, D.C.: Robert Armstrong, 1853), 993; Joseph C. G. Kennedy, *Population of the United States in 1860; Compiled from the Original Returns of the Eighth Census* (Washington, D.C.: Government Printing Office, 1864), xvii, xxvii, xxix, xxxi, xxxiii, 250–62; *Massacre in Minnesota*, 71–72.

9. *Dakota Eyes*, 8.

10. *38 Nooses*, 9–10.

11. *Dakota Eyes*, 23.

12. *Massacre in Minnesota*, 50, 73–77.

behalf. I ask only justice for a wronged & neglected race." Whipple explained that "dishonest" government agents and "ill conceived plans and defective instructions" had led to immense suffering on the part of the Indians. Indian agents were generally selected out of political considerations and "without any reference to their fitness for the place." As a result, they were often unfit for the position, and were "sometimes a disgrace to a Christian nation, whiskey sellers, bar room loungers [and] debauchers" who wasted supplies and defrauded the Indians of what was owed them. On top of that, Whipple explained that the Indians had sold their hunting grounds, and they were now left without protection or ways to improve their lives. According to Whipple, this "poor wronged people" was left with "only degradation and death." Whipple offered a series of six suggestions to deal with the rapidly deteriorating situation.[13]

Lincoln pledged to bring Whipple's recommendations to the attention of his secretary of the interior, but in reality, his administration was preoccupied with the Civil War.[14] And so the problems in Minnesota persisted. By August 1862, the federal government was several months late in paying its annuities to the Indians. Gold coin amounting to $71,000 arrived in St. Paul on August 16 and would have been distributed at the Indian agencies within a few days, but violence erupted on August 17—the same day that Buswell mustered into the 7th Minnesota—when four starving Dakota men murdered five white settlers in Acton, including four adults and a fifteen-year-old girl named Clara Wilson.[15] These killings sparked six weeks of war—what historian Gary Clayton Anderson

---

13. Henry B. Whipple to Abraham Lincoln, March 6, 1862 (two letters of same date), RG 48 (Records of the Office of the Secretary of the Interior), Entry 649 (Records of the Indian Division, 1828–1907, General Records, 1838–1907, Letters Received, 1849–1880), National Archives at College Park, Maryland (scan provided by the Papers of Abraham Lincoln).

14. Lincoln to Whipple, March 27, 1862, in Roy P. Basler, et al., eds., *The Collected Works of Abraham Lincoln*, 9 vols. (New Brunswick, N.J.: Rutgers University Press, 1953), 5:173.

15. *Dakota War*, 7–9; *Dakota Eyes*, 34–36. The best modern treatments of the conflict are *Massacre in Minnesota*, *Columns of Vengeance*, and *38 Nooses*. Numerous images of the conflict are available in *Dakota Uprising*. For an analysis of how the execution of the Dakota has been commemorated, see Melodie Andrews, "'That Derogatory Rock': The Contested Memory of the 1862 Hanging of Thirty-Eight Dakota in Mankato, Minnesota," in Brian Matthew Jordan and Jonathan W. White, eds., *Final Resting Places: Reflections on the Meaning of Civil War Graves* (Athens: University of Georgia Press, 2023), 102–15.

calls "the most violent ethnic conflict in American history." Under the leadership of Taoyateduta, or Chief Little Crow, many Dakota warriors mobilized for war, attacking the Redwood Agency, or Lower Sioux Agency, on August 18, killing twenty whites and capturing another ten.[16]

Over the next few weeks, huge swaths of Minnesota territory were virtually depopulated as white Minnesotans fled eastward to cities in Minnesota, Wisconsin, and elsewhere, seeking safety. The Dakotas killed more than six hundred white settlers and seized hundreds more as captives.[17] Stories of rape, murder, and pillaging abounded in the press and in private conversations, some of which were true, and others of which were exaggerated. Fear permeated the area. "Did you ever contemplate how horrible it is that young, respectable females, like yourself and your friends, are in the hands of savages who have *not the least restraint, either moral or physical, upon their conduct toward their victims?*" wrote one man to his sweetheart in September 1862. "To the horrors of death and captivity they add every possible torture and outrage. I believe I could yield my life willingly to see these savage devils exterminated."[18] Extermination became a watchword among many of Minnesota's leaders. Journalist Jane Grey Swisshelm, for example, crowed, "Shoot the hyenas and ask no odds of any man. . . . Exterminate the wild beasts, and make peace with the devil and all his host sooner than with these red-jawed tigers whose fangs are dripping with the blood of innocents! Get ready, and soon as these convicted murderers are turned loose, shoot them and be sure they are shot dead, *dead*, DEAD, DEAD! . . . kill the lazy vermin and make sure of killing them."[19] Buswell's hopes of fighting Confederates were dashed as his unit was now needed for fighting Indians on the home front.

Buswell reported on many of the key events of the Dakota War, including the Battle of Birch Coulee (September 2, 1862) and the fighting at Wood Lake (September 23, 1862). He also participated in the Sibley Expedition in the Dakota Territory in the summer of 1863, which included the battles of Big Mound (July 24), Dead Buffalo Lake (July 26), and Stony Lake (July 28). Along the way, he witnessed the most controversial moment of this dark episode in American history—the execution of

---

16. *Dakota War*, 5, 14.
17. *Massacre in Minnesota*, 110, 146–49, 157–59.
18. James Madison Bowler to Elizabeth Caleff, September 27, 1862, in Andrea R. Foroughi, ed., *Go If You Think It Your Duty: A Minnesota Couple's Civil War Letters* (St. Paul: Minnesota Historical Society Press, 2008), 124.
19. Quoted in *38 Nooses*, 209.

thirty-eight Dakota warriors on December 26, 1862, the largest single-day mass execution in American history.

Buswell's writing is vivid. Following Birch Coulee, for example, he described the Dakota warriors advancing "stripped, nearly naked, painted and covered with grass and flowers, and crawling on their bellies towards the fort, and then shoot their flaming arrows into the fort."[20] Buswell tended to describe his Indian foes in condescending ways, using words like "fiendish devils," "bloody savages," and "treacherous dogs." After one encounter, he took "a ring from the dead injuns finger" as a trophy.[21] While Buswell attributed their rebellion to "their wild untamable nature," he acknowledged that the Native Americans were treated unjustly by federal Indian agents who used "artful deception and intrigue" to deny "the indians their just annuities" while also "supplying them with not the best articles of food & clothing but an inferior article."[22] He was appalled when white settlers attacked Dakota prisoners who were being marched through New Ulm in November 1862, writing that he "would have liked nothing better than to give the cowards [meaning the white assailants] a full volley, and only waited the order."[23] When he witnessed the execution of the thirty-eight Dakota warriors on December 26, 1862, he wrote with measured admiration that "they were all brave & fearless."[24]

Around the first anniversary of his enlistment, Buswell expressed dissatisfaction with his service in Minnesota. "Just one year ago I signed the papers that made me a soldier," he wrote, "have seen some hard service, and have not accomplished much either." Many Minnesota volunteers, he further noted, were "especially anxious for active duty, and something

---

20. Diary entry for September 3, 1862.

21. Diary entries for August 23, September 2, 6, 11, 25, 1862, July 24, 1863. While Buswell took a ring off a dead Dakota warrior's finger, Civil War-era soldiers were known to cut off body parts as well. On the taking of "trophies," see Joan E. Cashin, "Trophies of War: Material Culture in the Civil War Era," *Journal of the Civil War Era* 1 (September 2011): 339–67; Ari Kellman, *A Misplaced Massacre: Struggling over the Memory of Sand Creek* (Cambridge, Mass.: Harvard University Press, 2012), 11, 13–14, 24, 36, 174. In some cases, Minnesota soldiers mutilated the bodies of dead Dakotas in retaliation for the scalping and mutilation of white soldiers and civilians. See *Massacre in Minnesota*, 185, 262, 283–84.

22. Diary entry for August 23, 1862.

23. Diary entry for November 9, 1862. For secondary accounts of this horrific incident, see *38 Nooses*, 196–97; *Massacre in Minnesota*, 232.

24. Diary entry for December 26, 1862.

besides state or Indian service."²⁵ Soon he would have the opportunity to face a Confederate foe in the Western Theater, just as he'd wanted in the first place.

In the fall of 1863, the men of the 7th Minnesota Infantry were finally sent south, arriving at St. Louis on October 11. Buswell found himself guarding Confederate prisoners at Gratiot Street Prison and making excursions into Illinois and Tennessee in search of "butternuts" and guerrillas. When contemplating his future, he thought it would be "a good idea to learn something . . . so if I ever get out of the Army alive I may be prepared to take upon myself some more responsible position than a common menial." In January 1864, he decided to apply for a lieutenancy in a "colored" regiment. By this point in the war, the Union had been recruiting African American men into the army for about a year, and the nearly two hundred thousand black soldiers who enlisted would play an integral part in securing Union victory. After studying a great deal, Buswell went before a board of officers who examined him on tactics, army regulations, and other subjects. "I came away quite well satisfied," he wrote, "feeling that I had answered most of the questions correctly, and that I had my first war victory in the South."²⁶

Buswell knew that serving in a black regiment was "a very dangerous position as the Rebels are very bitter towards Colored Soldiers & their officers." Confederate policy was to kill African American enlisted men and their white officers, treating black units as slaves in insurrection.²⁷ In fact, many families were conflicted by the prospect of their relatives becoming officers of black regiments. When Daniel Densmore, one of Buswell's comrades in both the 7th Minnesota Infantry and the 68th USCT, informed his family that he had received an appointment in a black regiment, his Aunt Martha replied, "I can but rejoice and yet am sad at your promotion, sad to think of the many dangers to which you may be exposed as an Officer in a Colored Regt, and glad that you have proved yourself worthy the promotion." Two pages later in the letter, she added: "My heart *sickens* when I think of the dangers to which you will be exposed on having that place—was it not dreadful that last battle, where the negroes fought so desperately, Daniel I am sick *sick* of war. Would it

---

25. Diary entries for August 14, September 17, 1863.
26. Diary entries for January 6, 22, 28, 1864.
27. Lorien Foote, *Rites of Retaliation: Civilization, Soldiers, and Campaigns in the American Civil War* (Chapel Hill: University of North Carolina Press, 2021), chap. 2.

were ended and *our dear ones* at home again." Buswell's family may have had a similar reaction at the thought of their relative leading men of color into battle, although he reported in his diary that "they were glad to know of my success."[28]

After some delay, Buswell was appointed first lieutenant of Co. K, 68th US Colored Infantry. As he encountered the institution of slavery, and the men who had recently escaped from bondage, Buswell noted the "evil effects" of the peculiar institution. Nevertheless, he believed that black men "will make excellent soldiers" and should "assist in carrying on the war, not only to save the Union, but because the war has been the means of striking off their shackles." In May, he added, "Some have thought they would not make soldiers, but that idea is being exploded, as they have already proved good fighters."[29] Buswell's perceptions aligned with those of his fellow officers. In a letter home, Daniel Densmore noted, "I have not seen a more able bodied regiment either white or black. The men are uniformly large and muscular. They behave themselves very nicely too, and take hold of soldiering with a will. But I shall be very anxious to have them get a smell of the powder of blank cartridges, before we see any secesh." After the 68th had proved itself in battle, Densmore wrote to his brother, "All is good times having made 60 miles in just 48 hours—Niggers can march as well as fight."[30]

During the summer of 1864, the Union army engaged Confederate general Nathan Bedford Forrest in several battles in Mississippi in order to stop him from attacking the railroad line that supplied William T. Sherman's army outside of Atlanta. Buswell reported on the Union route at Brices Cross Roads on June 10. Writing from Memphis, he noted, "All was excitement in and around the City." Buswell heard rumors that Union general Samuel D. Sturgis "was drunk, that his men were put into the fight with Forrest by detail, and having suffered a succession of defeats, a panic ensued, and the army completely routed, and every man for himself, many regiments being cut all to pieces." Still, Buswell noted that the men of the 55th and 59th US Colored Infantries had fought with great bravery.[31]

---

28. Diary entries for January 9, February 17, 1864; Aunt Martha to Daniel Densmore, June 26, 1864, Densmore Papers. See also *Family War Stories*, 72–73, 79.

29. Diary entries for February 18, May 22, 1864.

30. Daniel Densmore to friends at home, June 2, 1864, and Densmore to brother, August 30, 1864, Densmore Papers.

31. Diary entries for June 12, 13, 14, 1864.

When Sherman learned of the Union defeat at Brices Cross Roads, he ordered Maj. Gen. Andrew Jackson Smith to attack Forrest, and so Smith's men—Buswell among them—departed Memphis on July 5. The armies met outside of Tupelo on July 14–15, and over the course of several days' fighting, the Union army prevailed over the Confederates, with Forrest being badly wounded in the process. Buswell described the battle in vivid detail in his diary. He remarked on the bravery of the Confederate soldiers, and how he "came very near paying dear for my service, as a bullet passed through my hair, a close shave, and a spent bullet struck my foot, which I stooped down and picked up."[32]

After returning to Memphis, Buswell wrote at great length about the upcoming presidential election. His experiences in Tennessee and Mississippi had changed his perspectives about race and politics. Southerners, he found, were generally "unrepentant Rebs, except the black race, which are almost universally loyal." When Union soldiers were hungry, they found that "their only friends [were] the blacks, who fed them." As a consequence, Buswell came to support the Republican Party even though he had been a Douglas Democrat before the war. As a soldier, he wrote, "I have studied up some of the great issues, the matter has revolved itself over & over again in my mind. That Slavery was certainly wrong, and ought to be stamped out, I was well determined upon, and the Republican party being what the Johnny Rebs called the Abolishionists, I was further determined that it was my party. Again Lincoln was the President in favor of prosecuting the war and restoring the Union." The election was vitally important to the future of the nation, and on election day, Buswell wrote, "the votes of the people will decide many great questions—Slavery or Freedom to 5 millions of human beings, honorable war or a dishonorable peace, Union or Disunion."[33]

One of the last events recorded in his diary was the execution of Confederate guerrilla Dick Davis. This was the third execution Buswell witnessed as a soldier—earlier ones had been the thirty-eight Dakota warriors (December 26, 1862) and three soldiers convicted of murder (December 16, 1864). (He also wrote in detail about three soldiers who were executed for murder and rape in June 1864, although he does not appear to have personally witnessed this execution.) These were difficult scenes to watch, and Buswell apparently closed or averted his eyes during some moments. But in the case of Dick Davis, Buswell felt differently.

32. Diary entries for July 14, 15, 1864.
33. Diary entries for June 8, 10, 11, 16, September 23, November 8, 1864.

"Such sights generally sicken me," he wrote. "I prefer not to see them, but this time I had no such sensitive feeling."[34]

Buswell's diary offers remarkable insights into the daily lives of common soldiers in multiple theatres of war—from the experience of combat (against both Native Americans and Confederates), to garrison duty in urban settings (in both a Border State and in the South), to the tedium of camp life in the field (in Minnesota, the Dakota Territory, and several Southern states). For two and a half years he kept a daily account of his life, offering insights into numerous aspects of the Civil War era that are often overlooked or minimized in the secondary literature, and that few published primary sources include.[35]

Buswell's diary also speaks to modern historiographical controversies over the nature of the Civil War itself. Some recent scholars have argued that the war was "not only a fight between white men over the right to own slaves, but also a series of conflicts between American Indians and Anglo Americans over the right to self-determination," to quote historian Megan Kate Nelson. She adds that the war "was fought over African American emancipation in the East, and American Indian subjugation in the West."[36] Buswell and the men who fought with him would not have recognized this characterization.[37] Indeed, Buswell's diary is an extraordinary record of *two* wars.[38] He takes readers through the Dakota War (which he saw as distinct from the Civil War), into Union prisons, onto picket lines where he searched the bodies of Confederate women suspected of smuggling, and into an African American regiment that saw both field and garrison service in the Western Theater.

In the final surviving entry, on New Year's Eve 1864, Buswell remarked,

---

34. Diary entry for December 23, 1864.

35. For the letters of an enlisted man in the 7th Minnesota who became an officer in the 68th USCT, see Richard S. Offenberg and Robert Rue Parsonage, eds., *The War Letters of Duren F. Kelley, 1862–1865* (New York: Pageant Press, 1967). Buswell's diaries have not been widely utilized, although they are quoted once in *Massacre in Minnesota*.

36. Megan Kate Nelson, "The Civil War from Apache Pass," *Journal of the Civil War Era* 6 (December 2016): 511, 530.

37. On this point, see Gary W. Gallagher, "One War or Two? The United States Versus Confederates and Indians, 1861–1865," in *The Enduring Civil War: Reflections on the Great American Crisis* (Baton Rouge: Louisiana State University Press, 2020), 27–34.

38. On September 26, 1863, Buswell described meeting with neighbors and having "a long talk about the *wars*" (emphasis added).

"The last day of the year, and I am fully discharging my duty not only to my country, but to myself, how many more years of such toil and excitement and suspense. May the time be speedy when this service shall terminate and peace once more shall reign upon and over a united Country."[39] Buswell's surviving diary ended with that statement of hope. Fortunately, he would live to see the war's end less than four months later.

39. Diary entry for December 31, 1864.

NOTE ON METHOD

Around June 1, 1868, George W. Buswell began painstakingly copying his Civil War diaries into three journals. The handwriting in these clean copies is uniform and generally legible, but it is not without its inconsistencies and irregularities. In transcribing Buswell's words, we have striven to keep them as close to the originals as possible. However, we made some interventions for the sake of clarity.

In several instances we silently corrected minor errors in spelling. (For instance, we silently corrected about twenty words in which Buswell inadvertently omitted a letter when he was copying his diaries into the journals, such as when he left the "d" off of "sword.") If a word was misspelled consistently throughout the text (such as "lowry" or "near by") or if a misspelled word possibly gives a sense of Buswell's speaking voice (such as "devlish" or "loosing"), we retained the misspelling. However, if a word was typically spelled correctly, or had a number of variations (such as "ordnance" or "reveille," which he spelled at least three different ways), we silently corrected the spelling to avoid confusion. In five instances when Buswell mistakenly wrote "by," we silently changed it to "my"; in five instances we corrected the spelling of "to" and "too"; and in eight places we corrected his confusion of "there" and "their." We omitted words that Buswell struck; however, when he appeared to write words on top of one another, we explain our transcription in a note. We also omitted words that he accidentally duplicated. When we believe he inadvertently omitted a word, phrase, or part of a word, we inserted what we thought was missing in brackets. In eight instances we inserted "[sic]" after a misspelling or grammatical error to alert the reader to an unusual mistake in the text. When we believe he wrote the wrong word, we inserted a guess in brackets with a question mark.

We standardized "A.M.," "P.M.," and "R.R." (for railroad) by always including periods after each letter; however, we retained "U.S." and "US" as he wrote them because he used these abbreviations in almost equal numbers. Buswell rarely used apostrophes in possessives and contractions, and we rendered them as he wrote them. When Buswell wrote a quotation mark (") after a number, we rendered it as a superscripted ordinal number.

Buswell typically did not follow standard grammatical rules. He tended to use periods and commas interchangeably, he often omitted punctuation, and his sentences at times run an entire paragraph. For the sake of readability, we silently inserted sentence breaks, and on some occasions we inserted or omitted commas.

Unless otherwise noted, the information in the footnotes was gathered from online databases, including Ancestry.com, ReadEx, Fold3, Newspapers.com, and Find-A-Grave. We also made extensive use of *Annual Report of the Adjutant General, of the State of Minnesota, for the Year Ending December 1, 1866, and of the Military Forces of the State from 1861 to 1866* (St. Paul: Pioneer, 1866), and *Minnesota in the Civil and Indian Wars, 1861–1865*, 2 vols. (St. Paul: Pioneer Press, 1890–93). When identifying Minnesota soldiers, we included their nativity so that readers can appreciate the scope of white migration to Minnesota in the years before the Civil War.

ABBREVIATIONS AND SHORT TITLES

38 Nooses	Scott W. Berg, *38 Nooses: Lincoln, Little Crow, and the Beginning of the Frontier's End*. New York: Pantheon, 2012.
CMSR	Combined Military Service Records, Record Group 94 (Records of the Adjutant General's Office), Entry 519 (Records of the Record and Pension Office, Carded Military Service Records, Volunteer Organizations, Civil War), National Archives and Records Administration, Washington, D.C.
Court-Martial Case File	General Court-Martial Case Files, Record Group 153 (Records of the Office of the Judge Advocate General [Army]), National Archives and Records Administration, Washington, D.C. (Each case file includes an alpha-numeric case number.)
Dakota Eyes	Gary Clayton Anderson and Alan R. Woolworth, eds., *Through Dakota Eyes: Narrative Accounts of the Minnesota Indian War of 1862*. St. Paul: Minnesota Historical Society, 1988.
Dakota Uprising	Curtis A. Dahlin, *The Dakota Uprising: A Pictorial History*. Edina, Minn.: Beaver's Pond Press, 2009.
Dakota War	Kenneth Carley, *The Dakota War of 1862: Minnesota's Other Civil War*, 2nd ed. St. Paul: Minnesota Historical Society Press, 1976.
Densmore Papers	Benjamin Densmore and Family Papers, Minnesota Historical Society, St. Paul, Minn.
Family War Stories	Keith P. Wilson, *Family War Stories: The Densmores' Fight to Save the Union and*

	Destroy Slavery. New York: Fordham University Press, 2024.
O.R.	*War of the Rebellion: A Compilation of the Official Records of the Union and Confederate Armies*. 128 vols. Washington, D.C.: Government Printing Office, 1880–1901.
Minnesota in Wars	*Minnesota in the Civil and Indian Wars, 1861–1865*, 2 vols. (St. Paul: Pioneer Press, 1890–93), vol. 1.
Pension	Civil War and Later Pension Files, Record Group 15 (Records of the Veterans Administration), National Archives and Records Administration, Washington, D.C.
USCT	United States Colored Troops

PART I
The Dakota War

I

"They Were All Brave and Fearless"

From Enlistment to Execution, August 13–December 26, 1862

⚭

THE MURDER of a white family by four starving Dakota warriors on August 17, 1862, ignited war between the Dakota Indians and white Minnesotans.[1] On the evening of August 17, Chief Little Crow reluctantly agreed to lead the insurgency, and on August 18 bands of young warriors spread throughout the area near the Lower Sioux Agency, or Redwood Agency, killing more than 150 unarmed, panic-stricken whites near Beaver Creek, Birch Coulee, and Middle Creek. Over the next few days, Dakota warriors attacked Fort Ridgely on August 19 and 22, as well as other settlements, including the town of New Ulm. Meanwhile, at the Upper Sioux Agency, or Yellow Medicine Agency, Sisseton and Wahpeton leaders, known as "friendly" Indians, resolved not to join in the attack against the whites.[2]

On August 19, Gov. Alexander Ramsey appointed trader Henry H. Sibley a colonel to lead the state's volunteers. Ramsey immediately pressured Sibley to relieve Fort Ridgely, telling him, "The eyes of the whole people are on Fort Ridgely." Ramsey further warned of "the intense anxiety" of Minnesotans, adding that if the fort were "lost it will cause lamentation throughout the land." On August 28, Sibley's forces reached Fort Ridgely, where approximately 350 white and mixed-blood refugees had been under siege. The colonel lacked the supplies he needed to push his army against the Indians, but he decided that he could at least reinforce

---

1. The resisters included the Mdewakanton and some Wahpekutes as well as individuals from two other bands.
2. *Massacre in Minnesota*, 80–111, 141–45; *38 Nooses*, 6–9, 13–15, 78–79.

Map 1. Locations of important sites in Minnesota during the US–Dakota War

the burial parties near Beaver Creek and Birch Coulee. Sibley placed Joseph R. Brown—an old friend and former Indian agent whose family had been taken captive on August 19—in charge of the expedition. Sibley neglected to tell Capt. Hiram P. Grant of the 6th Minnesota that Brown was in command.[3]

Over the next two days the troops buried scores of bodies. Then, at 4:30 a.m. on September 2, Dakota warriors attacked the sleeping soldiers at Birch Coulee. The initial attack killed a dozen men and nearly eighty horses that had been standing on the perimeter of the camp. "But once the men reached the dead horses," writes historian Gary Clayton Anderson, "hardly a man thereafter was killed. The sun slowly rose, and using

3. *Massacre in Minnesota*, 101–2, 108, 135–67 (quotation from pp. 145–46); *38 Nooses*, 110–13.

bayonets, knives, and the three shovels they possessed, the group dug rifle pits and prepared for a long siege." Throughout the day, the Dakotas fired occasional shots from a hundred yards away, rather than attack the entrenched US troops. Meanwhile, about twenty miles away at Fort Ridgely, Colonel Sibley sent Col. Samuel McPhail of the 1st Minnesota Cavalry to the scene of action. As McPhail's men headed toward the Lower Agency, they were attacked. Using a howitzer, they "dug in" and "kept the Indians at bay." The next morning, September 3, Col. William R. Marshall of the 7th Minnesota Infantry arrived about 10 a.m., bringing the thirty-three-hour battle of Birch Coulee to a close.[4]

Over the ensuing days, Little Crow's forces suffered from desertion, while Sibley's strength increased to about 1,500 men; however, several days of rain forced Sibley to delay his pursuit of the Indians. Sibley finally departed Fort Ridgely on September 18, marching up the Minnesota River Valley in pursuit of Little Crow and his men. After taking a day to cross the Minnesota River, the Minnesota forces marched sixteen miles on September 21 and fifteen miles on September 22, arriving just below the Yellow Medicine River at Lone Tree Lake. (The location was misidentified as Wood Lake and the subsequent battle there consequently bears the incorrect name.) Sibley ordered his men to prepare the place for defense, but a firefight broke out on the morning of September 23 when members of the 3rd Minnesota left their camp to dig for potatoes on farms near the Upper Agency. As one account later put it, "Soon the horizon became picturesque with Indians, some mounted and some afoot, single and in squads, advancing rapidly from the direction of the Yellow Medicine River." Little Crow, carrying a revolver that he never fired, rode out in front of his men during the battle "swinging his blanket above his head" while shouting loud "war-whoops." The two-hour battle ended in US victory, with seven white Minnesotans killed and roughly fifty wounded, compared with more than thirty Dakotas killed and "many more" wounded.[5]

About September 22, Little Crow's men transferred their white captives over to the leaders of the "friendly" Dakota tribes. On September 26, following the Battle of Wood Lake, the "friendly" Indians began releasing captives at a site that became known as Camp Release, about twenty miles north of the Upper Agency. By October 3, 107 "pure white captives" had been released. Meanwhile, over the ensuing weeks, Sibley arrested

4. *Massacre in Minnesota*, 167–70; *38 Nooses*, 110–13.
5. *Massacre in Minnesota*, 181–88, 212; *38 Nooses*, 155–56.

more than 1,700 Dakota men, women, and children, many of whom had been peaceful and had refused to join the Dakota uprising. (Buswell took part in these movements in mid-October.) Meanwhile, on September 27, Sibley established a military commission that, by November 3, would try 392 men and sentence 303 to death. White Minnesotans wanted all of the condemned to face the gallows, but Lincoln ordered that no executions be carried out until he reviewed the files. The president then had three lawyers in Washington review the cases to determine who had committed a war crime (such as rape or the killing of unarmed civilians) and who had fought on a battlefield (these would not be executed). In the end, Lincoln commuted the sentences of all but thirty-eight, and Buswell would see them hanged in the largest single-day execution in US history on December 26. Many white Minnesotans were dissatisfied that so few Dakota warriors had been executed. One white woman stated that she hoped the Dakotas "may have short lives, a happy death, and we be rid of them forever." Her brother remarked, "I wish Old Abe had a son or some kin or kine up there in danger" because then "he would begin to see 'a strong necessity for hanging the loathsome red devils.'" But Lincoln stood with resolve against this pressure. When Gov. Alexander Ramsey later informed Lincoln that the Republican Party would have been more successful in the presidential election of 1864 if he had executed more men, Lincoln replied, "I could not afford to hang men for votes."[6]

Wednesday, August 13, 1862. More than one year has past this rebellion & secession of which was considered of such small importance only 75000 men were called for three months to subdue it, and coerce those states which had become disorganized, destroyed their state governments, but from the determined resistance and extensive preparations made, it bids fair to be one of the most formidable rebellions ever on the face of the known earth. 300 000 have been called and have rallied to the seat of war, and now more are wanted. A call for 300 000 more is issued—every state legislature throughout the North and all the people are becoming interested [and] enthusiastic, their patriotism for this glo-

---

6. *Massacre in Minnesota*, 212–67; *38 Nooses*, 150–52, 164–74, 190–98, 212–42; *Family War Stories*, 23–24; Michael S. Green, *Lincoln and Native Americans* (Carbondale: Southern Illinois University Press, 2021), chap. 5 (Lincoln quote on p. 83).

rious old union is manifesting itself—money is appropriated and the cry "to arms" "to arms" resounds throughout. The interest, excitement prevails,—companies are formed, and there is a rivalry as to which company or regiment will first make its appearance, report for duty at the state rendevouz. Large Union mass meetings were held—I at the time am working on the Winona Court-House though quite young to [en]list, though my patriotism was aroused, our country was in danger, long had I meditated upon the subject, and finally resolved to enlist, slid from the roof of the Court-House and shortly enrolled my name for liberty and our glorious old stars & stripes, emblematical of the best country that ever existed, joining a company forming by Dr S. B. Sheardown[7] of Stockton, and immediately started for home to break the news to the family, to those I love. Remained but a short time, bid all a "Good bye" and left, promising to return before my departure from the state as was the usual custom.

Thursday, August 14, 1862. Left Winona at 12 ½ P.M. on board the good steamer Key-City amidst the tears and best wishes from the vast assembly of dear friends who had arranged themselves along the levee, with some excellent music which gave tone and cheer. With many a good bye we moved from the city and started on that passage, in the new career of a soldier, thinking solemnly that many of this gallant band may never return, forfeit their lives in the service of their country, with an occasional thought of those brave Spartans and their heroic mothers, "my son come home with your shield or on your shield." What patriotism, heroism, all for their children, their homes and their blessed country. Whom but tories traitors could manifest any other feeling.

This is my first trip up the glorious, proud Mississippi, so my thoughts must be in observing the towns, cities and hills and romantic dells along its banks, its grand scenery—fit pastime for an Italian artist. While some are thinking of the past and others the future, whether they will be crowned with success, become noted for bravery in action, or be shot in the back, and still others are thinking of promotion and conjuring up some method by which they may become Capt or Lieut of this company, whose officers we are to elect upon our arrival in St Paul, considerable lobbying is going on, others are humiliating themselves before him

---

7. Samuel B. Sheardown (1826–1889) was the surgeon of the 10th Minnesota Infantry.

who reigns supreme, praying that on leaving those they love and adore they may be carried safely through on this great three yr's journey—and directly opposite might be seen a group busily engaged, enjoy[ing] *themselves* taking a *simple* game of Euchre or Sledge,[8] what a striking contrast, while all are swiftly floating against the Miss tide. Passed Wabashau [*sic*] with a welcome cheer, amid floating of handkerchiefs and a "God speed" on our journey.

Friday, August 15, 1862. The weather is delightful. Passed through Lake Pepin, some 30 miles long by about 4 miles wide in widest place, surrounded by the most romantic scenery, an excellent spot for a first class artist to display their talents. The lake was named by a party of Frenchmen on an exploring expedition in honor of King Pepin of France.[9] Maiden Rock, towering perpendicularly nearly 300 feet, the scene of the famous historical Indian legend where one Indian maiden Winona jumped from the top of the rock and was dashed to pieces on the rock below, rather than remain to marry against her will, while she loved another, good grit.[10] Received tremendous cheering from the citizens of Lake-City while assembled on the point of land which indents the lake, which we returned appreciatingly and a tiger.[11] I retired early but the boat being pretty well crowded, my sleep was rather short.

Saturday, August 16, 1862. Passed Red-Wing rather early, before light. Took our breakfast on the boat, and having got well supplied went on the hurricane deck eagerly watching as we were approaching the Capitol,[12] where we arrived at 10 o'clock, not an unusual commotion by its inhabitants—as soldiers were nothing new. Left the boat and immediately marched through the streets to the capitol, and proceeded to elect our officers, which meeting, after a short time being rather quiet, not the

---

8. Euchre and old sledge are card games.

9. Lake Pepin was actually named for Jean Pepin, an explorer who settled near the lake in the late seventeenth century.

10. According to this Dakota legend, a young woman named Winona jumped to her death from the rocks in order to avoid a marriage arranged by her father, Chief Red Wing.

11. Adding "a tiger" to a cheer became common in the 1840s as "an intensive form of applause; an addition thought to embellish the traditional three cheers." See John S. Farmer and William E. Henley, *A Dictionary of Slang and Colloquial English* (New York: G. Routledge & Sons, 1905), 476.

12. St. Paul has been the capital of Minnesota since territorial times.

usual noise & bustle attending such meetings, resulted in the election of John W. Curtiss[13] of Winona, Captain, A. H. Stevens[14] of same place 1st Lieut, and A. A. Rice[15] of same place 2^d Lieut, and E. D. Eastman[16] of Utica Orderly Sergeant. By consent of the company the Captain was authorized to appoint the remaining non-com officers when J. W. Wilson[17] was appointed 2^d Sergeant, J. McDonald[18] 3^d Sergeant, John Hammond[19] 4th Sergeant, George Morrill[20] 5th Sergeant. A motion for three cheers for the officers was made and all joined in and made the hall ring, then adjourned and formed company for first time, and were marched by the new Captain—such marching—to the Winslow House,[21] where we soon supplied our inner wants from the bountiful repast which had been provided for us, then without any delay we moved to the levee and departed on steamboat up the Minnesota to Fort Snelling[22] which had for [a] time had considerable notoriety from the many things that infested

13. Capt. John W. Curtis (born ca. 1829), a native of Maine, commanded Co. B of the 7th Minnesota Infantry until he resigned on June 4, 1863.

14. Albert H. Stevens (1837–1884), a native of New York, served as first lieutenant in Co. B, 7th Minnesota Infantry. He was promoted to captain on June 4, 1863.

15. Archibald A. Rice (1839–1925), a native of Illinois, was second lieutenant of the 7th Minnesota Infantry, Co. B.

16. Ermon D. Eastman (1839–1911), a native of Maine, enlisted as an orderly sergeant in Co. B, 7th Minnesota Infantry, and rose to the rank of first lieutenant on June 4, 1863.

17. John W. Wilson (ca. 1830–1904), a native of Delaware, enlisted as a private in the 7th Minnesota Infantry, Co. B, in August 1862 and was quickly promoted to sergeant. In April 1864 he became a lieutenant in the 68th USCT.

18. James McDonald (1832–1882), a native of New York, rose to the rank of second lieutenant of the 7th Minnesota Infantry, Co. B. He was wounded at the Battle of Nashville and was discharged at Jefferson Barracks on May 12, 1865.

19. John Hammond (1833–1891), a native of Vermont, was later promoted to captain of Battery K, 1st Minnesota Heavy Artillery.

20. George E. Morrell (1831–1865), a native of Maine, was a corporal in Co. B, 7th Minnesota Infantry. He later served as first lieutenant of the 8th US Colored Heavy Artillery, Co. I.

21. Likely the Winslow House in St. Anthony, a luxury hotel established in 1857 that closed in 1886.

22. Fort Snelling (originally known as Fort St. Anthony) was built near the confluence of the Minnesota and Mississippi Rivers at St. Paul about 1819. Union regiments from Minnesota mustered in at Fort Snelling, and it became

its walls, arrived at 1 P.M. It has a large wall around it with two towers of stone masonry, not of much permanence as the design was only for a defence against the hostile indians, very many of whom inhabited this Territory[23] at the time, 1842. We were soon marched up to its gate, passed in by the sentinel, and we were under military restriction for the first time with no way of getting out but through the pass of a com'd officer. Soon had barracks provided for us, which answered the purpose very well, although not as clean, free from vermin as they might be. Took our supper, the first meal in what was rightfully named the "Slush House," large enough to seat about one company, a door on the side which led to the cook-house, and such dirty, greasy looking customers, the very sight of them was enough to choke and sicken one. At the end was the door at which we entered, passing in in two files separating at the end of the long table which was firmly fixed to the centre of the room, and passed down each side and took our seats by its side on low wooden long benches. The appearance of the table was sufficient to turn ones stomack, but we had prepared them for almost any emergency, covered with grease and dirt and tin dishes that you couldnt exactly see your face in, but were also greasy and dirty. Taking my handkerchief, I wiped mine, and left it. D[24] ye cooks, all black. Soon the soup or stew, for it was of beef boiled, then the bakers bread which I would have relished if it had been in any other place than the slush House. Having finished our *bountiful* repast we were hurried out to give room for more, it puts me more in mind of feeding hogs than anything else. Thus ended our first soldier meal, we survived it, but left the table hungry. Quite a number of companies had arrived before us awaiting their disposal and formations into regiments—the 6th Reg[t] was partially formed, and some [of] them were encamped outside and were under the instruction of drilling master, something which we expected in a short time.

Sunday, August 17, 1862. Beautiful Sabbath morning but as there is no rest for the weary soldier on Sunday, there is certain kind of work that must be performed. We were examined before an Army Surgeon, pass into his office, strip and if any defects the man is sent home, not mus-

---

a staging ground for troops going out to quell the Dakota resistance. The fort also held Dakota prisoners of war from November 1862 to May 1863. *Massacre in Minnesota*, 7, 18; *Dakota Uprising*, 34.

    23. Buswell originally wrote "state" and later changed it to "Territory" in pencil.

    24. Buswell appears to be abbreviating the word "Damn" here.

tered, not fit to endure the hardships and privations of a soldiers life. I passed in and was pronounced to be physically able. The company was examined and only one rejected. Our company taken together was considered as strong, able-bodied as any before examined here, they certainly were the cream of our country, most of whom being young, active, unmarried men. Were then mustered in by Col Nelson[25] Com of Musters, which initiated us into the U.S. Army, were tied to Uncle Sam for the defense & offense of his, for the term of three years. After dinner or slush received permission (how odd it seems to be obliged, like children, to ask permission to go any where) to be absent during the afternoon. Went to take a view of the celebrated Minnehaha Falls, beautiful scenery around and about them. The stream which forms them is about fifteen feet wide at the summit of the fall, it drops about 60 feet into a chasm below, a few feet out from the bank, making a fine passage behind it, a bridge below from which one has a fine view of it and the spray and rainbow, the whole in the sunshine forming a most grand imposing spectacle, well worth a visit by all tourists. Seven more companies from different portions of the state arrived with music and colors flying, all jubilant over the cause in which they were engaged. Part of our company returned home on furlough. As a few had to remain, I agreed to and will go when they return.

Monday, August 18, 1862. Delightful day. Have not received our clothing, although a vast amount is arriving. All is turmoil and confusion about. Ten more companies arrived today in response to the call of Father Abraham, two regiments will soon be equipped and dispatched to the seat of War. I trust it may be my fortune to be placed in a regiment that will be sent into the western department [to] deliver me from the Potomac Army, but however, the duty of a good soldier is to obey orders.

Tuesday, August 19, 1862. Pleasant as usual. The greatest excitement prevails, reliable reports that the Sioux Indians commenced depredations yesterday at Red Wood Agency[26] on the Minn River. Five companies armed & equipped and despatched for the scene of action. A portion

---

25. Anderson D. Nelson (1818–1885), a native of Kentucky and a member of the class of 1841 at West Point, had served in the regular army since the 1840s. He declined the colonelcy of the 6th Minnesota Infantry and for a time was a mustering officer for the US army.

26. The Redwood Agency, also known as the Lower Sioux Agency, was an administrative center erected on land ceded by the Dakota as a result of the 1858

of the 6th Minn now forming, a part of whom were without the proper U.S. Uniform.

Wednesday, August 20, 1862. Continues to be pleasant. No news of importance from the frontier in reference to the indian depredations, as to the extent &c. We are patiently waiting the hour when we shall receive orders to "forward march.["] We are not anxious until the remaining portion of the company, who have been sent for, shall arrive.

Thursday, August 21, 1862. Beautiful morning—more troops ordered to Ft Ridgely, the scene of action, nothing particular, some credulous persons believe it a hoax. Considerable excitement in Mendota, an indian scare, nobody hurt. We received orders to pack up and be ready to move immediately. This does not require much labor, as we have not drawn any clothes, arms or accoutrements, although I hope to get them.

Friday, August 22, 1862. Still continues to be pleasant. All doubts are now removed, and the first report confirmed, the indians are doing great damage to property and dealing destruction to its owners. Six more companies sent to the scene of action, with 50 Rifle Rangers.

Saturday, August 23, 1862. Pleasant as usual. No news worthy of note from the seat of the indian war. The cause of this struggle & desperation by those fiendish devils is hardly known, but many people as well as myself surmise that it is only their wild untamable nature manifesting itself, but some rather suspect the Indian Agents of using their artful deception and intrigue and not allowing the indians their just annuities and of supplying them with not the best articles of food & clothing but an inferior article. The indians have long been aware of it, and having probably been urged or incited by some whites, quarrelsome & mischievous, that not only the wild tribes, but those of a more civilized nature who have doffed the citizens garb for the war costume, breach-cloth[27] &c, and performed acts of hostility towards the whites, their enemies at heart.

---

treaty. It was located about thirty miles down the Minnesota River from the Upper Sioux Agency. The Dakota attacked the agency on August 18. *Dakota War*, 3–4; *38 Nooses*, 32–35.

27. Breechcloth was a piece of clothing that hung over a Dakota man's belt in both the front and back. They were usually about 10 inches wide and could be up to 5 feet long. Wearing breechcloth signified the rejection of white people's clothing. One missionary saw the abandonment of pants for breechcloth by Indians as part of "a retrograde movement." See *Massacre in Minnesota*, 51, 65, 70.

Sunday, August 24, 1862. Fine day—sky serene & clear. No news of importance. Expect the absent members of our company back today, as we expect to leave here immediately upon their arrival. Busied myself looking and walking around the fort and grounds taking observations.

Monday, August 25, 1862. Beautiful day, no great changes. On the evening boat from the city were a group of boys whom we had long wished to see, and shortly after its landing at the levee below the fort, they were among us. We greeted them with the good old pump handle shake, and many were the questions had we to ask, (of those who had arrived home, as a number of them got orders to return before getting home,) about the dear ones in whose midst they had been. My chance for furlough this time was rather poor, as we will probably leave before long for the frontier.

Tuesday, August 26, 1862. Pleasant morning. At 8 o'clock this morning our company received orders to be ready to march to Ft Ridgely. At 10 o'clock we were drawn up in line and received our guns—Endfields[28] and accoutrements, then with difficulty, as we were all green—we put the harness together. At 6 o'clock P.M. was again marched up to Quarter-Masters and received our U.S. clothing, and at once there was a strife to see who should first don the garb of blue. By this time we were soldiers indeed, clothed, armed & accoutered, and ready for active duty, although we were far from experienced in knowledge [of] U.S. Tactics, theory or practice, but this is useless—needless to war with redskins as we are destined to go at least for the present.

Wednesday, August 27, 1862. This beautiful morning received marching orders quite early, went to the bank of the Minnesota, ready to embark on the first boat, remained there most of the day, got supper and at 7 o'clock the long looked for boat, (which proved to be the sternwheel Pomeroy) appeared. We were soon on board and at a pretty fast rate moved up the river. The night being rather dark did not [see] the expected view of the beautiful river and its banks, so laid down on the deck and attempted to get some sleep and rest myself, preparatory for the march that we are to take on the morrow.

Thursday, August 28, 1862. This morning at 7 o'clock we debarked at Shakope[e] and marched to a vacant space near the Town Hall and

---

28. The rifled Enfield musket was invented by William Pritchett in England in 1853, and was used by both Union and Confederate soldiers.

stacked arms, uncoutred, and proceeded to get our breakfast, and having not become well accustomed to eating army food, we strolled around the town in search of bakeries and milkmen. Received ten rounds of ammunition and at 3 o'clock P.M. we fell in and started our eventful trip—through not the best country that I ever saw, marching ten miles and camping in a large wheat field.

Friday, August 29, 1862. This day—the weather still remaining pleasant—we passed across a beautiful prairie—with very fertile soil, and well indented with fine groves of elm, maple, walnut &c, and arrived at Belle-Plaine—and prepared our dinner, a small town with a very large hotel—beginning to be somewhat foot-sore. After eating *dainty* repast, we again took up our line of march, crossed the Minn River at Faxon,[29] and prepared ourselves a place for the night in a large barn on the bluffs side.

Saturday, August 30, 1862. This morning, clear without, somewhat refreshed, but with feet rather sore, we resumed our march and passed through a very poor country—sandy soil, and arrived at Henderson about noon where we took dinner. Feet beginning to be quite sore, got some liquor and placed in boots, and partaken of our frugal meal, accompanied with a variety of jokes by the [illegible word] & witty on the more sedate. We again started with our train, got pretty well wet through, the consequence of being obliged to march through a drizzling rain. Thus is the soldiers life, probably an inkling of what we may experience before the term of three years expires. Suffered very much from the ear-ache which hindered me from taking my regular sleep. Camped on the prairie—fertile soil, well watered, not thickly settled.

Sunday, August 31, 1862. The rain having fell to considerable depth during the night, and softened up the soil—somewhat retarded our progress, and we did not start until a late hour, and marched only about eight miles and camped at Mud Lake, where the owners of the farm having fled at approach of the indians, we helped ourselves to what corn that could be found in the fields. Went out with some of the boys and shot some ducks. Only thirty miles to the fort.

Monday, September 1, 1862. Pleasant morning but still rather muddy, and consequently the call to strike tents was blown at a late hour. Marched

---

29. Faxon, in Sibley County, was also known at the time as Walker's Landing. The town was founded in 1852 and for a time had considerable traffic because of its location on the Minnesota River, but by the 1870s was a ghost town.

8 miles further to another lake, called Swan Lake, near a large, beautiful grove in which was situated a small frame house which had from appearances been deserted but a short time previous. Was detailed for guard, the first time since leaving the fort. After being relieved, went and shot some ducks on the lake, nothing exciting, or news of importance from the fort or frontier.

Tuesday, September 2, 1862. This morning got up earlier than usual and started for Fort Ridgely. Saw Joe Browns[30] famous invention, the prairie engine & cars, which was constructed very large and powerful for the purpose of travelling across the vast prairies of the West, with a tender attached, it having proved a failure, was therefore laid up when we found it, about 4 miles from the fort. Halted here for a short time near a brook of pure sparkling waters. Between this point and fort is a high prairie, and while passing over it, there was a rumor of indians in the vicinity as several persons had not long since forfeited their lives by leaving the fort and crossing this high prairie for New Ulm or the settlements. This created somewhat of an excitement, though with quietude, and all our perceptive & imaginative qualities were put in use, and many an indian was perceived, but upon closer examination proved to be [a] tree or bush. Crossed the valley, fording the beautiful Minnesota River and passed up the hill on the other side on the top of which is the fort. The headquarters of the indian expedition marched out beyond the fort and camped in the vicinity of the 6th Regt Minn. Inft at 4 o'clock P.M., and prepared to get supper, feeling gratified to think that we had reached our journeys end for the present, being all tired out, and feet sore.

Ft Ridgely, composed of a few wooden & stone buildings, presenting more the appearance of barracks in a peaceful village than a fort upon the frontier, as a defense against trading post with the aborigines of the West, but not withstanding the apparent defenceless condition, had stood the galling fire—and the flaming arrows of the redskins for two days and nights, and then they not succeeding in accomplishing their hellish

---

30. Joseph R. Brown (1805–1870), a native of Maryland, married a Dakota woman and worked as an Indian agent in Minnesota. On August 19, his home was destroyed, and his wife and thirteen children found refuge with Little Crow. Brown was known for inventing steam-powered wagons. In December, he informed the condemned Dakota prisoners which of them would be executed. See *Dakota War*, 22–23; *38 Nooses*, 227.

purposes retreated up the river.[31] We here learn that the hostile indians are not only wild, but the majority of the civilized indians from Red Wood, Yellow Medicine[32] & the indian reservation, who had doffed the garb of a citizen and donned the garb of savage on the warpath, breach-cloth &c, and all under the command of one Little Crow,[33] a resident of St Paul. About 5 P.M. received orders to march to the front, as cannon, at intervals, could be distinctly heard, the prospects are for a squabble soon, the excitement at this moment was intense. It seems from what can be learned that Capt. Grants[34] Company A 6th Regt. Minn Inft were sent up the river some 16 miles per order of Gen'l Sibley.[35] Not much generalship according to my notion, to send a mere squad out when from every appearance there was a large force of savages in the vicinity, they having

31. By nightfall on August 18, more than 200 refugees, mostly women and children, had gone to Fort Ridgely for protection. The fort, however, had few defenses and no stockade to repulse an attack. Nevertheless, the Dakotas decided to attack New Ulm rather than Fort Ridgely, after receiving a false report from an Anglo-Dakota scout about the size of the US forces at the fort. This enabled Fort Ridgely to be reinforced with more troops. When the Dakotas attacked the fort on August 20 and 22, they were repulsed. *Massacre in Minnesota*, 140–45; *Dakota War*, 25–31; *38 Nooses*, 77, 150; *Dakota Eyes*, chaps. 6–7.

32. The Upper Sioux Agency, also known as the Yellow Medicine Agency, was an administrative center erected on land ceded by the Dakotas as a result of the 1858 treaty. The Upper Sioux reservation stretched along the Minnesota River from Lake Traverse to the Yellow Medicine River. *Dakota War*, 3–4.

33. Taoyateduta, or Chief Little Crow (ca. 1810–1863), reluctantly led the Dakota in the war. In the immediate aftermath of the killings at Acton, he encouraged his followers to seek peace, telling his men that "the Great Father had many soldiers, more than any Dakota warrior could fathom." Once he realized that he could not stop the push for war, he reportedly told them, "I will die with you." According to Joseph R. Brown's wife, Susan Frenier Brown, who was a mixed-blood captive, Little Crow said "in substance" that "his young men had started a massacre; that he at first opposed the movement with all his might, but when he saw he could not stop it he joined them in their madness against his better judgment, but now did not regret it and was never more earnest in his life." *Massacre in Minnesota*, 82; *38 Nooses*, 74; *Dakota Eyes*, 40–42, 130–35.

34. Capt. Hiram P. Grant (1828–1897), a native of Vermont, commanded the 6th Minnesota Infantry, Co. A. He was a member of the military commission that tried the Dakota warriors. *38 Nooses*, 166.

35. Col. Henry H. Sibley (1811–1891), a native of Michigan and a former fur trader, commanded the Union volunteers during the Dakota War. He had been the first governor of Minnesota from 1858 to 1860. *38 Nooses*, 108–10, 178–84.

been gone a few days and no dispatches being received, consequently the Gen'l was somewhat worried, and accordingly sent a reinforcement of some cavalry under command of Col McPhail[36] and a few pieces of artillery, and nothing being heard from them, with exception of the cannons roar, the Gen'l concluded to move the whole force, with exception of a sufficient number to man the fort, and to expedite matters, wagons were furnished for conveying the troop[s] to the scene of action. Went about 16 miles and arrived just in season to save the company from the horrible death which was already staring them in the face. The company had arrived in the vicinity of what was called Birch-Coolie[37] and were burying the dead, which were found per orders, and night coming on camped without having seen an indian—and feeling secure the guards, (there being but a few) were not expecting any, therefore were somewhat careless, and the first notice they had of the indians was the clash of fire-arms they [were] shooting into the tents, and nine were killed & wounded the first fire, and nearly every horse, some 96, fell to the ground either killed or wounded at the first fire. What a sad perplexity they must have been in. In a short time, a very few moments, all in the camp were aroused, and without delay took their places, behind the dead carcasses of the horses, and commenced to dig holes in the ground with their hands, bayonets, sticks &c to shelter and afford them a breastwork, to contest—severely—the field. Many a dusky Savage was made to bite the dust—their fiery demonical yell was heard all around them, and then would roll large logs towards them, crawling rather snaky behind, and occasionally would rise up and fire without stopping to take aim and then pop down as sudden. Col McPhail sent out hearing the contest, moved up and planted his

---

36. Col. Samuel McPhail (1826–1902), a native of Kentucky, commanded the 1st Minnesota Cavalry.

37. After federal troops successfully defended New Ulm and Fort Ridgely, Colonel Sibley sent troops out from Fort Ridgely, led by either Hiram P. Grant or Joseph R. Brown (this is a matter of some dispute), to bury settlers who had been killed near Beaver Creek and Birch Coulee, and to determine the whereabouts of the Dakotas. On September 1, these troops camped at Birch Coulee. Before dawn the next day, the Dakotas attacked the camp. From 16 miles away at Fort Ridgely, Sibley heard the fighting and sent Colonel McPhail with reinforcements. The Battle of Birch Coulee was the bloodiest engagement of the campaign for the Minnesota volunteers. They lost seventeen men and at least ninety horses, along with forty-three men severely wounded. *Massacre in Minnesota*, 167–69; *Dakota War*, 40–44. A number of accounts are in *Dakota Eyes*.

Col. Henry H. Sibley.
(Lincoln Financial
Foundation Collection)

batteries, (bear in mind, in a secure safe position) and opened upon the hellish crew. This was the cannonading that was so distinctly heard at the fort, but the company that had been so fiercely attacked were not relieved from their precarious situation until our arrival at the scene of action, and with a loss of 13 killed & 49 wounded. The whole force then headed for the fort, where they arrived about midnight pretty well tired out, having marched about 50 miles since morning.

Wednesday, September 3, 1862. Quite cloudy morning. Laid in and about camp most of the day, recruiting, went into fort and inspected it, took observations, bought some bakers bread, fresh, this was quite a rarity, the first since leaving Ft. Snelling, and with [it] did I listen to the narratives of those who [were] stationed in, and took part in the siege. Think of the red devils stripped, nearly naked, painted and covered with grass and flowers, and crawling on their bellies towards the fort, and then shoot their flaming arrows into the fort, and at times set buildings on fire, and then with daring bravery, some one would ascend, exposed to their fire, and with water quench the fire. Also made some improvements about the tent.

Thursday, September 4, 1862. Quite a cloudy morning. Was detailed for guard for the first time. My career, really as a soldier, has at last commenced. This is one of the most important duties, and this day was a thorough initiation, as we had quite a sprinkling of rain. Several reports from the scouts that large parties of indians are prowling around the camp and consequently the train which left the fort this morning returned, and during the night were cautioned to be quiet, though wide-awake and ready for an alarm or any emergency.

Friday, September 5, 1862. The rain purifying the air and made it much cooler, though the weather was beautiful. Went to the office (Post) as usual, and felt much gratified at the receipt of a letter from home, what [illegible word] a tendency to more satisfy—to cure one of that uneasiness, restlessness, and make a good & obedient, dutiful soldier than to know that you are remembered by dear ones behind. It cheers the very soul.

Saturday, September 6, 1862. This morning got up early, had a good bath, dressed up in my best soldier rig, and attended religious services at the fort. There was quite a large attendance, and considerable spirit was manifested, quite an interesting meeting. About noon towards the West on the prairie an object was descried by the sentinel on post, and was immediately communicated to H'd Qrs as it approached. It was found to be an indian on horseback carrying a flag of truce, probably with dispatches from the chiefs of the bands who were engaged in the massacre, and all our inquisitive propensities were aroused, eager to catch the first reason for his daring approach, some mere pretense probably & with a desire of estimating our force. They are treacherous dogs.

Sunday, September 7, 1862. Beautiful morning. Received orders from H^d Qrs to "fall in" and in we fell, and merely for the purpose of gratifying the wishes of this savage, who, a short time after the command had formed two lines, marched in company with Genl Sibley Comd'g and Staff, through, how ridiculous. Is this savage wild-man of the prairies capable of judging of our strength, or was this display for the purpose of amusing him. After dismissal the indian was escorted outside of the lines with his flag of truce.

Monday, September 8, 1862. Beautiful day. Nothing worthy of note in reference to indians, or their whereabouts. Rec'd orders from Col Comdg to fall in for drill, and in a short time armed and accoutered we were marched to the drill ground, first taking up the first & second parts of Caseys Infty Tactics.[38] We generally succeeded [as] well as expected,

---

38. Silas Casey, *Infantry Tactics*, 2 vols. (New York: D. Van Nostrand, 1862).

Col. Stephen Miller. (Minnesota Historical Society)

but the Capts & Lieuts being as green soldiers as any, many were the unsoldierly disputes as to the construction, Corpl Harrison[39] often being allowed to dispute with the Capt, and sometimes succeeded in convincing him[40] that he was right, he had studied, familiarized himself and from observations understood different movements practically. Now a

    39. Samuel H. Harrison (1837–1909), a native of Vermont, was a corporal in Co. B, 7th Minnesota Infantry, until his discharge on May 10, 1864, for promotion to lieutenant in the 65th USCT.
    40. Buswell originally started writing "the Ca" but then wrote "him" over it.

few words in reference to our field & Staff officers, as our company had been assigned a place in the 7th Infty, Company "B" with Col Stephen Miller[41] formerly of the 1st Minn as our leader, a real war horse, with a voice loud & commanding, next Lt Col Wm R. Marshall[42] who enlisted for the first time in this regiment as a high-private, then Major George Bradley,[43] the rotund, the consequences of using too much lager, as I am told. Surgeons, Smith[44] & Ames,[45] Chaplain O. P. Light[46] & Adjutant J. K. Arnold,[47] a list of men, who in my estimation are well calculated to fill those honorable, responsible positions, who I trust would not shrink from danger where duty called them.

Tuesday, September 9, 1862. Continues to be very pleasant. Was unexpectedly detailed for guard and reported prompt, was marched to Head Qrs, guard divided, and I was fortunate enough to form one of the camp guards. On guard, what an excellent place for concentrating ones thoughts and on the past, the present and reveries of the bright prospects

---

41. Col. Stephen Miller (1816–1881), a native of Pennsylvania, commanded the 7th Minnesota Infantry. He was elected the fourth governor of Minnesota in 1863 and served from 1864 to 1866. Miller would ensure that there was no drunkenness or frivolity among the Minnesota soldiers during the execution on December 26. *38 Nooses*, 212–13, 227–29.

42. William Rainey Marshall (1825–1896), a native of Missouri, enlisted as a private in the 8th Minnesota Infantry but was promoted to lieutenant colonel of the 7th Minnesota Infantry in August 1862. He became colonel of the regiment in November 1863. Following the war, he served as the fifth governor of Minnesota from 1866 to 1870. In 1862, he was a member of the military commission that tried the Dakotas. *38 Nooses*, 166.

43. George Bradley (1832–1879), a native of Maine, was a lawyer who served as speaker of the Minnesota house of representatives from 1857 to 1858. He joined the 7th Minnesota Infantry as a major and rose to the rank of lieutenant colonel.

44. Lucius B. Smith (1824–1864) was an assistant surgeon for the 7th Minnesota Infantry. He was killed when his division was ambushed by Confederate general Nathan Bedford Forrest's troops the day before the Battle of Tupelo.

45. Albert A. Ames (1842–1911) was an assistant surgeon in the 9th Minnesota Infantry.

46. Oliver P. Light (1828–1904) served as a sergeant in the 6th Minnesota Infantry before becoming chaplain of the 7th Minnesota Infantry.

47. John K. Arnold (1842–1906) was adjutant of the 7th Minnesota Infantry.

Lt. Col. William R. Marshall. (Minnesota Historical Society)

in the future. Quite a long train consisting of army stores arrived today from St Peter, an extensive preparation, probably for a campaign.[48]

Wednesday, September 10, 1862. Quite a cloudy morning. Crawled out quite early and went out to the drove of cattle and milked a cow, this drove having come in a few days ago, quite a luxury. It rained some during the day, flooded the ground, and our camp being on somewhat sidling ground, consequently we got some of our things wet. Two more redskins came into camp today, bringing with them four persons that they had recently taken captives, who were here released from captivity.

Thursday, September 11, 1862. This morning the air is rather raw and somewhat chilly. The bloody savages left camp and returned to the force they had left. This I did not believe in, take no notice whatever of a flag of truce, give them no quarter. Is there such a thing on record as that they ever respected a flag of truce.

Friday, September 12, 1862. The weather still remains quite cloudy and damp, although our company was put through in the manual. Towards

---

48. St. Peter is a journey of more than forty miles from Fort Ridgely.

noon a battalion of 250 men, members of the 3ᵈ Regᵗ Minn Infty, recently taken prisoners at Murfreesboro, Tennessee, or surrendered by the Col (Lester)[49] of the regiment to the Johnnies, and according to the laws of war, no quarter is given to soldiers taken prisoners, having been paroled and not exchanged, and more troops being needed in the indian campaign, these were sent, and consequently are pretty wild, almost unmanageable.

Saturday, September 13, 1862. The sky was all clear this morning, being much cooler, but prospects of pleasant weather. At drill hour we formed company and took our daily exercise in the manual & company movements, quite healthy as well as useful and of benefit to a soldier, and I am learning the movements with ease & dispatch. No news of importance from the front.

Sunday, September 14, 1862. Awoke up this morning and found it was raining quite hard. Was detailed for guard duty and at the required time was reported at Hᵈ Qrs.

Monday, September 15, 1862. Some pleasanter than yesterday, weather quite cool. Relieved from my post at the usual hour and immediately went to my tent and practiced cleaning my gun & accoutrements. A very long train arrived direct from St Peter, and I suppose that this expedition will take their departure soon.

Tuesday, September 16, 1862. Quite a rainy day. Drilled a short time in the afternoon. This is only just an inkling of what hardships & exposures we will be subject to before our military career is ended.

Wednesday, September 17, 1862. The long-roll beat at an early hour this morning, and all was excitement within and without, and instanter every man had his accoutrements on and rifle in hand sprung into the ranks,

49. Henry C. Lester (1832–1902), a native of New York, was a captain in the 1st Minnesota Infantry before being promoted to colonel of the 3rd Minnesota Infantry. He was dismissed from the service in December 1862 for having surrendered his regiment to Nathan Bedford Forrest at Murfreesboro, Tennessee, on July 13, 1862. Forrest had deceived Lester into thinking that he had a larger force than he actually did. See "Curator's Choice," *Minnesota History* 59 (Summer 2005): 268. A recent study demonstrates that Lester was essentially forced to surrender by his brigade commander. See Joseph C. Fitzharris, *The Hardest Lot of Men: The Third Minnesota Infantry in the Civil War* (Norman: University of Oklahoma Press, 2019), 4, 94–99.

Col. William Crooks. (Minnesota Historical Society)

but as there was a false alarm, we were shortly dismissed, and in a very few moments we were again in dreamland at a few knots at least per hour. Day rather misty, but took our regular exercise in drilling.

Thursday, September 18, 1862. Pleasant morning. The roll called quite early, and we received orders to be ready to at a moments warning to march to Lac-Qui-Parle on the Minnesota River, above Yellow Medicine, and in compliance therewith, tents were immediately struck and packed, and everything was put in readiness to move. The great expedition at last was about to move in search of indians and the hundreds of captives—white & half-breeds with them, and after taken [taking?] our frugal, hastily cooked dinner—the assembly sounded and in a short time we were in line with wagons loaded, and at 2 o'clock we departed, filing down the hill into the timber, which skirts the river, across the river, and on to the broad expanse of prairie, and which lies on the right bank of the river for some considerable distance, being a portion of the Sioux Reservation, which for ten miles in width and one hundred miles in length along the river, a rich, fertile tract, which at the expense of the Government, has been divided into small parcels, which are in a partial state of cultivation,

"Sioux Squaw and Pappoose."
(Library of Congress)

and with buildings upon them are apportioned amongst the indians, and supplied with a good stock of farming utensils. We found these farms all deserted, their homes burnt, their squaws & papooses sent westward out of danger, and the men with breach-cloth and club were on the war-path. The 6th Regt Col Crooks[50] comd'g was in advance with a small force of scouts & cavalry, the train came next with the remnant of the 3d Regt Maj Welch[51] comd'g as guard, and the proud old 7th brought up the rear with

50. Col. William Crooks (1832–1907), a native of New York, commanded the 6th Minnesota from 1862 until he was discharged along with his regiment in 1865. Crooks was a well-known railroad engineer who would later serve in both houses of the Minnesota legislature. In 1862, he was a member of the military commission that tried the Dakotas. *38 Nooses*, 166.

51. With the officers of the 3rd Minnesota Infantry being held in Confederate prisons, the regiment was commanded by Maj. Abraham Edward Welch (1839–1864) of the 4th Minnesota Infantry. Under the terms of their parole, the 3rd Minnesota could not fight against the Confederates until they were formally exchanged, but they could fight against the Dakotas in Minnesota. See Fitzharris, *Hardest Lot of Men*, 101–10.

a small battery of three field pieces. Marched five miles and camped near Lone-Tree Lake, a beautiful sheet of pure water on [the] Reservation.

Friday, September 19, 1862. Quite pleasant morning, but remained camped all day by this beautiful lake, for what purpose small fry know not, and took the opportunity to wash some clothes and go in bathing.

Saturday, September 20, 1862. Another beautiful morning and at an early hour were ordered to strike tents and prepare for our march onward. Moved about eight miles and halted by the roadside to take our noon rest and lunch, and an hour after received the order forward, having become somewhat refreshed, and moved about three miles and camped for the night, and with dispatch our tents were up and supper cooking.

Sunday, September 21, 1862. Moved out of camp at the usual hour and marched fifteen miles further to Red Wood Agency on the Minnesota River. Quite a number of the buildings had been [missing word], and others pretty well riddled. Below the village, which is built on a high hill, is the ferry, where about a month since (Aug 18th) Capt Marsh[52] was crossing with his company "B" of the 5th Minn Inft, when a large body of indians, who being aware of their presence had previously ambushed themselves, and at this critical moment while the company were in an almost defenseless position, attacked them from both sides of the river, and only two I learn escaped unharmed—24 killed & 5 wounded—to tell the tale. We found some excellent springs of pure limestone water trickling from the sides of the hill on which rests the village.

Monday, September 22, 1862. Pleasant morning. Roll-call early, got breakfast & started out of camp, indians ahead, several being seen by the scouts, who are always wide-awake. Camped at 2 o'clock at Wood Lake, there being a heavy grove of timber about it, three miles from Yellow Medicine, and two bridges on the road to that place were burning on our arrival here.

Tuesday, September 23, 1862. Reveille beat this morning at 4 o'clock in order to be ready to march early in accordance with orders from H^d Qrs, and we had just partaken of our breakfast when a party of indians

---

52. Capt. John S. Marsh (1829–1862) of the 5th Minnesota Infantry, Co. B, drowned in the Minnesota River while attempting to escape from Indians in August 1862. For more on his death, see *38 Nooses*, 27, 34–35; *Dakota Eyes*, 84, 93.

attacked a squad of the 3ᵈ Regt, who were in a wagon going up to Yellow Medicine for the purpose of getting some potatoes, when about a half a mile from camp. The driver turned the team about and started them on the run towards us, the indians throwing a volley after them. The longroll beat, the whole force were immediately in line awaiting orders. In the meantime the indians were coming out from every valley and hiding place in large numbers, front, rear and on all sides. The 3ᵈ Regt, always eager for the contest,[53] started out on the double quick and without orders, and in spite of the many orders of the col comd'g to remain quiet, until ordered, they moved boldly, bravely, with their front presented to the enemy. Now they cross the valley, and up the other side, and at the top were met by the wily foe, and who were reinforced to such an extent, that the gallant 3ᵈ boys were unable to withstand the fire, therefore retreated slowly and in order leaving several of their dead & wounded on the field to be cruelly, barbarously mutilated by them, and 2000 men remained in camp, not as reinforcements as we eagerly wished, but as witnesses. But at this critical moment the 7ᵗʰ Regt were ordered out as a support, on double-quick, two of the six-pounders were brought into position at the front and one in rear flank, and companys B & A were ordered to support the former, and while we lay in front of the pieces, they were groaning and belching fire & ball over our heads and amongst the devils, who were hooting and with the most hellish demonical yell, which had more of a tendency to cause panic than their fire. Shortly we were ordered to charge, which was done with a tremendous yell, the cannons taking a new position, arriving at the edge of the little valley, down which winds [a] stream of excellent water. There were many pretty severe claps of musketry, and occasionally, through the columns of smoke, could we see a redskin bite the dust. On we went up the hill, the other side of the brook, they scatteringly retreating, with about 30 killed and 40 wounded, and probably several more, as there is a superstition existing among them that they will never prosper if their dead are left in battle, so they often recklessly expose themselves to the fire of an enemy to carry away their dead, and our loss amounts

---

53. Fighting in Minnesota offered the 3rd Minnesota a chance for redemption. Despite their previous surrender, Sibley saw them as "disciplined" when compared with the "raw" recruits like Buswell's 7th Minnesota. At Wood Lake, they fought with great intensity to "redeem . . . their wounded honor" and to "protect the people from further outrages." See Fitzharris, *Hardest Lot of Men*, 109, 113–21.

to 4 killed and between 30 & 40 wounded, Major Welch of the 3ᵈ Regt being among the latter, and then left for camp, having been out about two hours. Thus ended my first experience in active warfare.

The hostile indians were estimated at 1500, mostly armed with shotguns, from which they threw leaden slugs of about an ounce weight, and a few were mounted on ponies. Took our dinner in quiet, and remained in camp here the remainder of the day. Towards evening two of the indians with flags of truce presented themselves before our picket lines for admittance, on a visit of business or curiosity to the Gen'l. After transacting their business they were escorted out of the lines and West they went to relate what they had seen within our lines. Such persons are generally hoodwinked, I believe, in order to prevent them taking details.[54]

Wednesday, September 24, 1862. Another fine morning. No orders to march today. Another flag of truce came into camp—and the report comes second handed from headquarters that the prisoners, some 300 in number held captives by the indians, will be delivered into our possession, and it is also rumored with probably some foundation, that there will be a general engagement soon. During the afternoon strengthened the rifle-pits around camp, and be prepared for any attack the enemy may make as treachery presents itself most prominent amongst the hostile foe, and extra guard was detailed, which nearly doubled it.

This morning had roll-call early, broke camp and resumed our march. Passed through Yellow Medicine, the Upper Agency, in quest of provisions, as this being an agency from which the annuities had been dealt out to the different tribes, consequently is a rendezvous for all classes of sharpers, and so a town of some dozen good buildings, mostly brick, but which were at present in ruins. Crossed the Yellow Medicine just above the town, the long bridge here had been burnt, also a saw mill. Went a short distance and camped, marching eight miles.

Thursday, September 25, 1862. Was one of the detail on picket last night, station on a point overlooking the valley. At early morning, I being on duty, an arrow passed my left leg and stuck in the bank. The two other pickets lying down were notified and we comᵈ firing in the brush—and the Indian fell—and was brot in—I took the arrow and a ring from the dead injuns finger as trophies.

---

54. For accounts of the Battle of Wood Lake, see *38 Nooses*, 155–56; *Dakota Eyes*, chap. 9; *Dakota War*, 59–63; *Dakota Uprising*, 174–75.

Friday, September 26, 1862. Pleasant as usual. Took an early breakfast and started at sunrise for Red-Iron Village, the camp of friendly indians, so-called under the control of the chief Red-Iron,[55] where it is reported the white and half-breed captives[56] are, the chief Red-Iron having succeeded in inducing Little Crow to allow them to remain with [him], without a thought that he would or intended to deliver them up to the Gen'l Comd'g. Arrived at the camp and camped about 2 o'clock P.M. near the river, and at once a guard was thrown around the indian camp, which was quite large, comprising some 400 tepees, with their warriors, squaws & papooses, and a large number of prisoners, who were so rejoiced at our approach that they acted more like insane than sane persons, and were ready to press us to their *bussumes*, and it was with difficulty that we resisted it, and from them we received information that Little Crow and his band with some others, and a few prisoners, had left the day before [for] the great prairies of the West.

Saturday, September 27, 1862. This morning got up early, and at about 9 o'clock A.M. a small force went into the indian camp (I one of the detail) and released the prisoners. Most of the females had been obliged by the indians to take off their citizens dress and don the squaw costume. They presented a sad, sorrowful appearance whose countenances although at this moment lit up with joy, traces of sorrow were yet visible. How thankful to know & feel that they were at last delivered from the hands of the devlish savages, with their lives, but having suffered almost death, dishonor and disgrace, and the Quakers of the Quaker City may cry Lo! the poor indian, dis-believing that there was even an indian war in existance on the frontier of the North Star State. Would that they had to experience one days suffering that those women have been subjected [to]. Soldiers have you sisters—cry vengeance and seek the life blood of

---

55. Chief Red Iron, also known as Mazaduta or Ma-za-sha, led a village located north of the Upper Sioux Agency. During the Dakota War, he was a leader of "friendly" Indians and would not allow Little Crow and his men to pass by his village. Following the surrender of the friendly Indians and the prisoners at Camp Release, Red Iron acted as a scout for Sibley as part of a plan to persuade the remaining Mdewankaton warriors to surrender. He also served as a "medicine man" for the Dakota prisoners at Camp Lincoln. See *Massacre in Minnesota*, 177–78, 187, 217, 242, 335.

56. For more on the captives, see *Dakota War*, 22–23, 63–67; Mary Butler Renville, *A Thrilling Narrative of Indian Captivity: Dispatches from the Dakota War* (1863; reprint, Lincoln: University of Nebraska Press, 2012).

the miscreants, be eager & watchful. They were taken to our camp, and tents were erected for them, and many were the soldiers who congregated around those tents and with fixed attention and eyes opened listen while they narrate their experience as prisoners. They numbered 105 whites, mostly women & children, and 165 half-breeds, and one negro,[57] who it is said, is more of a savage than those with him and boasts of killing some 16 persons. Some 60 indians were taken prisoners, brought to our camp and placed on trial.

Sunday, September 28, 1862. Pleasant morning. Several more indians arrested and put in the guard house with the others. The negro we arrested yesterday is reported to be the son of an indian squaw and an negro father, and lived amongst the indians at Lower Agency. When the outbreak occurred he donned the breach-cloth and was the most fierce, bloodthirsty character amongst them, although many of the rumors may be untrue owing to the prejudice existing by many against him. No church today, but the day was observed by most [of] the men through camp.

Monday, September 29, 1862. Still quite pleasant. Nothing of importance took place through the day.

---

57. Buswell pasted a 1909 newspaper clipping in his diary about Gusa (Joseph) Godfrey (ca. 1831–1909), "the negro whose name struck terror to the stout hearts of old pioneers in this region" and who was "hated and despised by redskin and paleface alike for his part in the Sioux massacre and its aftermath." The article recounted Godfrey's participation in the killing of white settlers and how he "turned state's evidence" to save his own life while sending "thirty-nine of his comrades to die on the gallows at Mankato."

As a young slave, Godfrey had been an errand boy for Henry Sibley. His was the first trial in Sibley's military commission, where Godfrey testified that one Dakota warrior told him "that I must fight with the Indians, and do the same they did, or I would be killed." Although Godfrey was convicted and sentenced to be executed, his testimony in eighty-two other cases proved useful—even though much of what he said was hearsay—and his sentence was commuted to ten years in prison (although he was pardoned and released in 1866). Historian Gary Clayton Anderson writes that Godfrey's leadership in the massacre is "very suspect," although he "seemed to be at the forefront as the party moved south." See *Massacre in Minnesota*, 94, 217–19, 227–28, 253; *Dakota Eyes*, 85–92; *38 Nooses*, 167–68, 192, 220–21, 229; Walt Bachman, *Northern Slave, Black Dakota: The Life and Times of Joseph Godfrey* (Bloomington, Minn.: Pond Dakota Press, 2013).

Gusa (Joseph) Godfrey. (Minnesota Historical Society)

Tuesday, September 30, 1862. Beautiful morning. Got our breakfast and immediately afterwards went by permission to visit the indians in[58] as they live in camp. We found it rather a filthy, nasty hole, and a lazerone[59] set. At about 11 o'clock P.M. the long-roll beat, and all were aroused from a sound sleep, and with accoutrements on, and rifle in hand, each company were soon in line, and "by the right flank," double quick reached the line, passed through, and into the indian camp, and then we were informed, too late, that it was a false alarm, and shortly were in camp and break ranks with a rush to our tents, and were again embraced in the arms of Morpheus, and all around was quiet with occasionally a halt, who comes there? from the sentinels, who were watchfully pacing to & fro.

Wednesday, October 1, 1862. Continues to be very pleasant. As some [of] the boys are outside of the lines everyday, scouting and seeking what they might devour, there were several went out to-day with thirty two horse teams, and towards evening returned with them loaded with

---

58. Buswell may have accidentally omitted a word after "in."
59. A lazzarone is a beggar from the southern Italian city of Naples.

potatoes & corn which the indians had buried on departing from their homes, and were found and dug up by our men, all of which we were very thankful for as army rations were beginning to be scarce.

Thursday, October 2, 1862. This morning we arose early, it having been intimated that we would before night be sworn to Uncle Sam for three years, which proved to be true as after breakfast were ordered to "fall in" and Lt Haight[60] Com of Musters soon had us united with the U.S. Army, in the great cause "Liberty, Union one & inseparable."[61]

Friday, October 3, 1862. We were again ordered into line and received, according to contract, our $25. advance bounty & first three months pay, which was very acceptable to us, and made the sutlers mouths water, but I think those foolish who will purchase trash of these goughes [gougers?] at such exorbitant prices, unless they have articles actually needed by them. But at this time our army rations nearly exhausted, no flour or hard tack, no sugar, a small ration of coffee, and not a particle of salt, this state of affairs we have long expected, and what bread, such as we have is made of meal from the indian corn that had been excavated and was ground in a large iron coffee-mill belonging to our company, which was obtained at Ft Snelling. This mill, singular enough, supplied the whole command with bread-stuff, and this with potatoes & fresh beef without any salt, constituted the food upon which we were to sustain life until the train loaded with rations shall arrive. Jolly old soldiering.

Saturday, October 4, 1862. Still pleasant. Enjoying ourselves generally grinding our corn and eating corn cakes. About 5 o'clock P.M. the assembly blew and at once we fell in and marched out on the color line formed on the centre for dress parade, lion-visaged Col Miller commanding. Were exercised in the manual, 1st Sergts reported officers to the front, parade being dismissed, they salute, any directions of the Col are here given, and a signal from the several company officers, the First Sergts march the companies to their quarters, and are dismissed. Thus ended our first dress-parade.

---

60. Probably Edward Haight (dates unknown), lieutenant and aide-de-camp, who mustered in the 6th Minnesota Infantry about this same time. See *Minnesota in Wars*, 312.

61. This was said by Sen. Daniel Webster of Massachusetts in 1830 while in debate with Sen. Robert Hayne of South Carolina. Webster's exact words were, "Liberty and Union, now and forever, one and inseparable!"

Sunday, October 5, 1862. Beautiful Sunday morning. Attended church, or rather religious services under the canopy of heaven. Wrote some letters to my friends behind. Had dress parade as usual. To[ok] a walk down by the river. The camp is named Camp Release[62] by the Gen'l, appropriate to the release of the prisoners.

Monday, October 6, 1862. A beautiful day. Were ordered out to drill at certain hours, and afterwards went up to prisoners camp to talk with them in regard to those many long, weary days they spent with the indians. They were completely heart-rending.[63] Quite a number of the boys were assembled in our company street intent on examining a pistol of a very curious character, carelessness as it was loaded, and it discharged its contents, hitting one D. Pierson,[64] member of our company, on the lower rib, which luckily caused it to rebound, the only damage being to knock him down. This is a lesson, much benefit is to be derived by it. Dress parade as usual at 5 o'clock.

Tuesday, October 7, 1862. Pleasant as usual. Some twenty indians, members of Little-Crows Band, came into camp surrendering themselves and five captives, wishing no longer to continue the war against us. Some of these too, are bad indians. They were given a camp ground and at short notice had their tepees erected, and were caged.

Wednesday, October 8, 1862. Beautiful morning, and pleasant all day. Drill at 10 A.M. as usual. No army rations, yet we are able to sustain life by eating indians food, and will fat on it. After dinner some 85 men, members of the 3ᵈ Minn Inft, arrived in camp from Ft Ridgely, mounted on good horses, and were well armed and equipped.

Thursday, October 9, 1862. Still the weather remains pleasant, what a beautiful fall. Minnesota will excel in this respect. Orders were received

---

62. Located near present-day Montevideo, Camp Release was the site where the Dakota freed 107 white and 162 mixed-blood captives in the final days of September 1862. By early October, some twelve hundred Dakota men, women and children were held there, and acts of cruelty took place against them. The first twenty-nine military trials took place there. *Dakota Uprising,* 202; *38 Nooses,* 179–80, 184, 191.

63. For a detailed analysis of the horrific experiences of white captives, which have been called a "fate worse than death," see *Massacre in Minnesota,* chap. 8.

64. Douglass J. Pierson (1842–1926), a native of Illinois, was a private in the 7th Minnesota Infantry, Co. B.

this day from H^d Qrs to build a jail, 20 x 60 feet, with an ell[65] 20 x 40 ft, the material to be of logs from the timber that skirts the river, for the purpose of containing the indians, and men were detailed from each company to prosecute the work.

Friday, October 10, 1862. Another beautiful day. The respective regiments were called out to drill as usual, and one man was accidentally shot, one of the mens guns being loaded went off and took effect. Had a frost this morning, the first of the season.

Saturday, October 11, 1862. Got up and crawled out this morning finding the ground covered with a white frost, and some water standing near was [illegible word] over with a thin ice. A man in the Tigers,[66] now company G, 7th Reg^t, shot himself through the hand, the general opinion is purposely, probably somewhat homesick.[67] At 6 o'clock P.M. the 6th Regt Col Crooks and the Rangers marched over to the indian camp, arrested 105 warriors, and took them to the jail.[68] Orderly Eastman was arrested per order Captain Comd'g Co. The long looked for train comprising 58 teams well laden with army rations and 120 head of cattle arrived, which caused a general rejoicing throughout the camp, having got tired and some were sick living on corn & fresh-beef without salt.

Sunday, October 12, 1862. Beautiful Sunday morning. Had an inspection in the forenoon, and after dismissal went over to camp of 3^d Regt

65. An ell is an extension to a building.

66. Buswell likely was referring to the Le Sueur Tigers, a unit organized in August 1862; however, they became Co. G of the 10th Minnesota Infantry, not the 7th Minnesota Infantry.

67. The company roster in *Annual Report of the Adjutant General* does not indicate the name of this soldier. Soldiers sometimes wounded themselves in attempts to be discharged from the service.

68. Historian Gary Clayon Anderson writes, "As the sun went down on October 11, the general ordered several hundred infantry troops to surround Camp Release and disarm the new group of four hundred men and women who had surrendered after October 4.... Over the next few days, some 101 Mdewakanton Dakota men at Camp Release and another 236 at Yellow Medicine were chained together, with the right leg of one man connected to the left of another.... The Dakota men in chains numbered 337, but only twenty-nine of this group had faced the military commission; a number of these had been released." See *Massacre in Minnesota*, 221–22.

and listened to an excellent sermon by its chaplain. I weighed 160 pounds this day.

Monday, October 13, 1862. A very cold raw morning. Received a new order the substance of which being to drill one hour before breakfast. After dinner our company received orders to be ready to march at 12 o'clock midnight, to what post we were bound was maintained in silence, so at once everything was placed in marching condition, and then for a short nap.

Tuesday, October 14, 1862. Before 12 o'clock we were all aroused from our dreamy slumbers at the appointed time in company with about 100 men from 3ᵈ Regt Inft, 50 cavalry, 50 men from 6ᵗʰ Regt Inft, 2 indians as guides, and a six pound howitzer, all under command of the gallant Col Marshall, with six days rations. Started towards the West,[69] took breakfast at Lac-Qui-Parle Crossing. Here remains a log-house in which resided an indian missionary before the indian war. At the outbreak he and wife were killed, and the wifes sister taken prisoner.[70] Marched 35 miles and camped on Red-Iron Creek, 6 miles from the Dakota Line, the Dakota Ridge towering up in the distance. Was on guard as it happened causing me [illegible word] fatigue.

Wednesday, October 15, 1862. Aroused early, struck tents, took our scanty half cooked breakfast and without delay were again dashing along. Crossed the line at 11 o'clock, over a fertile rolling prairie, well watered, but with great scarcity of timber. Marched about 30 miles and camped by a spring brook of excellent pure water, skirted by a grove, dense and beautiful. Four indians were seen and taken prisoner by the scouts, they report more in the vicinity, all on their way down to the big-camp (Red Irons). During the night indians were heard prowling around camp. The scouts went out and captured six more, but with considerable difficulty, knifes being brandished at a great rate.

69. Under command of Lt. Col. William R. Marshall, Co. B of the 7th Minnesota, Co. G of the 6th Minnesota, and a mounted detachment of the 3rd Minnesota headed west toward the Missouri River. Starting about midnight, the force marched thirty-five miles on the first day, making it close to the Dakota Territory. See *Minnesota in Wars*, 352.

70. Possibly Amos Huggins (1833–1862), reputed to be the only person killed near Lac Qui Parle. Huggins's wife, Sophia, however, was not killed—so Buswell may have heard false information. See *Massacre in Minnesota*, 206; *Through Dakota Eyes*, 247–48.

Thursday, October 16, 1862. Another fine morning. Started at daylight, passed down the coteau on the indian trail, very wide and evidences of its recent usage, then between Twin Lakes, beautiful but yet lonely, not a tree to be seen. The scouts report that the in[dians] camped here last night, they caused considerable excitement. Col Marshall here took the cavalry, howitzer & scouts, and pushed ahead faster than the infantry were capable. About 3 P.M. crossed a branch of the Sioux River, rather poor water, and on reaching the top of this branch of the coteau espied a lake in the distance, dazzling before the setting sun. Capt Valentine[71] of 6th Regt, Senior Officer, now comd'g, decided to move to the lake and camp.[72] Night came, the men being fatigued began to scatter, but continued to march until [al]most 10 P.M. when we camped near a pool of stagnant water on the barren prairie, hard tack & raw pork to satisfy our hunger and lay down to rest, and for two hours later men were coming in, marching about 35 miles.

Friday, October 17, 1862. Upon getting up in this morning, saw that we were yet about four miles from the lake, and felt much better with only sore feet to trouble me. Marched about 2 miles and crossed the Big-Sioux, though not very big here. Found a few willows and proceeded to cook some coffee, rations getting scarce, as usual under such circumstances, the 3ᵈ boys having eaten theirs all up or scattered it, and we having considerable, although we [were] magnanimous in giving them any, but Capt Valentine made us divide. This was the cause of much dissatisfaction amongst some of the men. 8 A.M. No return from the Col as yet. 2 P.M. Picked up a worn out cavalry horse. 4 P.M. Scout came back [and said] that they had been successful in capturing some 25 tepees of indians on ten-mile lake, surrounding and taking them by surprise. Marched about 12 miles and camped on Ten Mile Lake, east end, after camping [and] eating our hard tack, some went into the lake bathing, a beautiful sheet of water with many trees scattered on its banks, and a few proceeded to search the indians, finding several knifes, these with the 21 guns and sword taken from them by the cavalry were placed in the wagons and

---

71. Daniel H. Valentine (1827–1890), a native of Ohio, was captain of the 6th Minnesota Infantry, Co. G.

72. One member of Buswell's company reported that the men were "hoping to camp at Lake Kampeska," near present-day Watertown, South Dakota, "but failed to reach the lake, and bivouacked without wood or water." See *Minnesota in Wars,* 352.

guarded. Provision becoming short, and no means of obtaining any, as what we have must be divided with the indians, the Col Comdg despatched three cavalry men and a guide at 8 P.M. for the camp with orders to send rations without delay.

Saturday, October 18, 1862. Camp Captive, 12 miles west of Sioux River, and 14 miles to James River. Beautiful morning, struck tents, took our scanty meal, and with light hearts turned towards home, stopped to rest and take dinner at the Sioux River, very windy & dusty, marched a short distance further and camped on a branch of the Sioux. A cow was killed today which furnished us with fresh meat, but salt was rather scarce.

Sunday, October 19, 1862. Struck tents and started early, homeward bound. Another straggling indian came in today, he having been fishing while the others were taken. One of the scouts came in reporting having seen a buffalo cow & calf. Crossed the Dakota Ridge about noon, had one cracker and a piece of raw pork for dinner, a strong meal. Camped on one of our old camping grounds.

Monday, October 20, 1862. Arose early, took our scanty meal, and started at sunrise. Five more indians came into camp during the night surrendering themselves. Marched about 25 miles and camped at Lac-Qui-Parle, where we met the looked for train, and had plenty of rations tonight.

Tuesday, October 21, 1862. Started again quite early, and after a very disagreeable march through the dust made by the great prairie fire which preceded us, and arrived at camp at 3 o'clock P.M., immediately commenced putting up the tents, washed up &c. Then met Starr[73] & Jim Pope,[74] members of the 10th Regt Inft, which had been ordered up here. Enjoyed ourselves very much talking over affairs about home and since our last meeting.

Wednesday, October 22, 1862. No roll-call in order to allow us to rest our weary bones, having become quite sore & lame. Had dress-parade in the evening and received orders to march tomorrow morning at 8 o'clock, for what point we know not.

---

73. Ebenezer L. Starr (1838–1908), a native of Massachusetts, was a private in the 10th Minnesota Infantry, Co. C. He was later promoted to corporal. Buswell called him "Ed."

74. Pvt. James R. Pope (1839–1911), a native of Vermont, was a private in the 10th Minnesota Infantry, Co. C. According to the diary entry for May 2, 1864, Pope may have been a romantic interest of Buswell's sister Lucy.

Thursday, October 23, 1862. Struck tents, got breakfast, packed up and at 10 o'clock started in the following order.

1—The Renville Rangers.
2—The Artillery & train
3—The 3^d Reg't & train.
4—The 7th Reg't & train.
5—The 170 indians guarded by cavalry, mostly 10th Regt
6—The 6th Regt & train.
7—The Howitzer & Rear guard,

and marched towards home to Yellow Medicine 24 miles, and camped at this once pleasant, but now desolate village.

Friday, October 24, 1862. Got up early and at sunrise were enroute for Red Wood, 22 miles, where we arrived and camped near the large indian camp, guarded by two companies of the 10th Regt. Having got our tents up, Hayes[75] & Hopson[76] came over to see us and also Starr, and a joyful meeting was this. The sutler received an unusual run of custom that evening, oysters, lobsters, &c.

Saturday, October 25, 1862. Did not start as early as usual, bid good bye to the Beaver boys and started for Lower Agency, 8 miles, and camped near the old camping ground.

Sunday, October 26, 1862. Sunday morning, no preaching was held today, having not got well settled, took a walk around the place, most of the buildings burnt. Saw the ruins of the Episcopal Church erected by Bishop Whipple—principally for the indians benefit—and which was destroyed by them.[77]

Monday, October 27, 1862. Today our company was divided into messes, and a large mess-house was erected for the purpose of cooking provisions. Capt Hopsons Co arrived having in charge 207 prisoners.

75. James W. Hayes (1822–1902), a native of Maine, was a private in the 10th Minnesota Infantry, Co. C. He was eventually promoted to sergeant.

76. Albert S. Hopson (1823–1910) was first lieutenant of the 10th Minnesota Infantry, Co. C. He would later be promoted to the rank of captain.

77. Henry B. Whipple (1822–1901) was consecrated the first Episcopal bishop of the Diocese of Minnesota in 1859. Throughout his career he ministered to the Dakota population of Minnesota and in December 1862 he pleaded with President Lincoln to spare the Dakota Indians who were sentenced to be hanged. For more on Whipple's background, see *38 Nooses*, chap. 4.

Tuesday, October 28, 1862. Very pleasant morning—our regt. rec'd orders to have company drill, a flag staff was raised today and flag hoisted—13 guns fired.

Wednesday, October 29, 1862. Very fine day—we went at work today and raised our tent, built a sod foundation with a fire place, quite comfortable. Getting too well fixed to stay long.

Thursday, October 30, 1862. Very clear & warm—350 of the 3^d Reg^t Cavalry [Infantry] sent west today on some secret expedition. Capt Kennedy[78] of our regiment tried by a Court-Martial—was on guard today.

Friday, October 31, 1862. Rather cold today, quite a sudden change. Our Reg^t mustered today for pay. Hope the paymaster will make his appearance soon, we are all nearly out of cash.

Saturday, November 1, 1862. Continues cool weather—there was a light snow fell today, the first of the season. General washing day. This is needed bad enough, but many had rather go dirty then [sic] to do such work.

Sunday, November 2, 1862. Sabbath Day—quite cool—had preaching by our Chaplain—the first time that he has preached to us. After dinner went to see Hayes & the rest of the boys of 10th Reg^t.

Monday, November 3, 1862. A fine day. I was appointed cook of our mess. This the first time that I came into the cookship harness—took hold of matters like an old soldier—just imagine myself—master of the cook house—with sleeves rolled up and elbow deep in a pan of dough, for I was a baker also. It was baked—half burnt—& tough, and my messmates pronounced it excellent. Report in camp today that we will soon receive orders to go South.

Tuesday, November 4, 1862. Nothing of importance today, pleasant.

---

78. Capt. John Kennedy was court-martialed for disobedience for going to the Indian camp at Yellow Medicine, Minnesota, for five hours, against his commander's orders, and for conduct prejudicial to good order and military discipline for refusing arrest. He allegedly said to the captain, "You are a damned shitass and you may kiss my backside." He was also charged with being absent without leave for going with several women to Fort Ridgely, which was fifty miles away. He was found guilty of two of the three charges and was dismissed from the service. See Court-Martial Case File KK-516.

Wednesday, November 5, 1862. Rather cool today. Had myself weighed, the scales indicated 175 lbs. Rec'd a letter from my old friend Chas W. Coggin,[79] a citizen.

Thursday, November 6, 1862. Fine day. Two companies of 9th Reg[t] Infy left today for Fort Ridgely. Two deserters rec'd sentence of hard labor & confinement, not very severe.

Friday, November 7, 1862. Fine morning—our mess tent was burnt this morning—caught fire from sheet iron stove—while at breakfast. My overcoat, blankets and shirts burnt up—or ruined, tent destroyed—pretty severe loss. Rec'd a number of letters from home & elsewhere—what should we do without these kind missives to cheer us up while away from home & dear friends.

Saturday, November 8, 1862. Bugle sounds "strike tents" and down they go, rolled up & packed—knapsack packed and before sunrise were on the move towards Ft Ridgely as follows—

    1st   Renville Rangers—
    2d—4 co's 6th Regt Inf
    3d   The indians captives guarded on the flanks by cavalry—
    4th—5 co's 6th Regt Inf
    5th—7th Regt Inf
    6th—Rear Guard

halted for the night and cam[ped][80] near the reservation.

Sunday, November 9, 1862. Pleasant morning. Reveille sounded before daylight, cooked breakfast and started by day light, went through New Ulm about 10 o'clock. I had anticipated some sport passing through so I got permission to ride with Capt Hopsons Cav[81] who were guarding the indians—riding on the flanks. Upon arriving at New Ulm—saw a large crowd of men, women & children all armed with pistols, guns—knives & clubs and a great many with handfuls of rocks. The line of march

---

    79. There were two men named Charles W. Coggin in Lynn, Massachusetts, both of whom were born about 1840.

    80. The corner of the page is torn off; Buswell likely wrote the word "camped" here.

    81. Although Hopson was in an infantry unit, Gen. John Pope ordered Co. C to be mounted on horseback and armed with carbines, which is why Buswell refers to them as cavalry here. See *Minnesota in Wars*, 456.

was calculated to avoid them—but the boisterous crew crossed over to the line and commenced clubbing, knifing & stoning the captive indians while enroute. The cowardly dutchmen,[82] who when attacked filled the wells & cisterns through fear, now while the indians are captives—seek to destroy them as bold as lions. About a half a dozen indians were seriously hurt, but would have liked nothing better than to give the cowards a full volley, and only waited the order.

Passed through a very fine country, crossed the Big Cottonwood about 2 P.M. and camped near the Little Cottonwood. Recd orders that we were not to go South at present. Saw first white woman today. Was detailed on guard. What is there in the life of a soldier in the discharge of duties worse than after marching all day than to sit up—or rather stand up all night on guard, especially when a guard is not at all required.

Monday, November 10, 1862. Fine morning—up at starlight, took our meal and fell in before daylight and started on our march—passed through a very good country, down the wide Minnesota Valley, passed through South Bend, about noon, and camped on the Blue Earth River about a mile from Mankato. Here we shall remain for the present.

Tuesday, November 11, 1862. Some change in the weather, considerable cooler. Thirteen Winnebago Indians were taken and put in the guard house.[83]

Wednesday, November 12, 1862. Very cold morning—rec'd a pass and went to Mankato. Took dinner at the Clifton House. Had a good tramp marching about the city. Sent a letter to my mother.

Thursday, November 13, 1862. Quite cold day—but no severe storms as yet, hope that we will be caged in barracks or go South before they come. Orders issued that no furloughs be allowed at present for a longer time than three days.

Friday, November 14, 1862. Rather cool—but pleasant weather. The actions of the Indians indicated that they were going to rise and attempt to

---

82. Buswell's use of "dutchmen" refers to German immigrants, some of whom abandoned their wives and children when they fled New Ulm. See *Massacre in Minnesota*, 148.

83. Between ten and twelve Winnebago Indians were acquitted by a military commission in November 1862. See Carol Chomsky, "United States-Dakota War Trials: A Study in Military Injustice," *Stanford Law Review* 43 (November 1990): 13, 28, 53.

escape, an extra guard ordered. Four companies ordered to march next Monday to Ft Snelling.

Saturday, November 15, 1862. Warmer with quite a snow squall—was detailed on guard, my station was among the Indians—guns loaded plenty of ammunition, ready for them at any time should they attempt to rise. Had to be quite careful or we would get plenty of graybacks[84] as the Lo's[85] are alive with them. 4 P.M. still snowing. Rec'd orders today that our company would be stationed for the winter at Tivoli, 8 miles east of Mankato and near Winnebago Agency.[86]

Sunday, November 16, 1862. Sunday morning. About 3 inch snow. Two men in Co F our Regt were reprimanded before the regiment on parade for drunkenness—a lasting disgrace to them. Think of being brought up before 600 or 800 men to be dealt with, pretty severe.

Monday, November 17, 1862. Pleasant again. The 6th Reg^t left for their destinations for the winter. The cavalry also left. Capt Hopsons Co went to Ft Ridgely to barrack during the winter, but show is better than that. Was cook again today—and the way the slush was attended to was a caution.

Tuesday, November 18, 1862. Cloudy. Three companies of the 7th Regt left for their stations according to Gen'l Orders. Thirty men of our company left camp today for Tivoli to commence building barracks. Our company appeared on Dress Parade this evening with 15 men. One company of the 10th Minn Inf arrived here.

Wednesday, November 19, 1862. Pleasant but quite a frosty morning. Was on prison guard. Rec'd another overcoat. Rec'd orders to march tomorrow morning.

Thursday, November 20, 1862. Reveille sounded early, tents struck and started at 9 o'clock for our winter home. Stopped in Mankato about one hour, then proceed[ed] through the woods and arrived at our home at 2 P.M. The boys who preceded us had the foundation laid for our barracks, a much better location than we had expected—very few buildings

---

84. Lice.

85. Referring to Dakotas as "Lo's"—meaning Lucifers or Satans—was common. See *Columns of Vengeance*, 68.

86. The Winnebago Agency was located about one mile southeast of present-day St. Clair, Minnesota. *Dakota Uprising*, 304.

in the town, near a grist & sawmill on the Le Sueur River, heavy timber all around. Quartered for the present in an old log house & the school house.

Friday, November 21, 1862. Beautiful morning, Indian summer. Commenced work on the dam, it having went off—in order to get some lumber to complete our barracks. Drew clothing today.

Saturday, November 22, 1862. Fine—worked on barracks all day—Wm Newman[87] came back today. Sent a letter home.

Sunday, November 23, 1862. Pleasant day. Recd a box of good things from the ladies of Stockton. Went to meeting.

Monday, November 24, 1862. Continues fine—worked on barracks.

Tuesday, November 25, 1862. Very cold morning—put roof on the first building, and commenced work on 2^d building. Some of the boys went cranberrying, they got about four bushels. Four of our [men] taken sick with the measles. Am afraid that I may catch it, as I have never had it.

Wednesday, November 26, 1862. Pretty cold day, worked on 2^d building. Rec'd letters.

Thursday, November 27, 1862. Cold chilly morning with about 2 inches snow on the ground and still snowing. Thanksgiving day, but not improved by us.

Friday, November 28, 1862. Pleasanter, warmer, worked on the barracks.

Saturday, November 29, 1862. Pleasant day—some snow during the afternoon. Put roof on the 2^d building. Rec'd orders from H'd Qr's for Capt to grant furloughs, a few at a time.

Sunday, November 30, 1862. Pleasant Sabbath morning, about 4 inches snow fell during the night. 10 of the boys were granted furloughs and started this morning to be gone 15 days. Had meeting in the barracks.

Monday, December 1, 1862. A very cold morning day. Moved into part of the barracks—and pushed work on the others. The Capt started on leave of absence.

---

87. William Newman (born ca. 1841), a native of New York, was a private in the 7th Minnesota Infantry, Co. B.

Tuesday, December 2, 1862. Cold morning—& cold day. Put the roof on 2^d building. Dr Daniels[88] returned today from furlough, shall be glad to see the rest return—then it will come my turn.

Wednesday, December 3, 1862. Pleasant but cool. Completed the 2^d building and the remainder moved in. I built a table for our mess. The barracks were composed of two buildings made of logs with two apartments in each, making 4 messes in the company, one in each apartment, between the two at the west end was the Captains & Lieuts barracks.

Thursday, December 4, 1862. Fine morning, somewhat stormy in afternoon. Did not feel very well today, so did not work. This evening about 9 P.M., after a number of the boys had gone to bunk, a messenger arrived with an order for the entire company to proceed as soon as possible with arms & ammunition to Mankato. Considerable excitement for a short time, but soon the company was in line and moved a part of the time at double quick, being 1 hour & 10 min. in going to Mankato. Upon arriving found that crowds of people thronged the streets, some 300 or 400 had collected & armed were about moving to the indian camp for the purpose of releasing & murdering them. A large number of them were from New Ulm and up the Minnesota and principally Dutch. We went at once to the Indian camp near the Blue Earth River and were stationed with other troops who had arrived from St. Peter, Henderson & other places around the camp. About 12 o'clock the brave dutchmen approached the camp brandishing their clubs, knives & revolvers. Col Miller went out & met them—showed them the force around the camp and who if ordered would fire a volley into them. The dutch consulted a short time and then withdrew.[89]

Friday, December 5, 1862. We were on guard from 12 to 3 o'clock A.M. At 8 A.M., everything being in readiness, the whole camp including the Indians were moved into the city and took up quarters in log barracks erected for the purpose near Higgins Hall. Our company was then dis-

---

88. Jared W. Daniels (1827–1904), a native of New Hampshire, served as an assistant surgeon in the 6th Minnesota Infantry and later in the 2nd Minnesota Cavalry.

89. For accounts of the threats and violence against the Dakota prisoners by the citizens of New Ulm, see *38 Nooses*, 198–200; *Dakota Uprising*, 139; *Dakota Eyes*, 227, 234.

missed and we started for Tivoli about 10 A.M., arriving there about 1 P.M. Day warmer.

Saturday, December 6, 1862. Very clear & pleasant. Very little work of any kind done today, trying to get rested. 5 more of the boys started home on furlough. This day rec'd the company six mule team.

Sunday, December 7, 1862. Fine day. Sabbath—attended services in the school house near the barracks.

Monday, December 8, 1862. Clear pleasant. Have a very bad cold—no work done today by me.

Tuesday, December 9, 1862. Cloudy & warm, looks like more snow. Went to the store with a number of the boys, the store is about a mile away at the corners.

Wednesday, December 10, 1862. Pleasant day. We attended a magician performance given at the school house, had a good time. Recd a letter from home.

Thursday, December 11, 1862. Continues pleasant. Recd a report that 38 Indians[90] are to [be] hung, they having [been] convicted from the 150 prisoners, some are sentenced to prison for life, some for 20 years. Orders rec'd that no more furloughs be rec'd until further orders. This is quite unsatisfactory. We all want the same privilege. There was a dance in the evening at the village and I was invited & attended, had a very good time.

Friday, December 12, 1862. [No entry.]

Saturday, December 13, 1862. Cloudy & rainy—too muddy to do anything, stayed indoors and played old sledge.

Sunday, December 14, 1862. Cloudy morning—snowing before noon—Sabbath, attended services at school house.

Monday, December 15, 1862. Still cloudy, worked in the woods getting out fire wood. P.M. growing cold fast.

---

90. Buswell likely corrected this entry when he wrote the clean copies after the war. Originally 39 Dakota warriors were set to be executed but on December 23 one of the men received a reprieve so that only 38 were hanged. See *Massacre in Minnesota*, 258–59; *38 Nooses*, 227–35.

Tuesday, December 16, 1862. Very cold morning, a slight snow squall, had a bad cold as yet, have tried a number of balsams &c nothing will start it. Capt got back.

Wednesday, December 17, 1862. Pleasant but cold. Had a visit from two Winona gents. Had our first Lyceum this evening. The question, "Has the Negro more reason to complain than the Indian." Recd a letter from home.

Thursday, December 18, 1862. Pleasant & cool—prospects of fine weather. Went a hunting, shot some red squirrels. Recd orders that the Indians would be hung on the 26th inst and our company ordered to report at Mankato early in the morning.

Friday, December 19, 1862. Warm winter day—commenced drill four hours each day. Sent letter home.

Saturday, December 20, 1862. Cool & snowing, drilled as usual.

Sunday, December 21, 1862. Very pleasant, sabbath. Had inspection of arms, knapsacks, &c in the morning, afterwards went to meeting in the school house.

Monday, December 22, 1862. Pleasant morning, had a visit from Sheriff King[91] & others from Winona. Had a social chat with them about folks at home.

Tuesday, December 23, 1862. Cool, stormy—rained most of the day, quite unusual for Minnesota winters.

Wednesday, December 24, 1862. Clear & pleasant. Had a christmas supper. Enjoyed it finely, the kind ladies of Tivoli sent in some good things, a general good time, remarks & toasts by Capt & others.

Thursday, December 25, 1862. Cloudy, stormy. Orders to start tomorrow morning at 4 o'clock, making all preparations, ammunition given out, 30 rounds to each man.

Friday, December 26, 1862. Company had breakfast at 3 o'clock—and at 4 o'clock started for Mankato to attend the execution of the 38 Indi-

---

91. Lynch R. King (1824–1868), a native of Pennsylvania, was sheriff of Winona.

ans.[92] It was a very fine day. The gallows was erected on the levee, nearly in front of the Indians wigwam, was constructed in a square form for 10 on two sides and 9 each on the other two sides. A post was placed under each corner, and a large rope held it up, being passed over a post in the center and fastened to a post below. About 10 o'clock, the troops formed a square around the gallows—and two lines about 10 feet apart were formed, running from the wigwam to the gallows. The Indians marched through uttering a monotonous grunt, their death song, marched up onto the scaffold—were taken to their respective places, and the ropes attached to their necks, they were all brave & fearless. At a signal the props were knocked out—and at 14 minutes past 10 o'clock—the great rope was cut by Wm J. Duly[93] with a broad ax, the frame fell and the 38 treacherous Indians were swinging in the air—a very large assemblage of citizens but no disturbance whatever. The company arrived back at the barracks at 5 o'clock about tired out.

92. Soldiers, including the 7th Minnesota Infantry, were present at the execution to prevent outbreaks of violence, such as rock throwing at the condemned. See *Massacre in Minnesota*, 257–59.

93. William J. Duley (1819–1898) was chosen to cut the rope at the execution of the 38 Dakota warriors. During the Sibley Expedition of 1863 he served as chief of scouts with the rank of captain. For more about his wife's horrific experiences, see the April 23, 1863, entry.

2

"On Guard Again"

Furlough and Winter Quarters, December 27, 1862–May 12, 1863

In september 1862, following the misnamed Battle of Wood Lake, Little Crow fled westward into the Dakota Territory. White Minnesotans continued to fear an imminent attack, but in truth, the Dakota people were thoroughly defeated. Writes historian Paul N. Beck, "As a military opponent, the Dakotas were a shattered people."[1] Army leaders such as Gen. John Pope and Col. Henry H. Sibley did not yet realize (or perhaps better stated, acknowledge) this reality, but some of the enlisted men did. One member of the 3rd Minnesota wrote privately, "I believe the Indian outbreak to be fairly quelled, and little or no more fighting will be done. We might as well be at home as doing nothing here. Little Crow's band is all broken up."[2]

During this period of relative calm, Buswell received a brief furlough, which enabled him to see family and friends back in Whitewater. Then he and the men of the 7th Minnesota spent the early months of 1863 in winter quarters at Tivoli, a site about six miles east of Mankato, near the Winnebago Agency. Buswell periodically reported rumors of imminent attack, but most of the Native Americans he encountered, such as members of the Winnebago tribe, were peaceful.

The diary entries that follow reveal that Buswell was a skilled marks-

---

1. *Columns of Vengeance*, 48–53 (quotation from p. 48); *Massacre in Minnesota*, 274.
2. James Madison Bowler to Elizabeth Caleff, October 9, 1862, in Andrea R. Foroughi, ed., *Go If You Think It Your Duty: A Minnesota Couple's Civil War Letters* (St. Paul: Minnesota Historical Society Press, 2008), 126.

man. He received a copy of Silas Casey's *Infantry Tactics* (1862) in early 1863 as a prize for winning a shooting competition. He began studying its contents in earnest—a decision that would propel him toward being an officer by the end of the year.

∞

Saturday, December 27, 1862. Change of weather—pretty cold, the cold continues and is quite severe. I rec'd a furlough today to date from the 29th for 20 days—expect to have a fine time and shall try and get cured of my cough.

Sunday, December 28, 1862. Quite a pleasant day, packing my things up and getting ready to leave for home. Expected to go Tuesday but shall go tomorrow. Went to the store with Ed Metcalf[3] of Dearborn to stay until morning when we will take the stage.

Monday, December 29, 1862. Took the stage at the store at 4 ½ o'clock—took breakfast at the Winnebago Agency at 6 ½ A.M. Arrived in Owatonna at 2 P.M. and ate dinner—passed Rice Lake at 5 P.M. and ate supper at Wasioja at 7 P.M. Passed through a fine country today—especially Claremont settlement—by people from N.H. Arrived at Rochester at ½ past 1—stopped at the Cole House where there was a fine dance—with fine music.

Tuesday, December 30, 1862. Ate breakfast at St Charles at 9 o'clock, then started for home on foot—10 miles—took dinner at Barnes,[4] on the prairie, arrived at home at 2 P.M. The folks were quite surprised—not expecting me so soon—but they were very glad to welcome me.

Wednesday, December 31, 1862. Pleasant morning, got up and felt quite tired. Mother & I went to Beaver to see the folks—had a good visit & chat.

Thursday, January 1, 1863. New Years day, and I am at home with the folks all well and hearty except a very bad cough. It is now nearly two years since the war of the Union began. There have been some victo-

---

3. Edwin S. Metcalf (1841–1924), a native of New Hamphire, was a private in the 7th Minnesota Infantry, Co. B. He enlisted at Fort Snelling on June 11, 1861, and was mustered out with the 8th US Colored Heavy Artillery at City Point, Virginia, on May 16, 1865.

4. Possibly Thomas Barnes (born ca. 1804), a native of Pennsylvania who lived in Elba, Minnesota, a few miles from Buswell's home.

ries to be sure, but several disastrous defeats. The defeat at Bull Run was a bad one, and no doubt would have resulted in the capture of the National Capitol, had it been followed up by the Johnny Rebs, and might have terminated the war, but there seems at this time no immediate prospect of its close. The only victories of great importance being the fall of Ft Donelson and Shiloh, and the first clear victories of the war—of consequence, U.S. Grant,[5] a new man, formerly a West pointer, was the general in command, his name and his watchwords of an "Unconditional Surrender" are heard all over the north. May God speed the right and soon terminate this great rebellion. Much has been done in subduing the Indian, many whites have been released, but the Indian war has only commenced. This year it will be vigorously prosecuted. Spent the day at Beaver, attended the shooting match. Ate dinner at Mr Hopsons and in the evening attended the greatest ball of the season at Beaver. Enjoyed myself quite well. Take it all New Years Day was a very pleasant day and spent very pleasantly.

Friday, January 2, 1863. Quite a stormy day, not very cold as it snowed, and then turned into rain. Was invited to and attended a party at Alice Metcalfs.[6] Cough was quite bad.

Saturday, January 3, 1863. Pleasant day, but quite wet & sloppy under foot. Staid at home most of the day, cough being quite bad.

Sunday, January 4, 1863. Sabbath Day, and very pleasant, went to Beaver to church with Sister Lucy,[7] which was well attended.

Monday, January 5, 1863. Very cloudy and some snow. Sundogs show themselves, prospects of a severe storm.

---

5. Ulysses S. Grant (1822–1885) rose to prominence as a result of his victories in the Western Theater early in the war. On March 2, 1864, Lincoln promoted him to lieutenant general and placed him in command of all of the Union armies. Grant spent the remainder of the war in the Eastern Theater with the Army of the Potomac.

6. Alice Metcalf (born ca. 1829), a native of Maine who moved to Winona after the 1860 census was taken, was the sister-in-law of Obed, Edwin, and William Metcalf. She was married to Cyrenus Metcalf (1826–1913), a stonecutter.

7. Lucy P. Buswell (1844–1918) was Buswell's sister. She would marry George Knowles on April 20, 1864, and have one child and a stepchild.

Tuesday, January 6, 1863. Pleasant but quite cold today. Visited school at Whitewater with W[m] Metcalf.[8] Quite an Indian scare in the neighborhood, rumors that Indians had been seen in this vicinity, and several men went out to hunt for them. They were found and proved to be some poor harmless Winnebagoes enroute to the woods of Wisconsin. Attended a party at H. Wrights,[9] gotten up on my occasion, and spent a very pleasant evening.

Wednesday, January 7, 1863. Very pleasant morning, some warmer, and little snow. Staid at home trying to cure my cough before I return, if possible.

Thursday, January 8, 1863. Cloudy, looks like snow, somewhat warm. Went with W[m] and Cornelia Metcalf[10] to Winona, very pleasant ride over the hill, and arrived there at 4 ½ P.M. Went to Mr A W Gages,[11] who with his family were very glad to see me, staid at their house all night. Went to the Court House to see about the town bounty, did not succeed in getting it.

Friday, January 9, 1863. Cloudy threatening snow. Got things all ready, and we started home at 11 A.M. bidding good bye to my friends, and after a rough ride arrived home at 5 P.M., having enjoyed the trip very much, though did not notice a great many changes in the City. Cough troubled me some.

Saturday, January 10, 1863. Cloudy, stormy day, staid at home doctoring my cough.

Sunday, January 11, 1863. Cloudy, threatened snow. Went to Elba to visit with Dearborn,[12] took dinner with him at his uncles, had a fine time.

---

8. William Metcalf (1833–1905), a native of New Hampshire, was a farmer in Winona County.

9. Hiram Wright (1826–1876), a native of New York, was a farmer in Winona County.

10. Cornelia Metcalf (1831–1876), a native of Vermont, was married to William Metcalf.

11. Alvah W. Gage (ca. 1832–ca. 1885), a native of Pennsylvania, was a house builder in Winona County.

12. Alva E. Dearborn (1838–1914) was married to Marian Allen and suffered from sunstroke at Tupelo, allowing him to collect a disability pension. Dearborn was a private in the 7th Minnesota Infantry, Co. B. He was eventually promoted to the rank of sergeant major.

Monday, January 12, 1863. Cloudy, stormy day, staid at home and father went to Winona to see about my bounty.

Tuesday, January 13, 1863. Stormy, rain and sleet very icy. Was invited to a party at Beaver tonight, but the weather was such that I did not attend. Father returned from Winona and succeeded in getting the bounty for me, town bounty of $50. $25. in money and $25. in orders. This bounty was voted by the town of Whitewater to those who enlisted from the town and though voted after I enlisted, my name having been used to help make up the quota from the town, I was paid the bounty.

Wednesday, January 14, 1863. Pleasant, but cold. Went to Beaver to make a final visit with all my friends before returning to Tivoli, had a good time, bid them all good bye and came back as far as Stonings[13] where I ate supper, and staid there during the evening to a party given for my benefit. All the young people of the valley were there, had a grand time even into the wee small hours.

Thursday, January 15, 1863. Cold morning. My furlough being about at an end, I bid goodbye to the folks and started for the barracks carrying my cough back with me. Went to Elba, to Jerry Philbricks[14] where Dearborn was, ate dinner there and then Jerry carried us to St Charles where we ate supper, and at 8 P.M. got aboard the Concord Coach drawn by six horses. It was a very cold night, and there being no one on board except Alpha [Alva?] and I, we turned up seats and laid a buffalo robe at bottom, then we laid down and placed a buffalo robe over us. Thermometer 25 below zero, but we kept warm, riding all night, and frequently thought of the driver in his box on the outside, being so exposed to the intense cold, but they are generally well bundled up and keep warm. We arrived at Rochester at 1 ½ A.M.

Friday, January 16, 1863. Still very cold, 25 to 30 below zero. Were delayed at Rochester some four hours, [not] leaving that point until 5 ½ A.M., having changed horses and driver, and away we went, the horses on the jump. Arrived at Wasioja for breakfast, and getting well filled up and warm, away we went again, through Owatonna, Wilton and arrived at Tivoli Barracks, our soldier home at 1 ½ P.M.

13. George B. Stoning (1823–1906), a native of New York, was a farmer in Whitewater, Winona County.

14. Jeremiah Philbrick (1812–1881), a native of New Hampshire, was a farmer in Elba.

Saturday, January 17, 1863. Pleasant but cool. Was welcomed back by the boys, and all seemed glad to see us, though not many were permitted to leave at a time. Yet the life at the barracks, as it generally is, was rather a lazy one, very little guard duty, probably two to four guards stationed around the premises. Not much drill in cold weather, the fuel had to be got, and cooking had to be done, and we had to eat and then bunk. Some of the boys chatting in one corner, while in another were others playing euchre or old sledge or checkers and a few perplexed over a game of chess. My first duty upon my return was to clean up my gun, &c for inspection. Rec'd letter from Aunty.

Sunday, January 18, 1863. Pleasant Sabbath day, though somewhat cloudy and warmer. Had company Inspection, which is somewhat tedious, though a necessary requirement to keep a force in proper trim for service. Spent time in afternoon in writing letters. Sent one home & one to Aunty.

Monday, January 19, 1863. Cloudy, muggy day, January thaw. Was detailed as Company Cook today and entered upon its professional duties. Such a sight, with sleeves rolled up and an apron on, into the business I go. Under the regulations it is the rule for each soldier to take his turn as Cook, unless the Co should employ a regular cook. We had none such and so my turn came today, what success I shall make the boys will soon ascertain.

Tuesday, January 20, 1863. Warm, though quite stormy. Was into the cooking business, had beef soup, rice and tried my hand at making and baking bread. The soup and rice was pronounced No 1, and the bread considered fair for a beginner. Coffee first class.

Wednesday, January 21, 1863. Considerable warmer, quite muddy though it looks as though the thaw would catch a cold soon. The boys organized a Lyceum to take place once a week at the school house, a number of citizens joined, and the prospect is that it will be a success and be a relief to some extent to the monotony of barrack life.

Thursday, January 22, 1863. Warm day, done some cooking. There was a raising of a barn at Mr Harveys[15] about a mile from barracks and after work was done I went to the raising.

---

15. Oliver E. Harvey (1832–1901), a native of New York, was a farmer who had migrated through Ohio to Tivoli by 1861.

Friday, January 23, 1863. Some snow today, slushy. Had baked beans today which were pronounced excellent, baked more bread. Writing school established at school house, in charge of the teacher, Miss Harvey.[16] Many of the boys attended.

Saturday, January 24, 1863. Some cooler, but pleasant. Everything had to be cleaned up today, the grounds, barracks, bunks &c. Guns, knapsacks &c all ready for inspection tomorrow.

Sunday, January 25, 1863. Sabbath day, and my last day as boss cook, and am glad to get out of the cook's harness. Give me the ordinary soldiers duty, and privilege to eat rather than to cook. Company had inspection, and it was a fine day for it. Wrote letters home & to Aunty.

Monday, January 26, 1863. Very pleasant, though cool, quite dull today, nothing more than our general routine, cards, dice, checkers &c being the run.

Tuesday, January 27, 1863. Cold again, some like snow. Co rec'd orders to have target shooting by the whole Co, targets to be the size and shape of a man, and to be placed at a distance of 25 rods, and it commenced today. Had two targets arranged in rear of barracks and a prize was offered by Capt Curtiss of a copy of U.S. tactics to the best shot in the Company. The Co to practice for 10 days, then the best average of ten shots to decide.

Wednesday, January 28, 1863. Very pleasant, warmer. Had target practice, and the Lyceum took place in the evening.

Thursday, January 29, 1863. Cloudy, windy. Some snow. So stormy today, target practice was postponed. Was glad to hear from home.

Friday, January 30, 1863. Quite cool. Some snow, but not sufficient to prevent the target shooting. The boys generally enjoy this part of the service, learning how to shoot the enemy.

Sunday, February 1, 1863. Cold windy Sabbath, very icy. Inspection postponed, and no meeting today. The boys busied themselves in barracks reading the bible and other books, and telling wonderful stories, adventures.

---

16. Possibly Caroline Harvey (1832–1906), a native of Ohio who married Oliver E. Harvey in November 1861.

Monday, February 2, 1863. Very cold, coldest day of the winter, 30 below zero. All in doors, no target practice, no drill. Rec'd a letter from mother.

Tuesday, February 3, 1863. Very cold day. No target practice, drill was in barracks today, and all kept around the fires most of the time. Lt Stevens returned to barracks today, all glad to see him.

Wednesday, February 4, 1863. Some warmer, stormy and windy, no practice or drill, wrote letters.

Thursday, February 5, 1863. Pleasant again and warmer. Company again got out to target practice. I made some good line shots today.

Friday, February 6, 1863. Very cold, windy, so much so that target practice was postponed. Invitations rec'd to attend Military Ball at Mankato tonight. Some will go, but I shall not.

Saturday, February 7, 1863. Some warmer, a general washing day, besides preparations for Inspection tomorrow. Company signed pay roll.

Sunday, February 8, 1863. Cold cloudy Sabbath, looks like a storm. Co Inspection was had, the paymaster arrived. This distinguished individual is always welcome, especially when his money bags are well filled.

Monday, February 9, 1863. Warmer, about 3 inches snow fell during the night. After breakfast the Co was notified that the paymaster was ready with the chink, and the Co presented themselves one at a time and rec'd 3 ½ mos pay until Jan'y 1"/63. Rec'd letter from Aunty.

Tuesday, February 10, 1863. Very cold weather, nothing important. Target practice took place, and tomorrow the contest will take place which is to decide the victor. Sent letter to Aunty.

Wednesday, February 11, 1863. Very pleasant and warmer, target practice took place, the match for the U.S. Tactics. The Company, one at a time, took turns, first the Com^d officers, then Non-Com^d, then the rank & file by name alphabetically. It was certainly a trial, one that tried some of those [who] had boasted of their shooting. Each time I made what appeared to many as very good line shots. At last it was over and then the summing up, to ascertain the average, and it was finally decided that I had made the best average. Taylor,[17] who was next to me, and who had done

---

17. Maurice W. Taylor (1832–1903), a native of New York, was a private in the 7th Minnesota Infantry, Co. B.

considerable boasting of his great shooting, feeling somewhat chagrined at the decision, interposed an objection that it was a tie between us, and though the officers would decide in my favor, yet 2^d Lieut Rice stated that if Taylor and I would shoot off a run of 5 shots each, he would give the winner another Copy of Tactics, this being done to satisfy Taylor, of course I was quite nervous. I was then quite a hero among the boys, and they not knowing anything about my former shooting, and my line shots rather astonished them, and as I never claimed to be anything extra as a shot, consequently was in favor among them. At first I was rather inclined not to shoot again, but the boys urging and backing me, I braced myself up and boldly decided to meet him when called upon by the Lieut.

Thursday, February 12, 1863. Very pleasant. Went with some of the boys into the woods to chop and get out wood, and the mule drivers with their mules came down and hauled it out.

Friday, February 13, 1863. Cloudy, somewhat stormy. Rec'd a letter from Eddie Hodgkins.[18] He also is a valiant soldier for Uncle Sam in the Army of the Potomac.

Saturday, February 14, 1863. Warmer, slushy and some rain, and finally snowed. All hands kept in barracks, wrote letters, one to mother.

Sunday, February 15, 1863. Pleasant Sunday, but cool. Recd a letter from home, also papers. Had Inspection as usual.

Monday, February 16, 1863. Cloudy, quite a warm day. The shooting contest between Taylor and myself took place today, each to shoot 5 times alternately. I was quite nervous, and it was quite an ordeal for me to pass through, but I had decided to contest. So I braced and nerved up myself and went at it to win, and did win, beating Taylor very bad, quite a victory for me as well as for the boys who backed me.

Tuesday, February 17, 1863. Warm & cloudy, thawing considerable. Rec'd papers from Lynn, Mass. I was very glad to receive them as soldier boys away from home in barracks, and not much to do, are very thankful for reading matter, which is read and read over & over again.

Wednesday, February 18, 1863. Very fine day & still thawing.

---

18. Joseph Edward Hodgkins (1841–1916) was lieutenant of the 19th Massachusetts Infantry, Co. B. He later became a prisoner of war at Libby Prison, Belle Isle, and Andersonville.

Thursday, February 19, 1863. Pleasant day. Military school organized today. 1st Lt A H Stephens [Stevens] Teacher. We will now learn the tactics and regulations, more thorough than when perusing them on our own account. A great deal of benefit will come out of this school if kept up.

Friday, February 20, 1863. Very fine, quite like spring. Boys are now enjoying themselves on the Le Sueur River, skating, the ice is splendid.

Saturday, February 21, 1863. Very fine warm, got a pair of skates and went down to the pond, skating, enjoyed it hugely.

Sunday, February 22, 1863. Sunday and Washingtons Birthday, very pleasant and clear. Company ordered out and a Salute 13 guns fired, and the Co gave three rousing cheers for our country and its progress. Sent a letter to Sister Lucy and rec'd one from home.

Monday, February 23, 1863. Pleasant day, furloughs rec'd for the balance of the Co. John Hammond left us today for promotion in another reg't. Recd two more papers from Hattie.[19]

Tuesday, February 24, 1863. Very warm, thawing much like rain.

Wednesday, February 25, 1863. Pleasant as usual, took upon myself the cook harness again, for temporary.

Thursday, February 26, 1863. Cloudy, about 6 inches snow fell.

Friday, February 27, 1863. Misty and quite warm. Rec'd permission from Capt and went upon a trip to Mankato, had a fine time, saw the Indians in their wigwam near the Stone building.

Saturday, February 28, 1863. Cloudy, warm, some snow. Had gen'l Inspection today, and company was mustered for two mos pay.

Sunday, March 1, 1863. Pleasant and warm. It is pay day, but no paymaster, no pay. Wrote letters to mother & father.

Monday, March 2, 1863. Very pleasant, more snow, but melts about as fast as it comes.

Tuesday, March 3, 1863. Cool night, but thawed during the day.

Wednesday, March 4, 1863. Fine morning, clear. Rec'd letters from Aunty & Willie with photos.

---

19. Likely Harriet H. Newhall (ca. 1843–1887), who had been a neighbor of the Buswells in Lynn.

Chief Little Crow. (Library of Congress)

Thursday, March 5, 1863. Pleasant, nothing of importance. Wrote some letters, sent one to Aunt H with a photo of Little Crow.

Friday, March 6, 1863. Pleasant but cool. Rec'd some papers from Aunty.

Saturday, March 7, 1863. Windy & cold. Rec'd letter from home.

Sunday, March 8, 1863. Pleasant Sabbath, but windy & cool. Done some cooking again today. We were quite surprised today to see Old Bell[20] from Winona drive up to barracks with his pedlar cart. He opened up and sold some goods to the boys.

Monday, March 9, 1863. Very pleasant. Sun shines but it is cool. Recd a needle case and a letter from Lucy. Glad to get it, as we soldiers have many stray buttons to replace and many rents[21] to close up, will put it to a good use. Went with detail to woods chopping.

20. Possibly Peter V. Bell (1810–1865), a native of Virginia who kept a hotel in Winona.
21. We rendered this word "rents," meaning openings or splits, but it might be "vents."

Tuesday, March 10, 1863. Very pleasant, warm spring morning. Rec'd paper from Aunty.

Wednesday, March 11, 1863. Pleasant & warm. By order Capt Comd'g Co—the Command to have Camp guard, and I was on duty. A soldier on duty is an important character, and I always feel the responsibility.

Thursday, March 12, 1863. Pleasant, fine. Rec'd the Copy of Tactics from Capt Curtiss for being the best shot in target practice in the Company, inscribed "Study its contents," and having attended the military school of Lt Stevens and taken a great interest therein, I now shall learn more of the tactics & military drill. I shall certainly study its contents. Rec'd & sent letters home.

Friday, March 13, 1863. Cloudy & warm, though quite pleasant. Concluded to learn the game of chess, and today attempted my first game.

Saturday, March 14, 1863. Warm Spring morning. Snow melting. Cleaned quarters and guns &c preparatory to inspection tomorrow.

Sunday, March 15, 1863. Sunday, cloudy & cool. Came out on inspection, strictly according to Military rules. Had meeting at the school house, and I went with many others, the house was nearly filled by soldiers & others.

Monday, March 16, 1863. Pleasant, snow melting. Several of the boys went out in the timber, among the farmers, prospecting for butter, eggs &c. Went about 12 miles, ate dinner at Johnsons, and a good one too, and arrived back at barracks quite late. Rec'd papers from Aunty.

Tuesday, March 17, 1863. Pleasant, looks like fair weather now. On guard last night. Saw a thunderstorm off in the distance, the first of the season.

Wednesday, March 18, 1863. Beautiful spring morning. Sun shining brightly. Two Winnebagoes came down near our barracks, was one of the guards that went out to arrest them & report them back to the agency, which was done.

Thursday, March 19, 1863. Cloudy, cool, looks like rain. Co had skirmish drill this A.M., boys like it much better than ordinary drill. It rained this P.M. & then turned to snow. Le Sueur River rising.

Friday, March 20, 1863. Cloudy, cool. About 8 inches snow fell, more than we have had at any time on the ground this winter, but probably will not last long. No stage from the East today, blockaded by the snow.

Saturday, March 21, 1863. Pleasant & cool. River quite high. Snow thawing fast, quite a heavy thunder shower during the night, getting ready for inspection.

Sunday, March 22, 1863. Sunday, cloudy. Stormy looking, had Co Inspection, rained a portion of the day. Sent letter to Mother. Stage got through today, rec'd 3 papers from Hattie.

Monday, March 23, 1863. Pleasant. Cooler. Snow most gone. Cleaned gun & equipments, ready to go to Mankato. Bot a gold pen of S. H. Harrison for $3⁰⁰. Rec'd a letter from Aunty.

Tuesday, March 24, 1863. Cloudy, cool, turned out to be a very fine day. Sent letter to mother.

Wednesday, March 25, 1863. Pleasant & warmer, had some pictures taken of myself, also some groups. I weighed 181 lbs today. Rec'd a letter from Aunty.

Thursday, March 26, 1863. Pleasant, thawing, persons in the neighborhood getting ready to make Maple Sugar. Sap running, river very high. We were visited today by our Col Marshall [and] Surgeon Smith. Was very glad to see them, especially the Col. Nine of the boys myself included had a group taken, sent a letter to Aunty with a copy enclosed.

Friday, March 27, 1863. Pleasant day, a more beautiful one we have not had this spring. Saw the first birds of the season, blue birds. Had a sail on the pond. No drill today.

Saturday, March 28, 1863. Very pleasant. Made a call at Bennetts, pleasant, bought some new maple Sugar of some Indians. Was on guard today. Letter from Lucy.

Monday, March 29, 1863. Pleasant & clear, warm most beautiful weather. Letter to Lucy.

Tuesday, March 30, 1863. Pleasant fine, had a game [of] ball with the boys, a No 1 game, though some windy. It has the appearance of rain.

Wednesday, April 1, 1863. Very warm day, warmest this spring. The boys played all sorts of April fool games on each other, and all in good part. Rec'd letter from Lynn.

Thursday, April 2, 1863. Pleasant though somewhat cooler. Co getting down to drill lively. Co called out and roll called four times at 6 A.M., this is done to account for each man. Co called again at 9 A.M. for Co drill, again at 2 P.M. for Co drill, and again at 6 P.M. usual roll call. Heard from home today. Dearborn rec'd a box of goodies from home, which he divided with me.

Friday, April 3, 1863. Pleasant & warm. Went with some of the boys and had a sail on the pond. Rumors that our Co will not remain here much longer, the boys are about tired of this barrack life, we long for something more active.

Saturday, April 4, 1863. Pleasant, cooler, prospects of fine weather. Several Indians were here today from the Agency, boys had considerable sport with them racing, the Indians in nearly every case, being very expert runners, coming out ahead.

Sunday, April 5, 1863. Pleasant Sabbath, had inspection throughout. After noon took a walk down into the Sugar bush and got some Maple Sugar. Some of the boys went down to river and caught fish, they having commenced running.

Monday, April 6, 1863. Beautiful morning. Some like Summer. No drill today, as many went to Mankato to witness the presentation of a Sword and Sash by the Reg't to Col Miller. A large turn-out, and the Col made a fine speech. Saw where the boys got their liquor, a full prohibitory law having been established by order Col Comd'g, but it was well arranged in a back room of a building, the 2^d one from H'd q'rs. A boy wanting a drink would go up, no one there, and would help themselves, and then drop the money into a small box, simply a matter of honor, and for liquor men are generally honorable about pay, especially in defiance of law. The money was scraped up by some one, not generally known, and the bottles kept filled to the brim. This blind pig would continue for a while, and was found out & wiped out, only to appear in some other place.

Tuesday, April 7, 1863. Pleasant, some windy. Capt Curtiss took leave of absence and left for Winona this A.M. John Lighthall[22] also left the Co. Many of the boys played ball, and a large number went fishing. I must now mention the fine fishing at the Le Sueur River. I never saw such a place to catch them, and such a plenty, they would come up the river in large schools, the river being just full of them, and they got up to the

---

22. John Lighthall, Jr. (born ca. 1834 in Canada) was a private in the 7th Minnesota Infantry, Co. B.

falls and endeavored to go up into the pond above. The falls rise some 4 to 5 feet, rather rocky, and water not deep enough to interfere with our standing on the rocks most anywhere on the falls, and up the fish jump by the hundreds & while doing so we stand there and throw them out with pitchforks, kill them with clubs, and catch them with our hands. They are so thick and so bent on climbing the falls, they pay no attention to our fishing, pickerel, bass, pike, red horse & suckers. We caught so many today, that not having use for them, sent a large number to the Co's at Mankato. Gave orders for new clothing, and signed payrolls.

Wednesday, April 8, 1863. Beautiful day, warm, fishing again today was the main business, though had usual Co drill. A dance was held in the barracks in the evening, and had some good music. Recd letter from Lucy, also papers from Jacob & Sarah.

Thursday, April 9, 1863. Cloudy, windy & cooler. No drill today, quite a number of soldiers came up from Mankato [on] horseback to catch fish, and while the boys were fishing I took one of their horses and had a good ride. They went back in evening with a horse back load of fine fish.

Friday, April 10, 1863. Cloudy, cool, had games of ball today, looks some like rain. Co mustered today, for some purpose, we do not know. It rained in P.M. Some hail. Sent letter to Lucy.

Saturday, April 11, 1863. Cloudy & rainy, rained most all night. No drill, pleasant afternoon, and everybody got ready for Inspection.

Sunday, April 12, 1863. Sunday, very pleasant. No mail. Had inspection, guns, knapsacks, barracks &c &c. One of our boys, the first, Henry Mountain[23] died today of Pleaurisy [pleurisy], only sick four days. The boys have been uncommonly healthy, very little sickness, but we do not realize what may happen before three years are past.

Monday, April 13, 1863. Pleasant day. Rec'd permission and went to Mankato to spend the day. Took dinner with the boys of Co F, 7th Regt. Steamer Jeanette Roberts came in loaded down while there, with Army supplies, preparatory for another expedition. Ret'd to barracks at 7 P.M. Letter from Lucy, also papers from Lynn.

Tuesday, April 14, 1863. Cloudy, cooler, most beautiful afternoon. Poor Henry was buried today in the graveyard here, a military burial, the first

---

23. Henry Mountain (1842–1863), a native of London, UK, was a private in the 7th Minnesota Infantry, Co. B.

I ever attended. Had the Military Band from Mankato, a detail was chosen to fire the volley over the grave. Orders rec'd today drawing the lines closer, no one allowed outside of lines now without a pass.

Wednesday, April 15, 1863. Pleasant, warm, prospects of fine weather. Was on guard again, my turn seems to come quite often, while about half of the Co are absent. Three Co's of the 6th Regt were ordered to Yellow Medicine. Soon no doubt we will follow. Letter from home today.

Thursday, April 16, 1863. Cloudy, thunder shower today, went fishing, caught plenty. Our Co bugler got a new Silver bugle, expect he will make the welkin ring now and get us out earlier than usual. Letter to Aunty & one home.

Friday, April 17, 1863. Pleasant, orders rec'd for our Co. to detail five men to report at H'd Qrs to join the battery. I was not among them. Orders rec'd that the Co be ready to march at a moments warning, as Indians had attacked a party near Madelia.[24] All excitement. Everything being put in preparation to start.

Saturday, April 18, 1863. Pleasant, guard placed around the barracks doubled today, and owing to rumors of Indians in the vicinity, guard all called out, but proved to be a false alarm. Orders rec'd from H'd Qrs, Mankato, to at once build a stockade around the barracks, as not only a protection to ourselves in case of attack, but as a place of rendezvous for the settlers in the neighborhood, and a detail was made this day to cut logs, haul them &c and commence the work. A good many fish caught today. Rec'd letter from Ed Starr.

Sunday, April 19, 1863. Sabbath day, cloudy & cool, looks like rain. Co had inspection, except the detail on Stockade, which worked all day. Wrote some letters, one home & one to Ed Starr, recd Lynn papers.

Monday, April 20, 1863. Cloudy & rainy. No drill, work on stockade was vigorously pushed as Indian rumors cause us to think that we may yet need it, as it is somewhat expected that the Winnebagoes, only 12 miles from here, may be implicated with the Sioux, and that there may be an outbreak. On guard again, rained most all night.

24. On April 15, a Dakota raiding party, which reportedly was made up of "civilized Indians," attacked white settlers at Madelia, about twenty miles southwest of Mankato, killing two or three civilians and one soldier from Co. E, 7th Minnesota, and wounding several others. See *Family War Stories*, 28; *Minnesota in Wars*, 353.

Tuesday, April 21, 1863. Cloudy, rainy, were obliged to cease work on Stockade on acc't of rain. The Capt was welcomed back today.

Wednesday, April 22, 1863. Pleasant, no drill. Stockade was completed today. It was built with posts set in the ground close together, standing about 10 feet above the surface of ground as follows. [Buswell here drew a small sketch showing the officers' quarters and enlisted men's quarters as small boxes surrounded by a larger box that he labeled "Stockade."] It was large enough to accommodate about 300 persons. An accident happened to our teamster, the mule he was riding threw him off and the wheel ran over his arm, & the mule kicked & broke 3 ribs.

Thursday, April 23, 1863. Pleasant—14 of the Co myself included divided into reliefs and carried Danl[25] the teamster to Mankato, to the hospital, a long journey, some 12 miles. While in Mankato visited Wm J. Duly & family, he being the man who cut the rope that hung the 38 indians. I had not seen his wife[26] since she was rescued from Little Crow, she with her 3 children having been taken prisoners & with some others were taken by Little Crow & his band across the great Dakota prairie to the Missouri River last summer. She related [her] experience, and it was truly awful to hear. The Indians made her a Squaw, with squaw costume, and made her not only carry a pack, as squaws do—but also carry her babe, she having become footsore & weary, the Indians took the babe and smashed its head, to help her to keep up they told her. They also killed her little girl who was unable to stand the jaunt, and this before their mother's eyes. They went to near old Ft Pierre where a French Catholic Priest had her released, first purchasing her of Little Crow by giving him a pony and the kind priest had her ret^d to her home. What a sad experience, perfectly heartrending to listen as she related it, and yet they say "Lo the poor Indian." Duly will join the expedition this season as Scout with revenge foremost on his mind.

---

25. We have been unable to identify this teamster. Buswell appears to have written "Danl," but it may be "Dave."

26. Laura Duley (1828–1900) and her five children were taken prisoner by the Dakotas at the outbreak of the war. Three of their five children—William Jr., Isabella, and Francis—were killed by the Dakotas; a fourth, six-year-old Lillie "was struck on the head with a heavy stake by a Dakota woman" but somehow survived. William and Laura were reunited along with their surviving children on January 1, 1863, at the Yankton Agency in present-day South Dakota. For more information, see *Massacre in Minnesota*, 104–5, 126, 130, 207–9, 237, 262; *Dakota Uprising*, 147–48, 255.

Laura Duley and her children. (South Dakota State Historical Society, South Dakota Digital Archives, [2019-08-30-301])

Friday, April 24, 1863. [No entry.]

Saturday, April 25, 1863. Pleasant, a flag having been provided for our fort, a flagpole was erected, and the flag arriving today, it was duly hoisted to its place. A great number of pickerel were taken today.

Sunday, April 26, 1863. Pleasant Sabbath, though somewhat cloudy. Had Co Inspection, fully equipped, was on guard again, comes quite often. Meeting at school house, attended the same. Learn that 3 Co's of our reg't will leave for up Minn[a] River next Tuesday.

Monday, April 27, 1863. Cloudy, muggy day, looks like rain. Drill com'd again 4 hours per day. I studied tactics, considerably, and have learned a great many of the evolutions of the Soldier & Company.

Tuesday, April 28, 1863. Pleasant, we cleaned up all around the barracks today, cut down trees and cut out all underbrush, so in case of an investment[27] here, we will have clear ground for better execution. Col Marshall visited us today. The Col is well liked by all the boys, ever jovial, kind &

---

27. An archaic definition of this term is the surrounding of a place by a hostile force in order to besiege it.

pleasant, and we all think him a brave man. Company was ordered out and drilled in his presence, who complimented us. Rec'd Lynn papers.

Wednesday, April 29, 1863. Warm weather. Our Company rec'd a present from a Methodist Minister of a number of books, the nucleus of a Company Library.

Thursday, April 30, 1863. Pleasant. Had general inspection by Col Marshall, who was very thorough. Though we had been taken somewhat by surprise, the Co made a very good appearance. Was detailed as Cook again. Boys made a large haul of fish. Letter from Cousin Mary,[28] sent one to mother.

Friday, May 1, 1863. Pleasant & warm. Some rain in P.M., boys had great sport fishing and caught more than we knew what to do with.

Saturday, May 2, 1863. Cloudy, some rainy. I doing the cooking & the boys fishing, they caught about a 100 nice ones with hooks, bass, pickerel & perch, plenty of brain food, but not much brain work, though I kept up my study of the Tactics and also Regulations.

Sunday, May 3, 1863. Sunday. Cloudy & misty. Had inspection in quarters. Meeting at school house by our Chaplain O. P. Light. He preached an excellent sermon, boys like him very much.

Monday, May 4, 1863. Cloudy, misty, took off cooks harness and took up that of a guard, quite a change from that of a menial to that of a proud soldier. Surgeon Smith and Lieuts of Co's "C" & "F" and several others came up from the City to fish. They had good success and carried away about 60 fine pickerel. Drill as usual.

Tuesday, May 5, 1863. Pleasant though somewhat windy & cool. Nothing important except a party of boys came up from City to go fishing. Winnebago Indians rec'd orders from Washington to be removed from their reservation here to Ft Thompson on the Missouri River, and they commenced to remove them today. Many went by here.[29] Had reveille by drum & fife this A.M. & Drill.

28. Mary Cushman Waitt (1820–1892) lived in Malden, Mass.
29. In early May, 1,318 Dakotas, mostly women and children, departed Fort Snelling on two steamboats. In June, 2,000 Winnebago Indians—"completely innocent of any role in the uprising," writes Paul N. Beck—were also deported from the state. See *Columns of Vengeance*, 73.

Wednesday, May 6, 1863. Pleasant, boys kept up fishing today, with good success. I helped some about the cook house. Large number [of] Indians went by here, going to Mankato. Learned that two Sioux Indians were killed on the Winnebago reservation, near Lake Elysian, great excitement among the Winnebagoes and fears of an outbreak.[30]

Thursday, May 7, 1863. Very warm Summer morning. The long roll beat about noon, and the Company at once fell in, armed & accoutered, with 20 rounds of ammunition. All was excitement as it was reported that there was a prospect of an outbreak at the agency & the Co's there needing assistance, we went as lively as possible, part of the way some 4 miles on the double quick, and just before arriving there we saw a great commotion, which proved to be a scalp dance, and a genuine one. Such I never witnessed before, there were some 100 or more Indians in a circle, at the head the largest, and graded down to the smallest bucks, squaws & papooses, even to little ones, going around the circle. In the Center were two indians, each carrying a scalp, all stretched on hoops about a foot in diameter, with ribbons hanging, and dangling at the top of long poles, held in their hands, and the victors, the Indians who killed the Sioux and scalped them, were also in the Center jumping & dancing around, and each [had] tufts of white feathers fastened in their hair, and all besmeared with paint & blood from the victims, and on they went, around and around all chanting a song only peculiar to the Indians, a kind of a hum-drum-ding-dong song, and as they sung they stepped around the Circle, only a few inches at a time, and sideways, keeping time to the song and the music, kept up by a musical Indian, who beat upon an Indian drum, and now & then the fearful war-whoop would be heard. It looked quite exciting, as well as alarming, as the Indians were considerably infuriated to think they had got to leave their homes, the agency, and go away for ever, this as they supposed on account of the Sioux—and we learned that the two Sioux came down here from the West, to endeavor to make some treaty or alliance with the Winnebagoes, to assist them in their warfare against the whites, and the Winnebagoes thinking the

30. The Winnebago Indians killed and scalped two Dakotas who came into their reservation seeking protection because they believed the Dakotas were the cause of their removal from the area and, in the words of a *New York Times* reporter, they were "in hope of getting into favor with our people, so they might be allowed to remain on their reservation." See William E. Lass, "The Removal from Minnesota of the Sioux and Winnebago Indians," *Minnesota History* 38 (December 1963): 361; *New York Times*: May 22, 1863.

Sioux the cause of their removal, fell upon them at once and killed them and took their scalps. Took supper with Co F 10th Reg't at agency. A large picket force was kept out all night, 20 of our co was detailed, I among the number, and we remained out all night.

Friday, May 8, 1863. Cloudy, cooler. Got up about 6, took a walk with some of the boys down among the Indians, into their camp, no disturbance, all was quiet now. Provision came about noon, and about 1 P.M. our Co started back to the barracks, having had quite an adventure.

Saturday, May 9, 1863. Cloudy & warm, plenty fish caught today. Quite a thunder shower. By order each man in the Co drew 4 days rations. 700 of the Winnebagoes left Mankato today for Ft Randall, going by steamboat down the Minn^a & Miss and up the Mo. Rec'd letter & papers from Lynn.

Sunday, May 10, 1863. Sunday, cloudy, cooler, looks like rain. Had inspection as usual, no preaching today. So I busied myself reading the Bible and other good books, and wrote letters to Mother & Aunty & Lucy.

Monday, May 11, 1863. Pleasant. Had drill in slinging and unslinging knapsacks, the only especial good to come out of this is to make a show on Gen'l Inspection. Uniformity & regularity is what makes a soldier. Some of the boys tried fishing, but with poor success, they are about done biting this season.

Tuesday, May 12, 1863. Pleasant & warm. Our Co rec'd a new recruit today.[31] Rec'd a report today that Richmond is taken, great rejoicing had.[32] Rec'd orders that we march tomorrow. So we are actively at work getting things in shape to move, and now for a more active service. We have had about enough of dead soldiering, give us something lively, animated.

---

31. Henry Steinbeck (born in Germany ca. 1839) joined the company on May 12.

32. This false news report appeared in the *St. Paul Press*; however, Richmond did not fall to the Union until April 1865. For the spreading of this false rumor among the men, see *Columns of Vengeance*, 74–75. The word we rendered as "had" is scrunched at the end of a line and may be "held" or "here."

3

"An Attack Expected Tonight"

The Sibley Expedition, May 13–September 20, 1863

~

Between september 1862 and the spring of 1863, Little Crow attempted to form alliances with other Native peoples of the Upper Midwest, but none would join him as they all wanted peace with the whites. In April 1863, Little Crow traveled from Devil's Lake in present-day North Dakota (where he and his people had spent the winter) to Canada to seek support from the British government, but Canadian authorities ordered him to leave. Upon returning to Devil's Lake in May, Little Crow found that he had lost the support of most of his followers. Some remained with him only because they feared punishment if they surrendered to the US army.[1]

Meanwhile, back in Minnesota, Native Americans continued to suffer. At Mankato, 143 of the roughly two thousand Dakota prisoners died during the winter. In early 1863, Abraham Lincoln signed two laws seizing Dakota lands in Minnesota and forcing peaceful Dakotas further west. (In his diary, Buswell mentions seeing Native Americans being deported from Minnesota.) Clearly the Indians were no longer a formidable enemy for white Minnesotans. Nevertheless, white settlers and military leaders continued to believe that Little Crow and his warriors were preparing another onslaught. In February 1863, Gen. John Pope informed Henry Sibley, "As you know it has always been my purpose to make a vigorous campaign against the Indians as soon as possible this spring."[2]

---

1. *Columns of Vengeance*, 48–53; *Massacre in Minnesota*, 280–82.
2. *Columns of Vengeance*, 53, 71–73; *Massacre in Minnesota*, 268–70.

Sibley arrived at Camp Pope, near Fort Ridgely, on June 6, 1863. After several delays his men—Buswell among them—headed westward on June 16 in pursuit of Little Crow and other Indian bands. Facing intense heat and water shortages, the men moved slowly, crossing into the Dakota Territory about June 25, near Lake Traverse. (Meanwhile, Little Crow was killed on July 3 when he returned to Minnesota as part of a raiding party seeking horses.) Throughout July, the army continued to move westward, closer to Big Mound, where several thousand Dakotas were encamped hunting buffalo. Most of the Indians near Big Mound had avoided the war in Minnesota, but fighting would break out that would engulf even those who had pursued peace over the previous year.[3]

On the morning of July 24, the Dakotas saw clouds of dust in the distance that they presumed to be buffalo they could hunt. They quickly realized that unfortunately it was the US army on the march. Notably, the Dakotas did not paint themselves for war, indicating that they did not intend to fight. Native American scouts serving in Sibley's army made the first contact with the Dakotas, and they greeted and shook hands. Sibley sent word to Standing Buffalo that he had no intention of making war on peaceful Indians, and several Dakotas rode into the US army camp, where the white soldiers shared crackers with the hungry Dakotas. "Suddenly, only three hundred yards away, their hopes of a peaceful surrender were broken asunder with a senseless murder," writes Paul N. Beck. A member of Inkpaduta's band named Tall Crown shot Dr. Josiah S. Weiser, surgeon of the 1st Minnesota Mounted Rangers, in the back. (Buswell wrongly interpreted this moment as a "signal" for the Indians to attack.) News of the killing quickly spread and fighting began in earnest. Buswell's regiment was on the right flank of the US line along with the 1st Minnesota Mounted Rangers. The Indians were outnumbered and outgunned, and so they fought using defensive maneuvers that appeared to the US soldiers as a "constant retreat" but that was in reality "a skilled delaying action" intended to protect the Dakota women and children, giving them an opportunity to safely get away. (Unlike other soldiers, Buswell noticed that the Indians' manner of falling back "was evidently for the purpose of giving the squaws & papooses time to move themselves and camp away beyond danger.")[4]

The US soldiers pursued the Dakotas for eighteen miles. Near Dead Buffalo Lake, the Dakotas made their final stand before breaking off the

---

3. *Columns of Vengeance*, 77–100.
4. *Columns of Vengeance*, 100–107; diary entry for July 24, 1863.

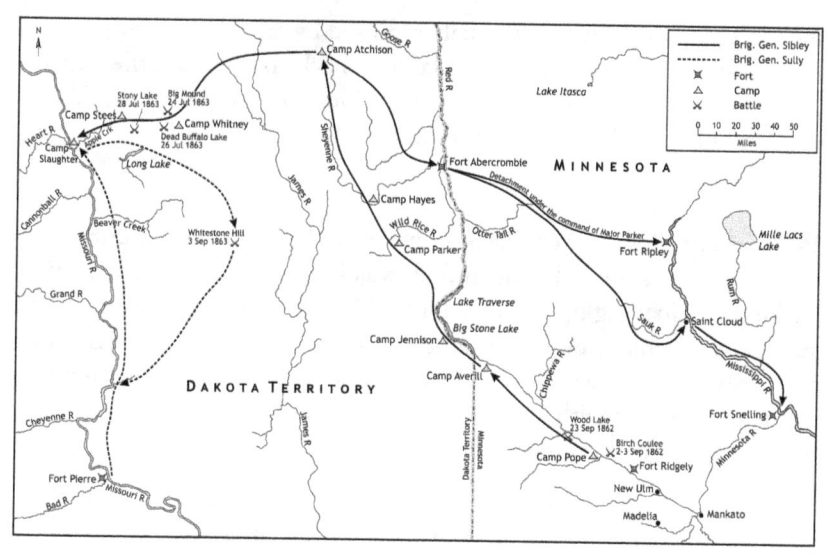

Map 2. Routes of the expeditions by Brig. Gen. Henry H. Sibley and Brig. Gen. Alfred Sully, June–September 1863

engagement. With night approaching, the US troops were now spread out, disorganized, exhausted, hungry, dehydrated, and in some cases, lost. Eventually, by the next morning, most of the troops made it back to camp. All told, US casualties were low: Dr. Weiser, a soldier who was struck by lightning, and two others. Estimates of Dakota casualties ranged from thirteen killed to more than forty casualties.[5]

After the Battle of Big Mound, pro-peace Dakotas led by Standing Buffalo fled to Canada, while the resisters continued moving westward toward the Missouri River. On July 26, the resisters, joined by several other tribes, attacked Sibley's forces near Dead Buffalo Lake. Riding on horses and ponies, the Indians assaulted Sibley's cattle herds in an attempt to reduce the food source of the US troops while also enabling Dakota civilians to retreat. After three hours of fighting the Dakotas were repulsed, although the US army was unable to pursue them since they were so fatigued and dehydrated from the earlier fighting and marching around Big Mound.[6]

The Battle of Stony Lake began two days later, on July 28, when several hundred Dakota warriors charged on horseback. They hoped to surprise

5. *Columns of Vengeance*, 107–15.
6. *Columns of Vengeance*, 115–19.

the US troops, but they were easily repulsed by artillery fire. Sibley then counterattacked and forced the Dakotas back. By July 29, the Indians had retreated across the Missouri River. Over the ensuing weeks, Sibley's forces would march back to Minnesota.[7]

                        ☙

Wednesday, May 13, 1863. Pleasant morning, but rained some during the night. Reveille sounded early and all was bustle and activity, arranging, packing and loading up, & at 8²⁰ formed into line, bid goodbye to Tivoli and its people, many of whom came out to see us start. Marched through the wet to Mankato arriving there about noon, moved up to the flat above town, and camped with other co's of our reg't. Had dress parade for first time. Camp called Camp Lincoln.

Thursday, May 14, 1863. Pleasant, was detailed for guard, & on Regt¹ guard mount for first time. My post was at the Winnebago Indian Camp in lower town, near the river. There were many Winnebago Indians camped who were awaiting transportation down the river & thence to Ft Randall [in the Dakota Territory]. Many citizens came down to see, and Indians had a scalp dance for their amusement. The steamer Pomeroy came tonight to transport them. Our Co was out on Battalion drill first time this season.

Friday, May 15, 1863. Warm & pleasant, was relieved from duty at 9 ½ A.M. Somewhat tired, not having slept much during the night, being on duty 2 hours and off 4 hours all day & night. Indians had orders to go aboard the Pomeroy. They were quite sad, being obliged to go away from their homes and to a place they know nothing about. They finally got aboard at about 11 A.M. [and] the boat pushed out and away she went down the river. Battalion drill and dress parade today. Witnessed a great wrestling match between Orderly Eastman and a citizen who has boasted of his prowess, and the orderly came out first best, and the 2ᵈ trial resulted the same, not only a victory for the orderly, but a victory for the soldier boys.

Saturday, May 16, 1863. Pleasant, cool breezes from the West. No drill today, but orders to get everything ready for gen'l Inspection tomorrow. Three steamboats arrived, bound up the Minnesota River, with supplies

---

7. *Columns of Vengeance*, 119–27.

to Camp Release. The Reg't rec'd a serenade tonight by the 7th Reg't Brass Band, boys have made a great improvement. Rec'd papers from home.

Sunday, May 17, 1863. Pleasant Sabbath, heavy frost this A.M. Reveille at 6, assembly at 8, and fell in and regiment had gen'l Inspection. Preaching by Chaplain Light at 11 A.M. I attended and listened to a good practical sermon. Three boats were on the bar opposite the Camp most of the day. Steamer Albany came and took a load of Indians and 25 men from Co F 10th Reg't as guard, and off they went down the river. Got excused from evening roll-call and went to church in the City.

Monday, May 18, 1863. Pleasant but cool. Guard boat came up about 9 A.M. The balance of the Winnebagoes left today going overland to St Peter, and there to take the boat. In consideration of the riddance of these poor devils, a salute of 13 guns was fired and the flag raised, and not much of a victory either. On guard again today.

Tuesday, May 19, 1863. Pleasant, came off guard, somewhat tired, for some reason there was no battalion drill or dress parade, to give us a rest I expect. Steamer Favorite came up today, and recd letter from Lucy.

Wednesday, May 20, 1863. Warm night & pleasant morning. Had Co drill in A.M., battalion drill in P.M. commanded by Lt Col Marshall, lasted about 3 hours. Having studied my Tactics considerably, I am getting quite familiar with Company & Battalion movements. The Capt frequently asks me as to the correctness of the position. Dress parade in the evening, Co drew blouses. In the evening attended a variety show given by some of the boys of our regiment, plenty of fun.

Thursday, May 21, 1863. Pleasant & warmer. Went with some of the boys in bathing in Minn^a River, first time this season. Had Batt^n drill & Dress parade.

Friday, May 22, 1863. Cooler & windy. Some rain. No drill or parade on account of same. Co "G" called the Tigers came in from Madelia, their winter quarters. Joined the Reg't and camped. Our boys were glad to meet the boys as they had camped near us most of the time last season.

Saturday, May 23, 1863. Stormy, wet & muddy, on guard again. Steamboat Ariel came down today from Camp Pope.[8] Her Capt says that

---

8. Located near Fort Ridgely, Camp Pope would become the rendezvous point for Sibley's expedition. See *Columns of Vengeance*, 71.

before leaving the camp, 15 Sioux Indians came in and gave themselves up, only a few less to fight us, and a few more to eat Uncle Sam's rations. Recd letter from Aunty.

Sunday, May 24, 1863. Pleasant Sunday, warm. Had meeting in the grove near, a large attendance. Dress parade with 7 co's, all in style. Col states that the paymaster is in St Paul enroute here to pay us our 4 mos pay. Boys are all getting short, as we have had to wait longer than usual. Letter to Aunty & Mother.

Monday, May 25, 1863. Pleasant & warm. Had Batt^n Drill & Dress Parade. Unusually warm and the boys sweat considerably. 4 co's 10th Regt Minn^a came in and camped at Camp Lincoln. We read of the war but nothing has been gained of great importance since Shiloh, but Grant and his gallant army are now pounding away at Vicksburg. It is the opinion of many that this time he will fail. We will wait and see.

Tuesday, May 26, 1863. Pleasant, warm, got up early and done my washing before breakfast, afterwards took a stroll about camp. Batt^n Drill & Dress parade. Letter from Lucy.

Wednesday, May 27, 1863. Pleasant, very warm. Recd orders today that we break camp and march West on Saturday next. Had severe Batt^n Drill & then Dress parade. Boys are breaking in well, and ere long will be full fledged, drilled soldiers, if they don't have the discipline.

Thursday, May 28, 1863. Pleasant, no drill. Orders to get things ready to march, and everyone is lively in getting things ready. The paymaster arrived and amidst the hurly-burly we sign the pay rolls, and the chink to come tomorrow. The ladies of the City gave 7th Reg't a fine supper, toasts & speeches were made, and 3 cheers were given by the ladies, and 3 cheers in return by the boys and a tiger in return. Letters to Lucy.

Friday, May 29, 1863. Pleasant, very warm, on guard. Regt rec'd 4 mo's pay, up to May 1st, sent $40. home per express, and letter to Mother. Had dress parade for last time here.

Saturday, May 30, 1863. Cloudy, cool, very heavy dew. Reveille at 6 A.M., got breakfast, and the call blew strike tents, at 8 A.M. packed up and loaded up & soon in line. Marched up to Hd qrs and gave 3 cheers for Col Miller, and started on the Campaign of /63 at 10 ½ A.M. Stopped to lunch near a stream of water above South Bend. Marched about 12 miles and camped on the high prairie.

Sunday, May 31, 1863. Pleasant Sabbath, tho some cool. Reveille at 4 A.M., breakfast, ate, all packed & started at 6 A.M. Stopped to rest at Butternut Valley at 8 A.M. and at Big Cottonwood, there we took dinner. Passed through New Ulm about 1 P.M. and camped, about 4 miles west of there. 20 miles today.

Monday, June 1, 1863. Pleasant, quite cool. Reveille at 4 A.M., left camp at 6 A.M., stopped to lunch on the prairie about 8 miles, passed "Travellers home" then Ft Ridgely on opposite side river about 10 ½ A.M. and took dinner at Lone Tree Lake, so named because there was a lone tree near the sheet of water. Went into camp about 4 ½ P.M. about 3 miles below the agency. 23 miles today.

Tuesday, June 2, 1863. Cool, some rainy. Left camp at 6 A.M. and arrived at Camp Pope at 11 A.M., a distance of 13 miles. Found it a beautiful place for a camp, on a gentle slope from the bank of the Minn^a River, back with timber plenty along the river. Sent letter to home & Aunty.

Wednesday, June 3, 1863. Fine day. Our Co was called upon for a detail for guard, I not being chosen, took my clothes down to the river and washed them. No drill or dress parade, but boys had a nigger dance[9] in the evening. During the evening witnessed the drill of battery and the firing of blank cartridges.

Thursday, June 4, 1863. Pleasant, had Co drill and dress parade. Witnessed target practice with shot & shell by the Battery, quite interesting. Col Crooks & Maj McLaren[10] of the 6th Regt and Maj Forbes[11] of Sibleys staff & W. J. Duly, scout, came in today.

---

9. White Union soldiers sometimes painted their faces black to reenact minstrel shows they'd seen in their hometowns. Some regiments, especially ones from urban areas, even formed minstrel troupes to regularly put on these performances. See Peter C. Luebke, "'Equal to Any Minstrel Concert I Ever Attended at Home': Union Soldiers and Blackface Performance in the Civil War South," *Journal of the Civil War Era* 4 (December 2014): 511–13.

10. Robert N. McLaren (1828–1886), a native of New York, was a major in the 6th Minnesota Infantry before being appointed colonel of the 2nd Minnesota Cavalry in 1863. For more on McLaren, see *Family War Stories*, 11, 15, 48–49, 65, 134–44.

11. William Henry Forbes (1815–1875), a native of Montreal, Quebec, Canada, moved to Minnesota to work as a fur trader in 1837, where he met Henry H. Sibley and worked as his clerk for ten years. When the Dakota War broke out in 1862, fur trading in the area largely ceased and Forbes joined Sibley's staff as

Friday, June 5, 1863. Pleasant & warm. Long roll beat at 1 A.M., soldiers got out lively, dressed, and with equipments on & guns in hand were soon in line and were shortly dismissed, rather provoking as it was done by Col Crooks Comd'g, just to try us. Commenced digging a well near our Reg't. Had drill & dress parade.

Saturday, June 6, 1863. Pleasant, was detailed for guard. Co "H" 9th Reg't & "F" 6th Regt came in today, also a detachment of the Battery, two Co's mounted Rangers also came into camp. Inspection of mules and wagons, which means that all mules and wagons in the command were brought out in one gen'l line and examined, both wagons, harnesses, mules and even the drivers.

Sunday, June 7, 1863. Pleasant, windy & dusty. Had inspection by Company. Paymaster came to camp with cavalry escort. Saw the 6th Regt on dress parade, made a very good appearance. Meeting today by our chaplain.

Monday, June 8, 1863. Pleasant & warmer. Co drill in A.M. & Batt[n] drill & dress parade. Small pox is reported in camp, and all precautions are taken against the spread of the disease.

Tuesday, June 9, 1863. Pleasant, 13 men of our Co detailed for guard. Co's "C" & "K" 10th Regt came in today. Saw Hayes, Hopson & others and had quite a fine chat with them. Genl Sibley Com[r] in Chief came in today, and all the troops were in line to receive him, and a salute 13 guns fired. The Com[r] having come and the troops coming in fast, the time approaches when this great expedition will move.

Wednesday, June 10, 1863. Cloudy, looks rainy, was on guard. Saw Loren Porter[12] today, had quite a chat. Co "I" 6th Reg't and a large number of mules came in today. Had Inspection at midnight, a fine time to inspect, or rather to ascertain who are asleep or absent.

Thursday, June 11, 1863. Pleasant, rather foggy morning, birds singing. No drill, boys amuse themselves having boxing matches, having got a pair of gloves. Battery fired shot & shell at target practice today.

---

commissary of subsistence. He acted as provost marshal during the military trials of the Dakotas. J. Fletcher Williams, *A History of the City of Saint Paul, and of the County of Ramsey, Minnesota* (Saint Paul: Minnesota Historical Society, 1876), 54–56.

12. Loren Porter (born ca. 1844 in New York) was a farmer in Milton, Dodge County.

Friday, June 12, 1863. Pleasant & clear, very warm. No drill, two boys hurt by mules, one of them died. 6 Co's cavalry came in today. Went in bathing in Minn^a River, 3 of the boys came very near being drowned, having got in beyond their length. Rec'd letters from home & Lucy.

Saturday, June 13, 1863. Warm & pleasant, rather dusty in camp. No drill, getting ready for Inspection. Many boys went fishing. Dress parade.

Sunday, June 14, 1863. Pleasant, on guard again. Regt had Inspection by Co's, my post of duty was outside of camp. Saw long train come in from Ft with supplies, preparations being made to start on the march, witnessed cavalry on dress parade. Today Capt Curtiss resigned which was accepted, he thinking that he would not be able to stand the long campaign. He got out easy, but not so easy for the rank & file.

Monday, June 15, 1863. Pleasant, quite hot. No drill. Capt Curtiss bid us all goodbye & left today for home, boys generally sorry to have him leave. Some strife about the new appointment, but 1st Lt Stevens is made Capt, 2^d Lt Rice—1st Lt, and Orderly Eastman receives the new appointment 2^d Lt. Rec'd orders to march tomorrow morning at 5 A.M. and all are getting ready for a long trip, how long we know not.

Tuesday, June 16, 1863. Pleasant, some cooler. Reveille at 3 A.M., got breakfast and struck tents at 4, and this Second Sibleys Expedition comprising some [blank space] men[13] and about 200 6 mule teams, loaded down with provisions, and quite a large herd of cattle. Started out in search of the Sioux Indians, marched about 8 miles and camped near the Minn^a River. Stood it quite well, tho eyes some sore. Our whole Co detailed for guard tonight, that is the hardest part. March all day, and then stand guard at night. Camp called Camp Crooks. The following troops comprised the force viz.

6th	Regt	Minn^a	Vols	Col	Crooks	Comd'g
7th	"	"	"	"	Miller	"
9th	"	"	"	"	Wilkin[14]	"

---

13. The expedition consisted of about two thousand men. See *Columns of Vengeance*, 81.

14. Alexander Wilkin (1819–1864), a native of New York, commanded the 9th Minnesota Infantry. Previously he had been an officer in the 1st and 2nd Minnesota Infantries and had fought in the Eastern Theater at the First Battle of Bull Run. Wilkin County, Minnesota, is named for him.

10th	"	"	"	"	Baker[15]	"
1st Regt Mounted Rangers				"	McPhail	"
3d Minnª Light Artillery				—	Capt Jones[16]	"
A Company Scouts & 200 wagons					—	
Genl H. H. Sibley Comd'g & Staff						

Wednesday, June 17, 1863. Pleasant. Reveille at 3 A.M., everything ready and started at 6 A.M., marched to Wood Lake & camped 12 miles. Was on rear guard and did not get to camp until 5 P.M. Camp Miller.

Thursday, June 18, 1863. Pleasant, but cool. Reveille at 3 A.M., struck tents and were on the move by 6 A.M., crossed Yellow Medicine River about noon, the long train being about 4 hours crossing, and camped near old Camp Mission about 4 P.M.—only 8 miles today, called Camp Baker.

Friday, June 19, 1863. Cloudy, cold for the season. Expedition did not move today, stopped for repairs to wagons &c, done my washing. Long roll beat by order gen'l comd'g to see who were missing. Wrote letters to mother & Aunty.

Saturday, June 20, 1863. Rainy. Reveille at 3 ½ A.M., struck tents at 5, & start at 6 in the rain. Soldiers must obey rain or shine. Passed old Camp Release at 1 P.M. and camped on the Minnª River 6 miles below Lac Qui Parle, 16 miles today. Beautiful prairie around called Camp McPhail.

Sunday, June 21, 1863. Sunday, cloudy, windy & quite cool. Some rain, no marching today. Heard preaching by Chaplain. Had Inspection, dress parade. Camp named Camp Ramsey.

Monday, June 22, 1863. Cloudy, cool. Reveille at 4 A.M., breakfast at 5, struck tents and at 6 on the advance. Crossed Inkpa[17] River about 10 A.M., left our old track here, camped on the high prairie at 2 P.M. at a lake called by the boys "Goose turd lake," nasty, filthy, thick water, so thick that it had to be strained through a cloth before being used, and yet many of the boys [were] so thirsty when they arrived here, just plunged into the

---

15. James H. Baker (1829–1913), a native of Ohio, commanded the 10th Minnesota Infantry and later served as provost marshal for the Department of Missouri.

16. John Jones (1824–1886), a native of England, was captain of the 3rd Battery Minnesota Light Artillery.

17. Inkpa River was another name for the Lac Qui Parle River.

water and drank the filthy stuff, but afterwards felt its effects. No wood near. 16 miles today, called Camp Averill.

Tuesday, June 23, 1863. Pleasant, warmer. Reveille at 4 A.M., start at 7, passed over very level country, saw the prairie on fire, camped at a lake about 30 miles South East of Big Stone Lake. Had our knapsacks carried today, quite a relief. 16 miles today, called Camp Marshall.

Wednesday, June 24, 1863. Clear, warm & pleasant. Reveille at 4 A.M., breakfast at 5. Start at 6, crossed a stream about 7, a branch of the Yellow Earth,[18] 13 miles, crossed Whetstone Creek and camped on banks of said creek, 16 miles today. Country poorly watered and no timber. Caught plenty pickerel in creek. On guard, called Camp Jennison.

Thursday, June 25, 1863. Fine, prospects good. Reveille at 4 A.M., left camp at 6, our Regt in advance today. No water for 9 miles, and being quite hot, were very thirsty. Camped at noon on a lake about 2 miles from Big Stone Lake, a beautiful lake, fine gravel shore, though scarcity of timber. Just before noon we saw three Buffalo, the first I ever saw. Some of the cavalry boys went after them and after an exciting chase which we witnessed, they finally killed one. 11 miles today, called Camp McLaren.

Friday, June 26, 1863. Pleasant, some like rain. Reveille early, left camp at 6, no water for 8 miles, camped on Minn^a River between Big Stone & Traverse Lakes, beautiful valley, though scarcity timber. Saw Indian burying ground on hill near by, some up in trees. Went bathing in Lake Traverse, the headwaters of the Red River of the North. Boys caught fish in the lake. 10 miles today.

Saturday, June 27, 1863. Pleasant, no march today, on guard again, done washing. Signs of about 40 Indians seen, but new [not?] enough to make much excitement. Some boys found about 200 bushels corn buried which was soon dug out & distributed around amongst the boys.

Sunday, June 28, 1863. Sunday, very cool. From here a train was prepared to go north to Ft Abercrombie[19] after more rations, we learn. Went upon one of the bluffs & with a telescope could see both lakes and a beautiful

---

18. Buswell likely meant the Yellow Bank River, a tributary of the Minnesota River.

19. Fort Abercrombie was, according to one historian, "a typical frontier post without walls or bastions . . . on the west side of the Red River of the North, better to guard the ox-cart trails north to Pembina and project U.S. power in the

view, and examined Indian burying ground. Some 75 to 100 were buried, and all either up on racks built of sticks above the ground, or placed in the crotches of trees, & all wrapped, or evidences of having been wrapped in blankets. Orders issued by Gen'l Sibley not to molest them.[20]

Monday, June 29, 1863. Fine morning. No marching, went fishing in Lake Traverse, plenty pickerel. Some Indians seen today by scouts, and there was considerable excitement in camp. A detail of cavalry & a section of battery were sent after them, great Indian trail found and some 20 fresh tracks. On dress parade.

Tuesday, June 30, 1863. Cooler, effects of a refreshing shower during the night. Train of 60 wagons being all prepared went to the Ft. with escort of 3 Co's Inf'y, 3 of Cavalry, and a section of Battery. Struck tents at 8 A.M., went up the bluff west of Lake Traverse, took a farewell look of the two lakes, went 8 miles and camped by a lake about 3 miles to timber. Had dress parade and was mustered for pay. Camp Bradley.

Wednesday, July 1, 1863. Cool, rather misty. Reveille at 4 A.M. Left camp at 5 ½, country well watered but some alkali. Marched 14 miles & camped at noon on the banks of a lake, alkali water, on the Coteaus [coteaux], the highest land passed over. Saw some 20 lakes today, bad stuff, mostly brackish water. Cavalry ret^d not overtaking the Indians. No timber as far as the eye could reach. Camp Crook [Cook].[21]

Thursday, July 2, 1863. Fine morning. Reveille at 3 A.M. Start at 5, night very cool, passed over the head of the Coteau about 9 A.M. Camped on a lake, beautiful surroundings at the head of Wild Rice River, about noon,

---

northern fur economy." See Joseph C. Fitzharris, *The Hardest Lot of Men: The Third Minnesota Infantry in the Civil War* (Norman: University of Oklahoma Press, 2019), 121.

20. Many of the soldiers destroyed graves at this burial ground, leading Sibley to issue orders to punish further vandalism. One soldier in the 7th Minnesota who approved of Sibley's order remarked that he was "sad to see" that "wherever there was a grave of an Indian the body was dug up and allowed to rot above the ground. With all the boasting of our civilization are we not almost as barbarous as they?" See *Columns of Vengeance*, 87.

21. In this and subsequent entries, we obtained the correct camp names from Susan Mary Kudelka, *March on the Dakota's [sic]: The Sibley Expedition of 1863* (Fargo, N.D.: McCleery & Sons, 2003), 61–71.

fair water. 11 miles today, picked some blueberries, dress parade. Camp Barker [Parker].

Friday, July 3, 1863. Fine with cool breezes from South East. Reveille at 3 A.M., left camp at 5. Crossed the Wild Rice River at 7. Marched 18 miles and camped by a lake of awful poor water, hottest day of the season, boys were most famished with thirst. Wells were dug from 20 to 30 ft deep before we could get drinkable water, and even this was strong with alkali. Camp Buell.

Saturday, July 4, 1863. Independence day, cloudy & some rainy. Reveille at 3. Start at 4 ½ A.M. Marched 8 miles & camped at noon, at Camp Hayes on the Sheyenne River, the long looked for stopping place where we will remain until the trains come from the fort with our supplies. While marching along the valley, a young elk came along on the jump and went headlong into the wagon train, and before it could get away, was captured. A beautiful place for a camp, plenty timber, and a spring of good water. After camping the command celebrated the 4th by hoisting the large flag upon a mast and firing a National Salute, and some fireworks in the evening.

Sunday, July 5, 1863. Pleasant & cool. Mail left here under escort for the fort, sent letter to mother. Whole command remains here until the train from fort arrives. Plenty of game, buffalo, elk, & antelope, & the river abounds in fish. So the boys are having plenty of sport. Dress parade.

Monday, July 6, 1863. Fine. Reveille at 5, cleaned guns &c and put everything in shape for Brigade review tomorrow. A few straggling Indians were seen today, though sufficient to cause an order from Hd qrs that trenches be dug around camp, a good idea to be cautious, as the Sioux are treacherous devils and might sweep down upon us while we are not prepared. A buffalo was killed. Saw the 10th Regt Lt Col Jennison[22] Comd'g on dress parade. It was somewhat singular to me to hear a Col swear on dress parade, but the boys say it is natural, and they are used to it.

Tuesday, July 7, 1863. Pleasant, took a number of officers & men up to the top of a bluff East of Camp, where there was a big mound, and with spade & shovel a number of the boys went at it, to dig it open. We dug

---

22. Samuel P. Jennison (1830–1909), a native of Massachusetts, was a lawyer in St. Paul before becoming lieutenant colonel of the 10th Minnesota Infantry.

down into the center of it about 10 feet, and finally struck some bones and the remains of two skulls. I took out one of them, only the outside rim left, and it at once dropped to ashes, yet the indentation of the skull was plain to be seen in the earth, where it was taken out, the remains of some very ancient people no doubt. The Indians that we had with us said "ugh!["] meaning that they know nothing about it. We were then shown an old Indian battlefield, where the Sioux & Mandans had a great fight as long ago as 1836. Found a beautiful spring of clear running water and drank hearty of it. Had dress parade, orders issued that all Co's have skirmish drill at 8 A.M. each day.

Wednesday, July 8, 1863. Cloudy, looks like rain. Skirmish drill in A.M., boys enjoy this drill exercise very much, especially by bugle. A portion of the supply train came today from camp, and a mail, but none for me. Was quite disappointed, as we will not probably get any mail again for some time.

Thursday, July 9, 1863. Very hot day. The balance supply train came from Ft, Co "D" 7th Minn with it, also a number of Red River half breeds. They report Little Crow & his band at the James River. Had skirmish drill and dress parade.

Friday, July 10, 1863. Very smoky morning, Indians no doubt having set the prairie on fire, though none were seen. Quite windy & dusty in P.M. Sent letters to mother, Lucy & Aunty. Had dress parade, and orders were rec'd that the entire camp move tomorrow at 3 A.M.

Saturday, July 11, 1863. Very cool. Reveille at 2 A.M., this is getting a fellow out lively, broke camp and started at 4, passed over a barren prairie, neither wood, water or grass, everything appears dried up, nothing for stock to eat except now & then some rushes on the margins of sloughs or ponds.[23] Marched 12 miles and camped near the Sheyenne River at 1 P.M. Report that if we do not encounter Indians in a week we will turn back. Some signs were seen by scouts today.

Sunday, July 12, 1863. Pleasant Sabbath, no marching. Inspection at 8 A.M. Gen'l Review at 4 P.M. Our camp is in a beautiful valley called

---

23. Another member of Co. B reported passing through "a grasshopper district south of the Sheyenne, where only stiff straw of the marsh grass was left—all the blades of grass eaten away. The hoppers threatened to defeat us by leaving no forage for our mules and horses." See *Minnesota in Wars*, 353.

Camp Wheaton [Wharton], plenty of wood for fuel, and good sweet water. Had dress parade. More signs of enemy seen. Rec'd orders to entrench at night.

Monday, July 13, 1863. Cool, boys had overcoats this A.M. Reveille at 2 A.M., got started at 4, passed a fine lake to look at. Some timber, marched 10 miles and camped at 9 ½ A.M. at 3 fine lakes, water good, though no timber. Carried our wood on wagons, rather hilly and dry country, though some grass around & between these lakes, an oasis in the desert. Saw millions of frogs here, which we [went] at with clubs & sticks, and caught a great many, taking off the legs which the cooks fried, also made frog soup. They looked like young chicken meat and when cooked it was difficult to distinguish the difference, and we ate them with a good relish, my first trial. Camp Wiser [Weiser].

Tuesday, July 14, 1863. Cool morning. Reveille at 2 ½ A.M. Start at 4 ½, passed over a very poor country. No water or wood. Soil loamy. Camped on a bluff near the Sheyenne, nearly 1 ½ miles to water at noon, having marched 18 miles. Many teams are wearing out, poor water, and very little feed, not much grass, is wearing on them. Camp Sheridan [Sheardown].

Wednesday, July 15, 1863. Beautiful day. Reveille at 2 ½ A.M. Start at 4 ½, passed a lake, which we tried, & it was very salty. Marched over a very fair looking country, though no good water & no timber, and camped at a salt lake at 9 ½ A.M.—8 miles today. Was detailed to help dig trenches around camp. Boys killed two elk. I had some of the meat, very good, quite a change and a relish. No wood, and built first fires with buffalo chips—or dried Buffalo dung—makes a very fair fire but the soup must look out for the cinders. It burns up to ashes and with a gentle breeze will fly quite a distance, and frequently causes our beef & pork to taste like a young buffalo. Camp Smith.

Thursday, July 16, 1863. Smoky morning. Reveille at 2 ½ A.M. Start at 4 ½, marched 18 miles over a very broken country, crossed the Sheyenne River at 11 A.M. Saw an elk, and a cavalry chase after him, and who finally run it down & killed it with their sabres, also caught a young elk. Camped at a lake 5 miles west of the Sheyenne, very poor water, brackish terrible stuff to drink or even use. Chips for fire, dug wells, & dug trenches. Camp Corning.

Friday, July 17, 1863. Pretty cool. Reveille at 2 ½ A.M. Start at 4:15, passed over a hilly country well watered with lakes of brackish water & no timber. Marched 15 miles and camped beside a lake, water some better than last night, was on guard. Signs of Indians seen, two half breeds[24] came in who report Standing Buffalo's Band[25] about 60 miles ahead. Camp Depope [Pope].

Saturday, July 18, 1863. Cool rainy, was on guard. Slept out all night. Reveille at 2 ½, breakfast ate & everything packed and start at 4. Marched 12 miles through a heavy rain & camped beside a lake at 10 A.M., water better and plenty feed and some timber here. Cavalry man shot by his 2ᵈ Lieut here in an affray.[26] Camp Atchison.

Sunday, July 19, 1863. Rainy morning but cleared up before noon. No marching today, done my washing and mended up generally & rested my feet & legs. Orders recd this P.M. that we leave here tomorrow on a forced march for 15 days. All sick and unable to travel to remain here where camp is to be established until the forces return. Scouts report Indians ahead some 30 miles and all is excitement. Our whole force about 2300 with 6 p's[27] cannon.

Monday, July 20, 1863. Cool and clear. R. at 4 A.M. Start at 6 A.M. I was detailed for cook. Went over a very level country for 18 miles and camped near a camp of Red River Half breeds who were here hunting buffalo. There were about a 100 of them came into our camp and reported having seen Little Crow & the Indians and that they were a few days ahead towards the West. They brought with them a boy that they purchased from Little Crow with a pony. I saw him, he was a very smart looking white boy about 14 years old and was in [the] charge of a French Catholic,[28] and

---

24. There were actually three mixed-blood Chippewa men. See *Columns of Vengeance*, 95.

25. Standing Buffalo (ca. 1833–1871) was the leader of a Sisseton band. In mid-1862 he met with Little Crow and voiced his opposition to war. He also wrote to Sibley that "neither I nor my people took part in all those massacres" and that "I always loved the Americans." *Dakota Eyes*, 291–97.

26. Lt. Albert R. Field (1836–1866), a native of Massachusetts, of Co. G, 1st Minnesota Mounted Rangers, shot a mixed-blood private in Co. L who was waving a sword at him. Field was acquitted at trial. See *Columns of Vengeance*, 96.

27. Six pounder cannons.

28. Father Alexis Andre (1832–1893) led a contingent of about one hundred mixed-blood Chippewa hunters along with "several hundred women and children." See *Columns of Vengeance*, 97–98.

"Gen. Sibley's Indian Expedition," sketched by George H. Ellsbury of the 7th Minnesota Infantry, *Harper's Weekly*, September 12, 1863. (Lincoln Financial Foundation Collection)

singular enough the boy felt quite at home with them. No wood, used chips for fire, my first experience in cooking with buffalo chips. It looks this P.M. as though we would have chips for Supper, the wind blowing considerably. Camp Forbes.

Tuesday, July 21, 1863. Lowry, looks some like rain. R. at 3 A.M. Start at 5, passed the half breed camp at 6 ½, quite a large camp, about 600 in number. They had a large number of oxen, ponies and carts. Boys traded with them for furs. Crossed the James River at 9 A.M., then turned our course to the South and camped at 11 A.M. on the James. 10 miles today. Camp Olin.

Wednesday, July 22, 1863. Beautiful morning, rained some during the night. R at 3 A.M. Start at 4 ½. Mail came in during the night, rec'd 8 letters and some papers. Glad to receive them, not only to hear from home, but to learn that Genl Grant has been victorious in the capture of Vicksburg, but that Gen Mead[e] also has defeated Gen'l Lee at Gettysburg. Cheers on all hands over these splendid triumphs of our forces. Mail is brought by mounted carriers, three together generally and well mounted on fast ponies and well armed, who ride night & day from Ft Abercrombie. Marched 15 miles and camped along a creek near the Coteaux de Missouri, chips for wood. Camp Kimball.

Thursday, July 23, 1863. Pleasant. R at 3. Start at 5, marched over a rough hilly country. Got water at a mineral (iron & sulphur) spring, best water we have seen for some time, & very palatable if not stirred too much. Marched 20 miles today and camped on the Coteaux near a lake where there was some grass, first we have seen for some time, and stock got a good feed. Had chips for wood. Camp Grant.

Friday, July 24, 1863. Beautiful. R at 2 ½. Start at 4^{15}, marched 15 miles when the cry Indians! Indians!! was heard along the lines, and went like a flash from front to rear guard, & orders were at once issued for the train to corral near a lake (salt water) at about noon, and to entrench at once, and a heavy detail was made who went at work to throw up trenches around the train & camp. The Indians, a large number estimated at 3000 warriors, were espied by the Scouts encamped just over the Big Mound on the Coteaux, and who had no knowledge of our approach until our force was very near. All was excitement to at once go up, plant the cannon on the hill overlooking their camp, and give them a cannonading, & then charge into them, but Gen'l Sibley, extremely cautious, ordered the command into camp, and to entrench and endeavor to treat with them.

About 2 P.M. the camp being only partially entrenched, many Indians showed themselves along in front of our lines. A number of soldiers went out to parley with them, amongst them Surgeon Weiser[29] of the 10th Reg't on horseback, accompanied by his servant who also was on horseback. The Indians evidently supposing the Doctor to be the Commander owing to his gay dress and caparisoned horse & equipments, and a shot was fired at him, hitting him, tumbling him off his horse. At this signal, the Indians began to rise up as it were out of the grass, having crawled up and secreted themselves under cover of the grass without being discovered in any number, but there was a plenty of them and they at once com'd firing at the squad who with the Dr had advanced beyond the lines.

The bugle was sounded to fall in, and the various Reg'ts were soon in line and were ordered to the front, some as skirmishers. Our entire regiment was sent out by company, and detachments as skirmishers in ad-

---

29. Josiah S. Weiser (1832–1863), a native of Pennsylvania, was surgeon of the 1st Minnesota Mounted Rangers. The Dakota warrior may have mistaken Weiser for Sibley. For more on this moment, see *Columns of Vengeance*, 103–4.

vance with six companies of cavalry and a section of artillery. We charged and chased, the Indians falling back from time to time until we got near where the Indian Camp was, and upon looking down the hill, discovered that they were gone, and also discovered that the attack made upon our lines was evidently for the purpose of giving the squaws & papooses time to move themselves and camp away beyond danger.[30] Indian strategy and well carried out, we had them in a pocket only we did'nt.

At this discovery, Genl. Sibley gave the order for the Mounted Rangers Col McPhail Comd'g, and a section of Battery, was ordered forward at double quick time. The cannon frequently firing into the retreating foe, the cavalry charging and the Infantry close behind, while upon the charge a small cloud was seen overhead and from it there came a flash of lightening and a peal of thunder and one of the Cavalry boys in front of our company was seen to fall from his horse, and upon examination was found to be dead, showing marks of the stroke which felled him.[31] We chased and fought the bloody savages, a running fight for some 15 miles, killing the 14 that we know of that the foe were obliged to leave behind, we were pushing them so lively.

We kept on during the night until quite dark, and at 10 P.M. gave up the chase, and infantry camped, or rather laid down on the ground for the night, being without food or water, excepting the dried buffalo meat thrown away by the Indians during their hasty exit, which we picked up and ate or rather chawed, the command having first been set the example by our brave Col Marshall, who not favoring the theory that it was poisoned, but that the hot pursuit caused them to throw it away as well as many other useful articles, tents, tent poles, robes &c, that he ate of it and counseled the boys to eat, and this was all we had and nothing but brackish water on all sides. Very many were nearly famished for water, my tongue & lips were swollen badly, and I actually cried water, water. One of the Lieuts seeing my distress, gave me a swallow of liquor from his flask, which he always carried, which to some extent quenched my terrible thirst.

I finally fell asleep, and a large percentage of our boys were asleep, when the cavalry, who had been farther in advance of us, returned and then Col McPhail, the Senior officer, consulted with Col Marshall, and

30. Historian Paul N. Beck observes that the Dakota warriors fought in ways that allowed Dakota civilians to retreat. See *Columns of Vengeance*, 106–7, 116–17.

31. John Murphy (ca. 1843–1863), a native of Indiana, was a private in the 1st Minnesota Mounted Rangers, Co. B. See *Columns of Vengeance*, 108.

he gave orders that we return to camp at once. Col Marshall was opposed and thought we had better remain where we were all night and let the provision trains come up in the morning, but Col McPhails order was imperative, he thinking it dangerous to remain there with such a small force as the Indians might return and wipe us out. The boys were then all tired out, sore, and most of them asleep and out of their troubles when the bugle was blown, when we fell in, and started upon the march back to camp, 15 miles away, no road and a terrible dark night. We followed the trail easily back to the Big hills when men and commanders differed as to the direction to camp—orders were given for the artillery to fire signal guns in hopes of receiving an answer from camp, but no answer came, only the reverberating echoes of our own cannon throughout the hills and valleys of the Coteaux. We were lost, everyone realized it, officers as well as men were excited, and the whole command became divided into squads, infantry & cavalry all mixed up, each hunting for camp according to their own idea. The command was lost and could not be kept together. Some got to camp about 4 A.M. next morning, but the squad I was with, about 40 of us, some Infantry and some cavalry boys, travelled incessantly and finally reached camp at 8 A.M. next morning, tired, hungry, thirsty and foot sore. Camp Whitney.[32]

Saturday, July 25, 1863. Pleasant morning, though I do not feel very pleasant, being nearly worn out, and now while resting in camp, we contemplate the perilous position that we were in during the night. Several times the boys saw what they thought were Indians, nearly everybody seen were Indians, as they viewed it, so tired, lost & frenzied, but those we saw were only stragglers same as ourselves, and had a few guns been fired by one party or the other, many men would no doubt have been killed before it was known who they were. At 9 A.M. tents struck, and camp moved 4 miles to a mud lake, though the water was such that we managed to use it. Indians were again seen today, but the large force of them are no doubt enroute to the Missouri Valley to gain the timber, and had we been this morning where we were last night, as desired by our Col, we would have cut them all to pieces today, but to cover 30 miles and catch a running Indian is too much for one day and more too.

32. For accounts of the Battle of Big Mound, see *Columns of Vengeance*, chap. 5; *Dakota Eyes*, chap. 10; Kudelka, *March on the Dakota's*, 27–29, 33–35; Arthur M. Daniels, *A Journal of Sibley's Indian Expedition, during the Summer of 1863, and a Record of the Troops Employed* (Winona, Minn.: Republican, 1864), 11.

Sunday, July 26, 1863. Quite cold & windy. The boys had overcoats on in the morning. R at 4. Start at 6. Indians seen ahead about 8, the Indian trail very wide, and their winters provision, buffalo skins, deer skins, tents, poles &c &c strewed all along the trail. Orders given and the long train closed to 12 deep, and guard thrown out on both sides, two Co's of 6th reg't were sent ahead to deploy as skirmishers. Went a few miles and camped by a lake called Buffalo Lake, because a dead buffalo was found out in the lake, the mud holding him up in position, it was yet warm, evidently been recently killed, an arrow was sticking in him just back of the fore shoulder. We had just got into Camp when the Indians came dashing down on the other side of the lake where the horses & cattle were feeding, on their ponies, and commenced firing. The 6th Reg't & the left wing of our reg't were ordered out on the double quick and the battery wheels into position and fires upon them, driving them back, but before night they returned again & charged down on North Side of lake where a cavalry Co were guarding them when the Co "M," Lt Miller[33] Comd'g, met the Indian charge, killing five Indians, one cavalry man being shot through the bowels & who died, and thus routed them. It was a fine sight as the skirmish was upon the side of a hill in full view, while I was with my Co about ½ mile away. The 6th Regt went to the assistance of the cavalry Co, & the 7th & 10th Regts fell in ready for orders. The Indians kept up a running & retreating fire for about three hours and then disappeared as mysteriously as they had appeared, though obliged to leave the 5 dead in our hands, and the boys soon had trophies, taking their scalps, though not in a genuine skillful-Indian manner. An attack expected tonight, and the camp is being heavily entrenched, our company slept in the trenches. Twenty six scalps have thus far been taken by our boys, though a larger number of Indians have been killed. Today is the Sabbath but there is nothing special to indicate it.[34]

Monday, July 27, 1863. Rainy & cloudy. R at 3 A.M. Start at 5. Our reg't in the advance, the position of honor. Indians seen ahead about 7, stopped at a lake to water, & then continued on marching twenty miles over a very level country, very dry, no grass, and camped at 3 P.M. by a lake of

---

33. It is unclear who this is. Infantry regiments did not have a Co. "M," and there was no Lieutenant Miller in the 1st Minnesota Cavalry.

34. For accounts of the Battle of Dead Buffalo Lake, see *Columns of Vengeance*, 116–18; Kudelka, *March on the Dakota's*, 35–37; Daniels, *Journal of Sibley's Indian Expedition*, 11–12.

good water, though no feed, was called Stony lake owing to the many stones that show themselves on its margin. Near here saw a large herd of buffalo, the country looked black with them to the South of us, and was estimated to be about 5000. Camp Schuman [Schoenemann].

Tuesday, July 28, 1863. Cloudy & foggy. R at 3 ½. Start at 6, as about to leave camp the advance were surprised by about 1000 Indians riding down upon us, on their ponies at full speed and firing as they came.[35] The train was in great confusion for a time, nearly stampeded, but they finally got together 10 deep. The 10th Reg't being ahead were at once deployed as skirmishers, four Co's of our reg't were deployed on the left, and nearly all the Cavalry force were deployed. The Indians came on dashing down upon us, near enough for us to get a good shot, but when they saw we were ready on all sides for them, after a contest of about an hour & a half, the six pounders shelling them, they disappeared, and were not again seen until they assembled together upon the top of a high hill about two miles away. The train moved on. About noon an Indian was overtaken and taken prisoner, he says, "me Teton." The Tetons I learn are a band of some 7000 who never saw white people, who have their homes upon the Hills & in the vales of the Rockies, and use the bow & arrows for weapons. As a general [rule] they are rather small in stature. He says, The Indian train only a short distance ahead, and that many of the Tetons have joined Little Crow to fight the whites. Indians were seen in almost every quarter of the horizon today, but not near enough to do us any harm, or for us to get a shot, though eight were run down & shot by the cavalry. Marched 20 miles and camped on a stream of water which empties into the Missouri River. Camp Stees.[36]

Wednesday, July 29, 1863. Fine morning, on guard all night. Did not get but a wink of sleep during reliefs as we were among the bloody redskins, and we have already learned that they appear upon us when we least expect them. R at 2 A.M. Start at 4. Cavalry and Battery went ahead. Soon heard the cannons boom, and we arrived in the Missouri Valley and got a sight of them, who had got across the river upon the bluffs the other side,

---

35. Sibley estimated the number as between 2,200 and 2,500 warriors but another soldier "more accurately," according to historian Paul N. Beck, placed the number between 100 and 150. See *Columns of Vengeance*, 121–22.

36. For accounts of the Battle of Stony Lake, see *Columns of Vengeance*, 119–22; Kudelka, *March on the Dakota's*, 37–40; Daniels, *Journal of Sibley's Indian Expedition*, 12–14.

and defied us to catch them. We marched down to near the timber which borders the river and halted on the flats, in the extreme hot sun. Several men were sunstroke. A detail scoured the woods, I among the number, to the rivers edge. The Indians mostly were on the other side, and down the river about ½ mile we saw some at the waters edge, who fired at us while we so extremely dry—almost—plunged into the water, and got a good drink, the first since leaving Minn, while others returned the fire of the Indians. We could see them upon the bluffs making signals, Little Crow comd'g his forces by means of looking glasses, in the sun-light. The banks of the river was strewn with wagons, carts, and other materials which they were obliged to throw away & leave behind in their hasty exit from this side of river. The Indians were seen to have three white flags. Finally orders were rec'd to return from the river, another good drink and our canteens full and the whole force, after laying around in the hot sun for several hours, marched down the valley about 5 miles and camped upon Apple Creek. Six men sun stroke, teams nearly worn out. The camp was located principally upon a high ridge overlooking the valley & river, which was at once well fortified. Lt Beaver,[37] a member of Sibleys staff, and his escort are reported missing tonight. He was ordered by Gen'l Sibley to carry despatches to Col Crooks, who was comd'g the force at the river, and they have not been seen since. Camp Slaughter.

Thursday, July 30, 1863. Beautiful morning. R at 5. About 1 A.M. the whole camp were aroused by Indians firing into camp, and they had set a fire to the grass—endeavoring to burn us out. The reg'ts all fell into line, the breastworks were lined with men, and details were made to put[38] out the fire by setting back fires. We remained in line about an hour, then broke ranks, and all to our tents again except Co's G & K who remained out as add'l guard until morning. At 11 A.M. our company was ordered to be ready to march. At 1 P.M. we left camp, in all 9 Co's Infantry, 2 Co's Cavalry, and 3 cannon, and went to the river at the point where we were yesterday, for the purpose if possible of finding Lt Beaver. We went down through the timber & brush, fighting the Indians, destroyed over a hun-

---

37. Frederick John Holt Beever (1830–1863) was a wealthy Englishman who had attended Oxford University. *Harper's Weekly* reported on September 12, 1863, that Beever had served during the Crimean War "and finally came to this country in search of adventures.... He fell into an ambush and was murdered. One side of his face was hacked off with a hatchet while he was still alive."

38. Buswell appears to have written the word "put" over the word "fight" here.

dred carts and many other things that the Indians had left behind, being unable to take across the river, and finally found the remains of Lt Beaver and his escort, one of the cavalry boys who had been detailed as orderly.[39] Beaver's body had two bullet holes and 2 arrows fast in him, and not having any hair to speak of and being a man with fine whiskers—one side was scalped, and carried away as a trophy. We took the bodies and carried them to camp, arriving there about sun down.

Friday, July 31, 1863. Very pleasant. R at 5, went with others down to the Mo river, sandy beach on both sides, quite large stream, wide but not very deep. Got our canteens filled and a good drink besides, though it was very muddy, yet good drinking water, and the only water we can find about here fit to drink. Apple Creek where we are camped is so strong with alkali that it is fairly soapy when a little grease is added, so much so that we took our greasy haversacks into the creek and washed them without any soap, and made a good suds, and washed them clean. Lt Beaver was buried here with military honors and also his orderly. Had dress parade and recd orders that we leave here homeward bound tomorrow, and which caused many a cheer from the ranks.

Saturday, August 1, 1863. Cloudy and smoky. R at 3 ½. Start at 5 ½, homeward bound, boys all gay as larks and we started out of Camp to the tune of old "John Brown's Body." About 12 last night the whole camp was aroused, as signs had been seen that indicated an attack, and all laid behind the trenches, on our arms for 2 to 3 hours, and then retired to our tents, it being a false alarm. Marched 16 miles. Camp Brainard [Braden].

Sunday, August 2, 1863. Pleasant. R at 3 ½. Start at 5 ½, scouts took a new and nearer route across the country. Passed old Camp Amber at 11 A.M., marched 18 miles & camped by a lake at 2 P.M., fair water, but no grass. Saw a large herd of Buffalo near here. Camp Banks.

Monday, August 3, 1863. Beautiful. R at 3. Start at 5 ½ A.M. Passed over a very level country, marched 15 miles and camped by an alkali lake at noon, though near by found a spring sweet water though quite a taste of iron. Saw 3 buffalo quite near the train. Cavalry chased and shot one. A heavy thunder shower in the P.M. Camp Kennedy.

39. Nicholas Miller (1842–1863), a native of Germany, was a private in the 6th Minnesota Infantry, Co. K.

Tuesday, August 4, 1863. Rainy, a northeaster. R. at 4. Start at 6. Passed over a beautiful looking country, north of old trail, and a better country, better water, and more grass. Struck old trail at old Camp Sibley and followed it to the camp and camped at 1 P.M. 18 miles today, between two lakes, fair water. Camp Willis [Williston].

Wednesday, August 5, 1863. Fine, no marching, stopped to rest the command, plenty water & feed. 8 A.M. rec'd orders to be ready to march in one hour, as Indians were reported near, the first alarm since leaving the river. At 9 A.M. orders countermanded as the supposed Indians proved to be half breeds coming to meet us with the U.S. Mail. Rec'd some letters and was quite glad to get them so far away from home, rec'd papers but no great victories for our forces since Vicksburgh & Gett[y]sburg. I expect we will before long be down in Dixie to help to fight it out. Camp Bracket.

Thursday, August 6, 1863. Cloudy with slight rains, quite a hurricane last night. Sand flew and many tents blew down. R. at 3 ½. Start at 6. Left old trail, went to the South of it, leaving old Camp Grant to the left. Marched 16 miles and camped by a lake on the Coteau, good spring water with sulphur in it near, chips for fuel. Camp Gilfillan.

Friday, August 7, 1863. Fine, our company on guard. Slept in trenches all night. R at 3. Start at 5 ½, passed over highest point of Coteau at 7 and stopped here to rest, good [could?] see for miles & miles and yet no sign of timber any where, mules & stock turned out to feed. Marched 13 miles and camped at a lake on old trail at 2 P.M. At 4 P.M. saw a party coming from a distance which proved to be some of our scouts, with 17 Indians, who were a part of Little Crows Band, and who gave themselves up. Saw timber on Devils Lake quite distinctly. Camp Hall.

Saturday, August 8, 1863. Fine, but a very heavy dew. R at 3. Start at 5. Went to the north of old trail, passed over a rolling country, well watered by beautiful lakes, crossed a branch of James River at 9 ½ A.M. Crossed another branch at 10 ½ and camped at 11 A.M. 12 miles today, very good water. Trial of Indians com'd, heard trial of 3 this P.M. Camp Carter.

Sunday, August 9, 1863. Beautiful Sabbath. R at 5, rest today, no marching, was on guard, my beat being that of guarding the mules. Half breeds came and camped about 3 miles away, many of the boys went over to trade. Outside of my guard duty I took a good rest.

Monday, August 10, 1863. Cloudy, heavy rain during the night. R. at 3 ½. Start at 5 ½. Was witness of quite an affecting [scene]. The 3 Indians who had their trial yesterday were held and were too [to go?] along with us, under guard, and the squaws & papooses were left behind, and such a bewailing time I never saw, and the squaws &c were determined to go too. They were without provision and they were given about a ½ bushel crackers and 50 lbs meat and without arms they were left behind to the tender mercies of him who provideth all things. Marched 22 miles and arrived at Camp Atchison, which seemed pretty near home, here meeting the boys left behind and the general camp.

Tuesday, August 11, 1863. Very pleasant. R at 5. Boys here were glad to see us. An expedition went to Devils Lake and captured Little Crows Son,[40] he was found near the lake with a musket in hand watching a wolf's hole, and had only the one cartridge, then in his gun, and nearly in a starved condition, and terribly lousy. He stated that after his fathers death he had started west, had followed the expedition, living upon what could be found left in the camp, had picked up the musket in one of the camps, and the cartridge. Upon returning had quite a menagerie, Little Crow's Son, a young elk, an eagle, and some white swan. Upon arrival at camp, Little Crow['s] Son was taken to the lake, stripped, his rags thrown away, washed thoroughly and some clean clothes placed upon him. Was on guard duty. Mail came today and bro't me some newspapers from Aunty, glad to get them, though the first for some time.

Wednesday, August 12, 1863. Cold & blustery. R at 4. Start at 6 towards home. A battalion of cavalry was sent to Snake river in search of Chief White Lodge[41] and his band. We followed old trail 16 miles and camped on a beautiful lake about 5 P.M., very passable water. Camp Burt.

---

40. After the Battle of Wood Lake, Little Crow and his band fled to the Dakota plains. At some point in early 1863, he and his son, Wowinape, or Thomas Wakeman (1846–1886), returned to Minnesota. On July 3, while traveling together, they encountered two white men who shot and mortally wounded Little Crow. Wowinape describes his father's death and his own capture twenty-six days later in *Dakota Eyes*, 279–82; *Columns of Vengeance*, 97–98. Little Crow's son was later tried before a military court. See Court-Martial NN-3132.

41. Chief White Lodge was the leader of the Sisseton band that captured Laura Duley and several others. See *Dakota War*, 24.

"Little Crow's Son. Wo-Wi-Na-Pe," also known as Thomas Wakeman, taken at Fort Snelling on February 24, 1864. (Smithsonian Museum of the American Indian)

Thursday, August 13, 1863. Misty & foggy. R at 3 ½. Start at 5. Stopped at old camp Corning at 7 to rest and water, crossed the Sheyenne about noon, Mt Bottineau on our left, marched 16 miles and camped at 4 P.M. at a lake of good water & plenty feed, rather dusty. Saw 5 antelope gliding past, a beautiful sight. Camp Libby.

Friday, August 14, 1863. Cold. R at 3. Start at 5. Scarcity of water, marched 14 miles & camped on a lake, passable water. Just one year ago I signed the papers that made me a soldier, have seen some hard service, and have not accomplished much either. Rec'd mail, a letter from home and one from Aunty. Camp Arnold.

Saturday, August 15, 1863. Cold & blustery. R at 3. Start at 5. Passed over a beautiful level country, no timber as far as the eye can reach, plenty grass, scarcity of water, marched 12 miles & camped at a lake very poor water. Camp Stevens.

Sunday, August 16, 1863. Cold, no marching today, wrote letters home & to Aunty. Was taken sick with bilious fever and kidney trouble and was taken to hospital. My back felt as if it was about broken, had my feet soaked, vomited considerable and such terrible green looking stuff came up. The Drs say it is the effects of drinking the Alkali water. Many of the boys are beginning to feel the effects of it, but it effects [sic] them differently. Camp Stevens.

Monday, August 17, 1863. Pleasant, but some windy. R at 3. Start at 5, rode in ambulance, two of us in one lying flat on our backs, my back aching terribly. Went 16 miles over a very level country, and camped on Maple Creek at noon, plenty timber and good water. The boys all rejoicing at once more getting into a country where we can see timber and get good water. A great many boys & teams nearly worn out, a hard march we have had on poor water, though plenty rations, very hot. Camp Ambler.

Tuesday, August 18, 1863. Cloudy, thunder shower, no marching, men & teams too tired, and stopped to rest. Boys improved the time by going into the timber & brush and getting plums & cherries on the bank of the Creek, which is a branch of the Red River of the North.

Wednesday, August 19, 1863. Cooler. R at 2 ½. Start at 4 ½, not well enough to walk, though feel better, though my kidneys trouble me. Passed over a beautiful level prairie country for about 18 miles and camped at the Sheyenne at noon, plenty timber and good water. A party came from Ft Abercrombie, which is not far off, with the mail.

Thursday, August 20, 1863. Fine gen'l Inspection in A.M. by Col Marcy,[42] U.S.A. Mail came in from Pembina. The Commissary train for the fort went across the river this A.M., and we struck tents at noon and marched about 4 miles to a lake [of] good water & camped. Feel some better, ¼ rations issued. Camp Arlington [Edgerton].

Friday, August 21, 1863. Beautiful. R at 3. Start at 5, feel about the same. Passed over a beautiful level country, & crossed the Wild Rice at 10 A.M. and arrived at the Fort [Abercrombie] about noon, 14 miles today, and camped near it. In the P.M. I with some others went into the Fort, found it merely a stockade, with some good frame buildings inside, but on the outside near the gate saw a camp of half breeds who had a train of Esquimaux dogs, the first I ever saw. Saw the Steamer International in the

---

42. Randolph B. Marcy (1812–1887) was father-in-law of Maj. Gen. George B. McClellan and served as inspector general of the US army. For an account of his inspection of the 10th Minnesota Infantry, see *Minnesota in Wars*, 460.

Red River, and went aboard of her, a long very narrow steamer, quite well built, and navigates this very narrow, crooked though quite deep river from here—down to Winnipeg. Camp Hackett.

Saturday, August 22, 1863. Beautiful, rather cool, no marching. Remained here for a few days for rest & for orders, so we learn. Left the hospital and care of the Doctors today & reported for duty, feeling considerable better, though entirely stought [stout?]. A Salute was fired today of 13 guns in honor of the presence of the Gen'l Comd'g, had dress parade.

Sunday, August 23, 1863. Rainy & cold, heavy shower, rainy nearly all day, no Inspection. Co "H" 9th Regt and one cavalry Co detailed to remain here at the fort. Am glad it is not our Co, too far on the frontier to soldier it, especially in a fort. I prefer going South.

Monday, August 24, 1863. Pleasant, rather muddy, mule teams loading with rations for 25 days. Mail came in, rec'd some letters, also papers. The civil war still continues & not much prospect yet of the end.

Tuesday, August 25, 1863. Pleasant. R at 4. Start at 8, we cross the Red River, marched 10 miles and camped on the Red River at 1 ½ P.M. Wood & water plenty, but grass rather scarce. Camp Phelps.

Wednesday, August 26, 1863. Very cold. R at 3 ½. Start at 5, was on guard. Reached Ottertail River at 8 A.M. Passed the ruins of Breckenridge, there were several brick buildings here, but were burned by the redskins. Passed a very good country for 16 miles & camped at noon on Ottertail River at the Crossing. Was more tired than usual being on guard duty, brought wood with us for fire, caught plenty fine pickerel here, & had quite a fish feast. Camp White.

Thursday, August 27, 1863. Cloudy, like rain. R at 4. Start at 5 ½. Passed over a beautiful country, well watered by lakes, some timber and fine feed. Marched 15 miles & camped at a beautiful lake, headwaters Pomme de Terre River, excellent water, plenty wood & fine grass. Camp Sullivan.

Friday, August 28, 1863. Cold, windy. R at 4. Start in rear column at 7. Passed over a beautiful country, many fine lakes, good water, good soil, plenty timber, & feed. Went 13 miles, crossed the Pomme De Terre River & camped upon a lake, being the widening of the River, near a nice grove timber, good water & such grass, how the stock did go for it. Camp Heath.

Saturday, August 29, 1863. [No entry.]

Sunday, August 30, 1863. Pleasant, warmer. R at 5, no marching, had inspection at 8 A.M. Plenty game here, also plums, grapes, and now & then a marsh of cranberries. Mail came, rec'd a letter from Eddie Hodgkins. Dress parade.

Monday, August 31, 1863. Very fine. R at 4. Start at 6. Pass over beautiful country, 17 miles, and camped beside a lake & clump of timber at 1 ½ P.M., quite tired. Reg't was mustered this P.M. for 2 mos pay. Camp Jones.

Tuesday, September 1, 1863. Very pleasant. R at 4. Start at 6. Pass over a beautiful country, and through quite a body of timber, 14 miles, and camped beside a beautiful lake & grove at 2 P.M. on the townsite of Weston, buildings all burnt, quite lame. Camp Beaver [Beever].

Wednesday, September 2, 1863. Cool & misty. A mistake being made, R was at 2 ½ instead of 3 ½, everybody out, though we did not start until nearly 6. Marched 12 miles over a fine country and saw the first of Civilization, an improved farm and some people, which did certainly look good to us. At 10 A.M. passed Sauk Center, and camped at 1 P.M. below & near the town. Got some potatoes, the first for some time which we certainly relished. Had quite lame back. Had dress parade. Camp Rubles.

Thursday, September 3, 1863. Beautiful. R at 5. No marching. Was glad to hail the approach of the provision train from Ft Snelling, as our rations have been quite short. Mail also came and good tidings from home, boys all feeling well as we are nearing home. We parted with the 10th Reg't boys here, who were ordered to scour the big woods and report at Ft Ridgely. Great many people came from town & the county near to see us. Had dress parade.

Friday, September 4, 1863. Warm and cloudy, like rain. R at 4. Start at 8, bid good bye to 10th Regt boys at 7, passed fine farms, through timber & clearing 17 miles and camped on a bluff at 5 P.M. which overlooks the Sauk River, was on guard. Camp Wilson.

Saturday, September 5, 1863. Pleasant. R at 4. Start at 6 on advance guard, got quite tired and rode part way, went 16 miles & camped near Richmond at 1 P.M., beautiful place, fine lakes with gravel shores, good place to come fishing & hunting. Senator Ramsey[43] and many others

---

43. Alexander Ramsey (1815–1903) was Minnesota's second governor (1860–1863) before serving in the US Senate (1863–1875).

from St Paul met us here, whole command was reviewed at dress parade. In the evening the band serenaded Sibley, Ramsey & others, and many fine short speeches were made. Bishop Whipple also spoke, he is a man of ability. Camp Austin.

Sunday, September 6, 1863. Beautiful. R at 6. In camp all day, command reported unfit for duty, there being a lack of supplies. Bishop Whipple preached. I went and heard a very interesting sermon. Had dress parade. Rec'd orders from Gen'l Pope Comd'g, very complimentary to the Command stating that we should have a wider field to range in.

Monday, September 7, 1863. Very pleasant. R at 4. Start at 6. Pass through heavy timber and brush nearly all the way down the Sauk Valley, principally settled by Germans. Crossed the River and camped at 2 P.M., 18 miles today, St Cloud in the distance, begin now to have a plenty of visitors. Gen'l Sibley & Staff left us at 4 P.M. for Ft Snelling in advance, and the command now under Col Marshall.

Tuesday, September 8, 1863. Pleasant. R at 4. Start at 7. Pass through St Cloud—a fine location overlooking the Miss River from a high bluff, and rather a pretty place. Water in the Miss low, teams forded, men cross on a fence, went 10 miles and camped at 1 P.M. beside the river bank. Did not feel well and was reported [to] quarters. Mail came, and many more visitors, who though anxious to look into camp life yet were afraid to try it. Camp Daniels.

Wednesday, September 9, 1863. Cool & misty. R at 3 ½. Start at 6. Passed over very sandy country, covered with stunted pin oaks, & not much settlement for 22 miles and camped at 3 P.M. at Big Lake in the bushes. Saw the village of Monticello across the Miss River. Big Lake is a beautiful sheet of water and abounds in fish, game plenty. Not feeling well, my back troubling me, I rode in ambulance most of the day. Will soon be at the end of our march for the present, then for home and friends, then possibly to Dixie. Camp Anderson.

Thursday, September 10, 1863. Pleasant. R at 3 ½. Start at 6. Passed over more sandy country, very thinly settled by Yankee people, oak openings, marched 16 miles and camped at 2 P.M. on bank [of the] Miss River, 2 miles from Anoka, rode in ambulance today though feel some better, back trouble[s] me. Plenty of visitors from Anoka & vicinity. Camp Davy[s].

Friday, September 11, 1863. Cool. R at 3 ½. Start at 6. Pass over rather uneven, sandy country, through Anoka across Rum River at 7 A.M., rather a pretty place, quite a milling town. Marched 15 miles and camped on Miss River 4 miles above St Anthony at noon. Billy Stevens[44] met us here. Rode in the ambulance most of the day. Had plenty visitors who came out from St Anthony to meet us. Camp Rice.

Saturday, September 12, 1863. Cool, misty. R at 5. Start at 7. Passed through St Anthony, across the Suspension bridge & through the streets of Minneapolis at 9, had a fine view of St Anthony Falls. The people of the place were out in large numbers to see & greet us, plenty ladies, a beautiful place, much more so than St Anthony. Marched 11 miles & camped near Ft Snelling at noon, a great many visitors came out from St Paul. Now we rest for a time, after our tedious and long campaign, and though many thousands of dollars have been expended, yet the expedition has accomplished but a very little—other than to destroy the Indians equipments, wagons & their winter supply. They were driven across the Missouri River, but it dont take long for them to come back, of course they are no doubt discouraged, as Little Crow supposed he had force enough to whip the whole world. Met Col here. Camp Steele.

Sunday, September 13, 1863. Pleasant. R not very early. Company Inspection at 9 A.M., plenty visitors today. John Morrison[45] & Gil Tucker[46] from Winona, now belonging to Hatch's Battalion, came over to see us. Had a good time chatting over the people at Winona, the Indian & Civil war. No dress parade. In fact we were not in shape for dress parade before such a crowd of visitors. Orders rec'd that Comd^{rs} of Regts grant furloughs ¼ at a time until Oct 1st. So we will have a chance to go home again & then where will we go.

Monday, September 14, 1863. Beautiful, up early before sunrise & went down to the Ft. Took quite a tramp around, went into the old slush house w[her]e we got our first soldier meal, and one that I never can forget. They were still slushing it out in the most approved style. Had dress parade, when Col Marshall took command of the Reg't and said that he would stay with us during the war, that we would have 12 to 15 days fur-

44. William Stevens (1832–1918), a native of New York, was a private in the 7th Minnesota Infantry, Co. B.
45. John C. Morrison (1842–1927), a native of Canada, was a corporal in Hatch's Cavalry Battalion, Co. C.
46. Gilbert R. Tucker (1841–1924), a native of Canada, was a private in Hatch's Cavalry Battalion, Co. B.

lough, and should probably be at the taking of Richmond. After breaking ranks, 3 cheers were given for our Col Marshall and the furlough.

Tuesday, September 15, 1863. Pleasant, very warm night. I was on guard. The entire regiment rec'd new clothing, and I rec'd my clothes from Mankato, which were left there during the expedition. Very heavy wind, and the sand about here flew considerably. Col Miller takes command of the Ft today. Genl Sibley & staff came up from St Paul & made us a visit.

Wednesday, September 16, 1863. Pleasant warm night, turned out to be a rainy day. Report is that we get paid off tomorrow. We signed pay roll & some of us will soon be off on the furlough, & then for down South.

Thursday, September 17, 1863. Cold, rainy morning. Stormy all day, no pay today. Rec'd report that the 7th, 9th & 10th Regts after short furloughs will go South, but where is not stated, the 6th Reg't to remain in the State, which created many a cheer by our boys, who seemed especially anxious for active duty, and something besides state or Indian service.

Friday, September 18, 1863. Cold morning. Sprinkled snow, but finally cleared up by noon. Was on police duty today, this is a duty that a true soldier ought not to be called upon to do. The U.S. Soldiers are the only ones put to such menial service except as a punishment. Co's "C" & "K" paid off and furloughed for 12 days.

Saturday, September 19, 1863. [No entry.]

Sunday, September 20, 1863. Pleasant, warm. Inspection at 9 A.M., rec'd letters from home, made a visit to the fort to give it one more good look before leaving here. A good many boys got furloughs today with orders to report at Winona. I expect to go tomorrow.

PART II
The Civil War

4

"Away To Dixie"

Travels in Missouri, Illinois, and Tennessee, September 21–December 21, 1863

Henry Sibley considered his expedition into the Dakota Territory a great success. He cruelly reported that he had seized "vast quantities of subsistence" that would leave "many, perhaps most of them, to perish miserably in their utter destitution during the coming fall and winter." The corpses of "many of the most guilty have been left unburied on the prairies," he continued, "to be devoured by wolves and foxes." To his troops, he proclaimed, "You have routed the miscreants who murdered our people last year ... and driven them in confusion and dismay across the Missouri River," although he wished "these remorseless savages could have been pursued and utterly extirpated, for their crimes and barbarities merited such a full measure of punishment." Of course, many of those who suffered had been women and children, or people from peace-seeking tribes, who were caught up in the destruction and killing.[1]

Buswell had not enlisted to fight Indians, and he was glad when his time fighting in the Upper Midwest came to an end. In October 1863 he and other members of the 7th Minnesota boarded a train bound for Chicago and then St. Louis, where they were housed in Schofield Barracks. It was in St. Louis that Buswell finally encountered "the first rebels I ever saw"—prisoners of war who had been captured in Arkansas. After several weeks of touring the city and attending services and lectures at various churches, Buswell and a contingent of men crossed the Mississippi River into Illinois to suppress the disloyal activities of antiwar and pro-Confederate Democrats, known as Copperheads, who were suspected

---

1. *Columns of Vengeance*, 125–26.

of being members of traitorous secret societies. From November 21 to December 3, he pursued Copperheads, bushwhackers, and deserters in the Prairie State. Then, on December 7, Buswell was detailed to go on special guard duty to Nashville. He enjoyed his time touring the Tennessee capital, much as he did in the city of St. Louis.

༺༻

Monday, September 21, 1863. Beautiful, our company rec'd pay—I got $40^{05}, rec'd furlough, & started at 7 P.M. for St Paul. Put up at Whitchers Hotel[2] on 4th Street, and after roaming about the town for a while, went to the Hotel and to bed.

Tuesday, September 22, 1863. Fine. Slept well, the first time in a bed for about 6 months. Got breakfast, paid my bill 75 cents, went to the levee and got aboard the Steamer Cutter with some of our boys, and at 10^{20} A.M. left St Paul, down the Miss. Changed boats at Red Wing at 9 P.M., got a state room and went to bed.

Wednesday, September 23, 1863. Pleasant, slept finely, got up at 5 A.M., found that the boat was lying at Wabasha, having been there two hours. Left there at 6, got a good breakfast, and at 8 A.M. arrived at Minneiska and here went ashore. Soon saw Porter the mail carrier and he took Alva E. Dearborn and myself up the valley. Arrived home at 10 ½ A.M. and took the folks completely by surprise. They were heartily glad to see us & we were glad to get home.

Thursday, September 24, 1863. Cool, cloudy, went to Beaver with mother & visited the folks there, ate dinner at Mrs Hayes,[3] had a pleasant time, all seemed glad to see me.

Friday, September 25, 1863. Pleasant, at home all day, telling the folks about the expedition, the Indians &c. Was invited & spent the evening at Mrs Hiram Wrights,[4] had a pleasant visit.

2. Sylvester C. Whitcher owned a livery stable at the corner of Robert and 4th Streets. The 1863 city directory lists several hotels on 4th Street, but none called Whitcher's.

3. Probably Laura A. Hayes (born ca. 1822 in New York), wife of James W. Hayes.

4. Lovisa (or Lavina or Louisa) C. Herring (1831–1915), a native of New York, married Hiram Wright in 1848 in Wisconsin.

Saturday, September 26, 1863. Pleasant, though windy, remained at home with folks all day. Had some calls from neighbors, and had a long talk about the wars.

Sunday, September 27, 1863. Pleasant, went to meeting with folks at Beaver, attended the funeral sermon of Mr Herring[5] at the school house in the P.M.

Monday, September 28, 1863. Pleasant, staid at home all day, tried my hand at a little work, helped father stack hay in the P.M.

Tuesday, September 29, 1863. Fine, helped father in with one load of hay, then went to Elba to spend the day with Alva. Saw no change in Elba to amount to anything. Ate dinner with Alva at his uncle Jerry's, then made calls & returned home. Upon arriving there found an invitation to spend the evening at Obed Metcalfs,[6] which I accepted.

Wednesday, September 30, 1863. Cloudy, threatens rain. Alva came down and we went to Beaver. Saw Starr, Hopson & others who had got home. Took dinner at Hopsons, had a No 1 time, made several calls.

Thursday, October 1, 1863. Cloudy, rainy, was at home during the A.M. In P.M. went to Beaver. Saw Robt Rolfe,[7] Dan'l Winter[8] & Jim Pope who had got home. On my return visited at Stonings & Warners & spent the evening at Warners.

Friday, October 2, 1863. Cloudy, cool, remained at home, rec'd a call from Robt Rolfe, was invited to a party at Jacobus Hall, accepted and went and danced into the wee small hours of the night. Quite a number present from Plainview. Had a very pleasant time and got home about daylight.

Saturday, October 3, 1863. Cloudy, rainy, staid at home all day, and in the house, reading and talking about the future prospects, as my furlough

---

5. Henry Herring (1797–1863), a native of New York, was the father of Lovisa Wright. He lived with his daughter and son-in-law.

6. Obed Metcalf (1831–1910), a native of New Hampshire, was a farmer in Winona.

7. Robert Rolph (1840–1876), a native of Illinois, was a farm laborer in Winona County. He enlisted in the 10th Minnesota Infantry, Co. C, and rose to the rank of sergeant.

8. Daniel Winter (born ca. 1837 in Indiana) was a private in the 10th Minnesota Infantry, Co. C.

nearly out, and have to report soon and away to Dixie, a new and a different field of action. When I shall be home again is a hard question.

Sunday, October 4, 1863. Pleasant, was at home most of the day, had visit from Mr & Mrs Hayes, and a very pleasant time.

Monday, October 5, 1863. Pleasant, prospects of fine weather. Took dinner with Mr Whites folks and tea at Obed Melcalfs, and engaged my passage with William Metcalf to Winona.

Tuesday, October 6, 1863. Pleasant. Bid good bye to all the folks and as a bold soldier boy left for Winona, with William, when again to return is difficult to tell, possibly never, possibly to be shot down, wounded or perish with some fell disease. Many such thoughts occur to my mind as departing from my home & parents on this occasion. Had a pleasant trip over & arrived at Winona in the P.M. Some of our Co had already reported. Saw Mr Gage and I had to go home with him, he & his folks were glad to greet & entertain me, and I accepted their very generous hospitality.

Wednesday, October 7, 1863. Pleasant morning. Our company with others of the 10th went into camp near Winona Lake back of the City, no guard, and we had the full liberty of the City, a friendly feeling seemed to be everywhere. Staid at Mr Gages, had dress parade in the evening to the amusement of the citizens more especially and who turned out en-masse.

Thursday, October 8, 1863. Some cloudy, but came off pleasant. Rec'd orders that we be prepared to leave here this P.M. At 1 P.M. struck tents, and moved to the levee, and at 5 P.M. went aboard the Northern Belle. Nearly the whole town turned out to give us the Shake and "God speed" with many a good bye and warm kiss, & away we went for Dixie Land. Found the balance of our regts on board, had a very pleasant trip down to La Crosse [Wisconsin] arriving there at 10 P.M. At once went aboard the cars, and staid in them all night.

Friday, October 9, 1863. Had very little sleep, if any, and nothing but the back of the car seat—worse than a canteen—to lie my head upon. Remained here, being very poor management, until noon. Had an opportunity to see this city, on the Sand bar, and it was truly a Sand bank, it having been dry, and wagons to sink into the hubs in many places. At noon the train started and away we went for Chicago.

Saturday, October 10, 1863. Cloudy, sprinkled rain. Slept a little though some of the boys quite noisy. Arrived at Chicago at 9 A.M., changed cars and were soon enroute by a special train for St Louis, Mo. Did not have much time to see Chicago, but crossed the Canal which connects the Miss with the lake.

Sunday, October 11, 1863. Fine morning, passed over quite level country, with very large corn fields. Passed Springfield [Illinois] the capital at 5 A.M. and arrived in St Louis at dark in a rain storm. Crossed the river on a ferry boat, and up through the City, and were soon housed at Schofield Barracks, nearly in the heart of the City. Got a bunk and went to bed.

Monday, October 12, 1863. Cloudy morning, got a pass and went out to see the City. Quite a large, fine, and busy looking place. Our Reg't moved into the new Schofield Barracks near by today, this suited us better, good clean quarters. The 9th & 10th Regts came in today and went to Camp Gamble, about 3 miles out, and went into camp.

Tuesday, October 13, 1863. Smoky morning. Had a pass and went down to the river to see the Monitor Ozark, a new monitor just built, and the first I ever saw. A very curious looking craft, no wonder the monitor was called a cheese box as it certainly resembles one as it floated upon the water. Went aboard and was shown around by an officer, the movable turret contained two large guns. Went below into the machinery departments, all machinery being below the waters edge, a very wonderful invention and wonderful that Ericson[9] should have developed it at this particular time. Then went up to the Lindell Hotel and went through its spacious apartments, said to be the largest hotel in the U.S. It certainly was very large, covering over half a block 7 stories high, and fitted up in magnificent style.

Wednesday, October 14, 1863. Very dull morning. Was called out on special detail at 6 ½ A.M. and went with others to the levee and assisted in bringing or guarding up 330 rebel prisoners, recently taken at Little Rock, Ark,[10] the first rebels I ever saw, and they were butternuts sure,

---

9. The USS *Monitor*, an ironclad vessel designed by Swedish inventor John Ericsson (1803–1809) in 1861, fought against the CSS *Virginia* in Hampton Roads, Virginia, on March 9, 1862. After its successful trial in battle, the Union ordered other monitors. See Anna Gibson Holloway and Jonathan W. White, *Our Little Monitor: The Greatest Invention of the Civil War* (Kent, Ohio: Kent State University Press, 2018).

10. Little Rock, Arkansas, had fallen into Union hands in September after a two-month campaign.

their uniform if it was such, being ordinary cotton cloth, dyed with butternut, native cloth & native dying, which made a uniform color, and they were a dirty, shabby looking sett. We took them through the streets with considerable pride to the Gratiot Street Prison, the principal prison in this City, and then we were relieved from duty.

Thursday, October 15, 1863. Clear overhead, but a raw air. Got a pass and took a walk about the City. Our Company rec'd orders to take 3 days rations in knapsacks, to go West on some expedition, and all was excitement over our first initiatory expedition in rebeldom. Had dress parade near the barracks at 5 ½ P.M.

Friday, October 16, 1863. Got our breakfast at 1 A.M., quite early for breakfast & everything in readiness we marched to the Pacific R.R. Depot, and at 5 A.M. got aboard the train bound to Washington, Mo, as we learn to coerce some militia men who had been ordered out by the Governor and who refused to obey orders. Arrived there at 11 A.M. after a fine run along the many windings of the Missouri River Valley, Washington being situated on the river & rather a fine looking place. Took up our quarters at the City Hall though we were not very welcome, as the people here, quite generally, were sympathizers with the fractious "melish" and the Johnny Rebs in general.[11]

Saturday, October 17, 1863. Very pleasant morning, took a ramble around the town, met some people who were Union at heart, though they were generally afraid to utter their sentiments. Got plenty of grapes. I never saw such a sight before, grapes grew everywhere, seemed like a spontaneous growth. We expect to have to go into the interior in quest of the "melish," but our presence has already begun to have a mellowing influence, as they are beginning to assemble. Was on guard, though guard duty here is an easy one.

Sunday, October 18, 1863. Pleasant, went to the Catholic church, this is the leading denomination here. Took a walk after church, got plenty [of] apples & grapes, and some of the boys went into the woods and got pawpaws, a fruit shaped like a banana, but quite green color, fair fruit to eat. I relished them.

Monday, October 19, 1863. Pleasant morning, we rather enjoy it here. Went to hear a Union speech, there were some believers in Secession

---

11. The Missouri State Guard was a pro-Confederate militia in the state; the Missouri State Militia was the pro-Union organization.

present, and they talked considerably, and but for our presence there would have been a disturbance. This evening a dance was held in the Washington House, many of the boys attended.

Tuesday, October 20, 1863. Very fine morning, the militia having come and now ready to report. Our work being ended, we were ordered back to St Louis, and bidding good bye to our short timed though many dear acquaintances, we got aboard the train at 9 A.M. and were soon in the barracks at St Louis. Sent letter to mother & Lucy.

Wednesday, October 21, 1863. Pleasant day, was on guard duty. Saw Hopson and some of his boys, they were guarding skiffs on the river, and I was guarding on a steamer.

Thursday, October 22, 1863. Cool morning, snowing, and it fell to the depth of 3 inches, a slight drizzle all day, and froze up at night. Sent letter to Aunty and Geo Knowles.[12]

Friday, October 23, 1863. Very cold morning, rather cold snap this early in the season & in this section. On guard again, this time on Washington Av[e.] guarding gov't warehouses, where our rations are stored. Very pleasant evening, had a city watchman for company. Recd two papers from Lynn.

Saturday, October 24, 1863. Pleasant, but rather cool. Was relieved at 10 A.M., cold snap thawing out and it is quite muddy.

Sunday, October 25, 1863. Warmer, was detailed for guard, my post being on the walk outside barracks, but had not been on my beat long before my back gave out and I fell on the walk, was picked up and taken into the barracks [and] relieved from duty. In the P.M. towards night took a short walk. Rec'd two letters from home, glad to hear from them, & they glad to know where I am.

Monday, October 26, 1863. Pleasant day, got a pass and went out in P.M., went down to the Court House, and after going through it, went up in the dome, had a fine view of the City & country around. Spent the balance of the P.M. in the Museum,[13] quite extensive and many rare curiosities. Enjoyed the day finely.

---

12. George Knowles (born 1834 in New York) was a farmer in Winona County who married Buswell's sister, Lucy, on April 20, 1864.

13. The Academy of Science in St. Louis, which was established in 1856, operated a museum in the city.

Tuesday, October 27, 1863. Pleasant, was on guard, my station was at the Schofield Barracks Prison. My back troubled me considerably. This prison is more especially for our own soldiers who do not behave themselves and today there were 18 in it.

Wednesday, October 28, 1863. Pleasant day, got a pass and went out for a tramp, went up on Broadway among the residences. Some very fine.

Thursday, October 29, 1863. Rainy morning, on guard again at the gate, Regimental Hd'qrs. Here is where a soldier learns soldier etiquette, it being necessary to Salute every officer who passes in or out, even though one pass[es] every 5 minutes, or be reported [for] neglect of duty and disobedience of orders and like as not to the guard house.

Friday, October 30, 1863. Snowy morning, snowed most of the day, was not relieved until quite late. My back still troubles me, that alkali water I fear will always trouble me.

Saturday, October 31, 1863. Pleasant but cooler, had regiment mustered for pay, this is what the boys want. Soldiering in a city requires pay quite often and more of it. In fact a soldier ought to have more pay while stationed in a city, more style and it requires more expenditure for clothes to keep it up.

Sunday, November 1, 1863. Rather wet and nasty. On guard again, our turns come quite often, this time at Cor 1st & Greene Strs, very easy time at this post, and a pleasant place.

Monday, November 2, 1863. Rainy, was relieved in good season. A circus came into City today, boys all excited and expect to go if passes can be procured for all who apply, probably not. Sent letter to mother.

Tuesday, November 3, 1863. Pleasant. Election day and I am on guard again. While on guard my back gave out again and I fell to the ground, was picked up by some of the boys and carried into quarters & relieved from duty, back troubled me much throughout the day & night. The Surgeon gave me nitre and something else.

Wednesday, November 4, 1863. Pleasant day. Slept some, but my back troubled me much and I laid in my bunk most of the day.

Thursday, November 5, 1863. Pleasant, when I awoke felt some better, though my back still aches, did not stir around a great deal today. Kept my quarters.

Friday, November 6, 1863. Very pleasant, felt much better. Rec'd two letters, one from my esteemed friend A. W. Gage of Winona, and one from Aunty. Dress parade.

Saturday, November 7, 1863. Pleasant morning, and old Sol[14] is out in all his glory, felt like myself again. The military burial of Maj Walker[15] took place today, quite an extensive funeral procession. Rec'd letter from Lucy, got a pass and took a stroll around the City. We rec'd the Company Records, a record of every man in the Co, his home, age when enlisted, where, and battles engaged in, all in a sheet for framing. Sent mine home.

Sunday, November 8, 1863. Fine day, went with some of the boys to the Union Methodist Church in the A.M. Yankee soldiers are quite welcome here. Such courtesies we will not forget. In the evening we went to the Unitarian, the people here seemed cold & distant, such a contrast, heard some beautiful singing.

Monday, November 9, 1863. Pleasant, wrote some letters the first thing, one to Lucy, A. W. Gage, & Aunty, then took a stroll around the City. Went to a gallery [of] paintings, some very fine, though I am not much of a judge of skill in Art, but they were quite a sight even for a greenhorn.

Tuesday, November 10, 1863. Pleasant, got pass & went to the Rooms Young Men's Christian Ass^n. Was well rec'd & had the privilege of many newspapers & periodicals, examined their free library and took a book with me to quarters, a fine arrangement especially for us soldiers, & we certainly appreciated it as a good institution and the means of doing much good.

Wednesday, November 11, 1863. Fine day, on guard on board Steamer Dickerman guarding it & the gov't skiffs near by. Fell in with the cook and staid with him in the cook house most of the time, and had my rations cooked, fine place for guard duty. More rebel prisoners came in and were taken to the prison. Temperance Lecture at the Baptist Church tonight. Rec'd letter from home, glad to hear that they are well.

Thursday, November 12, 1863. Cloudy, morning looks like rain. Some of our boys got taken by the Provost Guard while returning from the lecture. I went to the lecture tonight, was quite interested upon this worthy subject, and quite a large attendance.

    14. Sol, the Roman sun god.
    15. We are unable to identify Major Walker.

Friday, November 13, 1863. Cloudy morning, prospects of foul weather. Was on guard again but upon reporting was excused, not feeling well, my back trouble seems to follow me. U.S. Inspector came today who will examine our equipage &c and condemn such articles as are worthless.

Saturday, November 14, 1863. Weather better than yesterday & warmer, boys getting anxious for their pay. The payments are behind but we will have to be patient. Masquerade Ball tonight and an extra guard detailed in consequence, guard was also doubled at the warehouses, for what reason, we know not. Common soldiers have no business to know, no rights except to obey orders.

Sunday, November 15, 1863. Pleasant. On guard at Schofield Barracks No 1, growing cold. In the evening went with some of the boys to the Wesley Chapel or Methodist Church (South) & certainly it was South, as there was not a syllable mentioned that indicated any sentiment in favor of the Union, not much like the Union Methodist.

Monday, November 16, 1863. Pleasant, prospects of better weather. Got our washing done up today, rather a tough job while living in a city.

Tuesday, November 17, 1863. Pleasant, so much so that I concluded to get a pass and go to the top of dome of the Court House, and went, after a tiresome tramp reached the top, but even today it was some smoky, hazy, in the horizon, and not as good a view as we had anticipated, and concluded to try again some other day. Thence to the gallery of paintings. Thence to the U.S. Cracker Bakery and saw how our hard tack is made. Quite an interesting process, ate some warm ones which were much better than those we get. They are manuf^d from flour and water and no salt, a simple process, but the secret I learned was in the baking. From what we could see good flour was used.

Wednesday, November 18, 1863. Pleasant, but rather lowry towards noon. Some of our boys gone as guard on a Steamboat to Vicksburg, a fine trip & one I expect we shall all take one of these days. Got a night pass and went to the Varieties Theatre, had a very good performance. Rained some during the evening and finally turned to snow. Pay rolls were ready & signed, & then the paymaster.

Thursday, November 19, 1863. [No entry.]

Friday, November 20, 1863. Cloudy & muddy. At 10 P.M. most of the boys were in bunk, & many asleep, when orders were rec'd for our Co to be ready to march at once with 40 rounds ammunition, and so all was hooray boys. Out of our bunks we jumped, and everything was soon in readiness, and we marched to the levee about 100[16] strong. Upon arriving there found 53 men of the 10th Regt. Minn. We took the ferry and over we went, staid aboard the boat all night as there was no train until morning. Fine arrangements, but we are soldiers, and supposed to stand anything. It was quite cold and some of the boys went out on the bank and built fires, but where are we going, I suppose our leaders know, but the rank & file are not supposed to know anything but to obey our superiors.

Saturday, November 21, 1863. Pleasant, but quite cold. Slept very little if any, much as we could do to keep warm. At 6 A.M. the train was ready and we jumped aboard, and it soon started and we had our hardtack for breakfast. About noon we arrived at Springfield, got a No 1 dinner here, and then got aboard the Great Western R.R. for Jacksonville and from here took a Branch R.R. to Manchester, Ill, it being pleasant, many of us, I with the rest, rode on the top of the cars. Upon arriving at Manchester we soon learned what we were sent here for. The union loving people were rejoiced to see us, and had everything prepared to provide for us. They had lived for some time in constant fear of their lives, and their property, the country around being full of the Knights of the Golden Circle, or Copperheads,[17] who were organizing a regiment to join the rebel army, drilling nights, and threatened not only the people and their property, but had actually fired into passing railroad trains, torn up the track, captured one train, and was a rendezvous for deserters from the Union Army, and this was the reason we were here. This state of affairs had been carried on for some time, the coppery fellows being more & more bold, until the Gov't were obliged to interfere, and our orders were to ferret out these men, the leaders, their rendezvous, and capture them if possible, and route the balance out of the Country. We were at once quartered about the town, a few in a place and a guard was put out. I was among those quartered at the Manchester Hotel.

---

16. Buswell later wrote "96" in pencil above the "100."
17. Republicans used the term "Copperhead" to refer to Democrats during the war. The Knights of the Golden Circle (KGC) were a Democratic secret society suspected of wanting to aid the Confederacy and overthrow the Union from within. While the KGC were particularly strong in the Midwest, historians disagree over whether they were a real threat to the Union or more of a paper tiger.

Sunday, November 22, 1863. Very fine morning. Slept well, got up quite early and was invited to breakfast by a Union Citizen. Had a No 1 joyful meal not only for myself, but they as well felt more secure with the US Soldiers so near, had plenty cider, apples & nuts. Went to the church in the evening. A large number of horses were brought into town for our use as we are to be mounted soldiers, and to scour this whole region in search of the Secesh & their dens, &c.

Monday, November 23, 1863. Pleasant morning, orders rec'd to start on the Scout today. We fell in and having chosen our horses, at 8 A.M. we mounted and away we went, rather new business, this horseback soldiering. I'll bet some of us will wish we had boofed it before this campaign is over, riding all day without any practice will be rather tough on us. We were divided into squads—35 in the first—31 in the second and 30 in the last, each to go in a different direction with a guide for each squad and all to meet at Franklin, as it was reported that it was the place of rendezvous of the hostiles in that vicinity. At noon our squad arrived at Athens, & here we met some boys of the 113th Ill who had been sent to this point a few days before. They had succeeded in capturing some deserters, and a few bushwhackers. Having got our dinner here at the hands of the citizens, we then turned down into Apple Creek Valley, a very lonesome obscure place. Here we saw several shanties, recently occupied, but now deserted, the owners thereof being the chaps we were after, having fled. A very wild dismal looking valley, heavily timbered, and no one living there excepting corn crackers, & most of them were Southern Sympathizers & negro haters. We stopped and looked into one log shanty, which evidently had just been vacated, not a window in it, shutters & door made of shakes, the ground for a floor, a stick & mud fire place & chimney, not a table, no stove, a few homemade stools, an old fashioned bake pan, or Dutch oven as some called it, and a few iron spoons constituted the entire stock household goods, & these were the people who would take possession of Egypt (Southern Ill) in the name of the Confederacy. About 6 P.M. we arrived at Franklin, a town of about 500 people, here we met the other boys and stopped for the night with some Union people. Nothing occurred of consequence this day, except that we got some pointers as to the characters we were after. One thing we noticed that what Union people we encountered throughout the day were much excited, being not only afraid of their property, but their lives. Rather sore from my first ride.

Tuesday, November 24, 1863. Very pleasant, much tired, horseback soldiering being new business, but slept pretty well. Got a fine breakfast, the horses were fed, and the bugle blew at 7 A.M. We mounted & were away, passed over some fine Country, ate dinner with some union people at Palmyra. We were on the lookout all day for a brush, as it was reported that the Johnnies intended to meet us, but let them come, we are ready and will give them the best in the wheelhouse. We finally got a track, and run down, shot at and finally arrested two notorious bushwhackers. Arrived at Fayette at 6 P.M. where we stopped for the night, being divided around among the Union families of the place. I got a fine place, feather bed, whoop what a Luxury, and plenty to eat, good cider, apples. Still[18] guard was kept.

Wednesday, November 25, 1863. Pleasant morning. Slept finely, got quite rested, though am quite sore. Had a fine breakfast, the best the country affords, and at 7 A.M. mounted our horses, and away we went again. Passed through Greenfield at 9, very kindly rec'd here and were invited to stop and partake of a collation[19] provided by the ladies, which we kindly accepted. They were so glad that we had come, having been nearly terror stricken by the bushwhackers, who had been out one night every week drilling & parading, terrorizing the people, that they were glad to see us, and it seemed that they could not do enough. We filled ourselves with the good things and bid them a good bye, and on we went, arriving in Manchester at 3 P.M. without any especial occurrence, other than to get the track of some of the leaders, and we were somewhat sore & tired.

Thursday, November 26, 1863. Very pleasant. Thanksgiving Day, went to thanksgiving services. One squad of our boys came in today, having had better luck than we did and brought in quite a number of prisoners. Lt Mannings[20] squad had quite a little fight, having learned that the two sons of an old man who were leaders and who were engaged in firing into the train & tearing up the track were in the vicinity yet, and having reasons to suspect that they were at their fathers log shanty, about midnight last night, went to the shanty, and called upon them from within to open the door, no answer, the demand was made again, and again, and still no answer. Finally the Lt told them that if the door was not opened at once, they would batter it down, and having procured a log for that purpose, and with it in the hands of several of the boys, the door not being opened,

18. Buswell appears to have written "Still" on top of "rested."
19. A collation is a meal, generally left ready for people to serve themselves.
20. Nelson H. Manning (born ca. 1831 in Canada) was second lieutenant in the 7th Minnesota Infantry, Co. K.

and nothing being said from within, bang the log went against the door, once, twice, the door began to give, when several shots were fired from within, and one of our boys was wounded. They returned the fire, the door was broken down, and in they went, and found therein the two sons which were at once taken prisoner. There were two daughters, the old lady and the old man also within, and the old man was wounded, two balls having taken effect. It was also ascertained that they were well armed having 9 guns & pistols, & that the girls had also fired in the first volley, they were brave enough possibly, but lacked discretion. The two leaders and some other prisoners were brought in and placed under guard.

Friday, November 27, 1863. Rather cloudy. Sent letter to Aunty, rainy & muddy in P.M., no scouting tonight. The 10th Regt boys here were ordered to Jacksonville, and at once went to the train, the report being that the rebel sympathizers threaten to burn the place.

Saturday, November 28, 1863. Rainy weather is past. All froze up this morning, quite icy, was detailed on picket tonight.

Sunday, November 29, 1863. Pleasant but cool, relieved from picket duty. It was rather cool, but I built a fire on the post and kept as warm as possible. Have a fine boarding place, a man by the name of Eaton,[21] has a fine daughter, plenty of apples & cider. Went to church in the evening.

Monday, November 30, 1863. Fine morning, rec'd my share surplus of the Company Fund, 60 cents. Had battalion drill Lt Col Clarke[22] 113th Ill comd'g. Went to hear a lecture on the Civil war, a benefit to the W. S. C.[23] Sum raised about $30.

Tuesday, December 1, 1863. Very fine morning. Assisted in chopping some wood this A.M., plenty cider & apples. Dress parade in the P.M. under Maj Cook,[24] a dance last night and another tonight. The people here desire to make it as pleasant & lively as possible.

21. Possibly A. G. and Lucy Eaton of Manchester, Scott County, Illinois, who had nine children, including a daughter, Margret, who was about sixteen years old at this time.

22. George R. Clarke (1827–1892), a native of New York, was lieutenant colonel of the 113th Illinois Infantry.

23. The Western Sanitary Commission was an abolitionist charitable society operated out of St. Louis that sought to aid the freedpeople.

24. Michael Cook (1828–1864), a native of New Jersey, was a major in the 10th Minnesota Infantry. He was wounded at the Battle of Nashville on December 16, 1864, and died on December 27.

Wednesday, December 2, 1863. Pleasant, rec'd orders that we leave here today, and so packed up, and having bid good bye to our recent acquaintances, having fulfilled our mission here, dispersed the rebels, captured some 60 and sent them to Camp Douglas and captured several deserters. At 2 P.M. we got aboard the train of freight cars, a fine day, I on top, and away we go. Arrived at Jacksonville and again left at 5 P.M., arriving at Springfield at 8 P.M., & stopped for the night in rooms of the ULA.[25]

Thursday, December 3, 1863. Pleasant, got breakfast at 8 A.M., moved to the depot and stacked arms, and then rec'd orders that we do not leave here until 5 P.M. Got my dinner, & then for a tramp around the city. Saw the home of our father Abe Lincoln, a rather plain square two story frame house.[26] This seems like a very pleasant place, though not very driving business, and the Capitol don't amount to much. Finally the train came, and we piled into first class cars, and at 6 P.M. we glided out of the depot for St Louis, where we arrived at midnight, crossed the river, and arrived at Barracks at 1 A.M. the 4th.

Friday, December 4, 1863. Very pleasant. Found our Reg't boys mostly well, and glad to see us. Rec'd two mos pay from Capt, $26. Was detailed as an escort to cross the river and receive some new recruits from Ill. Went across on ferry boat at 6 P.M., came back about midnight, train being late, with the prisoners, and did not get to bunk until 2 A.M. the 5th.

Saturday, December 5, 1863. Very fine. Did my washing, which needed it very much. Two boys from our Co were detailed on special guard to go to Memphis, Tenn. Had dress parade and wrote some letters to mother & others.

Sunday, December 6, 1863. Very pleasant, was on guard at what is called the rat holes, in lower portion of the City, where there is plenty of rats, plenty of hard places & plenty of hard characters, but they don't interfere with soldiers, if you do not give them a chance. Did not go to church for want of time. Some of the 10th Reg't boys riding on the horse cars.

Monday, December 7, 1863. Rather cloudy. Was detailed with two others from our Co with some from other Co's as a special detail to guard the

---

25. The Union League of America, or Union Leagues, were established as patriotic societies in the North to support the Union war effort and the Republican Party.

26. The Lincoln home at 8th and Jackson Streets in Springfield, Illinois, is the only home the president ever owned. It is now a historic site run by the National Park Service.

Steamer City of Pekin from here to Nashville, Tenn, she being laden with stores, and at 4 P.M. reported at the levee, upon board of the Steamer, all manned & equipped, but the boat not being ready to go until tomorrow, we reported back to the barracks & that evening we got a night pass and attended the Varieties Theatre.

Tuesday, December 8, 1863. Cloudy & cool. Packed up again, and went to the boat, and at 8 A.M. bid good bye to the City, and away we went down the river. The boat was heavily laden with government stores, and was barricaded with cotton bales, and besides the Co of soldiers on board, we had a cannon, the country from the mouth of the Cumberland River to Nashville being lined more or less with guerrillas. During the A.M. we passed Carondelet [Missouri]. Saw the shipyard where the gov't is building the gunboats, there being several in the different stages of construction. Just below this point the steamer ran aground where we remained all the P.M. Towards night a barge was brought down, as a lighter to take off a part of the cargo. Thinking to especially prepare myself for the trip, I bought a revolver paying $12. The boat remained on the sand bar all night.

Wednesday, December 9, 1863. Pleasant, had a good sleep, being stretched out on the Cabin floor. Roustabouts were out at 3 A.M. to change the freight, was aground all day. I with some others went ashore in a boat to help haul a line to shore. The line was pulled to shore & fastened to a tree and the capstan Com[mence]^d its noise and work to pull the boat over the bar. While they were at work us soldier boys went up to Jefferson Barracks,[27] got some apples & nuts, beautiful grounds, a great many soldiers here, sick & invalid mostly, many fine buildings, and has been gov't barracks for many years. Twas here they say that Grant was first stationed as a soldier.[28] At 4 P.M. the boat got over the bar but night approaching, tied up at 6 P.M. Saw several other boats in the same predicament as ours. Had dancing on the boat during the evening, and for music, darkeys with their banjoes, and it was lively.

Thursday, December 10, 1863. Somewhat rainy. Slept well. The boat started again at 6 ½ A.M., fine scenery along the route, thickly settled

---

27. Located south of St. Louis on the Mississippi River, Jefferson Barracks was established as a military installation in 1826. During the Civil War it served as a hospital and recruiting station.

28. Ulysses S. Grant was ordered to Jefferson Barracks in 1843, shortly after graduating from the US Military Academy.

on the Mo side. Passed Genevieve, Mo, about noon, passed a good many boats. Saw Gloster, Ill, at 3 P.M. Laid up for the night at a wood yard where wood was taken on at 6 P.M., 50 miles above Cape Girardeau, quite misty & rainy. Went up to a house near the landing and got some apples. We are free yet, no guard required.

Friday, December 11, 1863. Lowry morning. Start at 6 A.M. & at 9 got stuck on a sand bar, in Co with ten other boats, did not get over the bar until 5 P.M., then tied up for the night at Ransoms landing. Went ashore and up to a small store where we saw the corn cracker fed Missourian.

Saturday, December 12, 1863. Rainy, quite foggy. The boat started at 7 A.M., arrived at Cape Girardeau at 9 ½ A.M. Saw fortifications along the shore, and Union soldiers in them. At 11 P.M. [A.M.?] laid up on account of the fog on the Ill shore, but it finally cleared up, and away we went again. Stopped at Rodneys Landing at 2 ½ P.M. to load 870 sacks of oats and to take on more wood, tied up here for the night. Saw some guerrillas for the first time, being apparently on picket or watch, but not near enough to have any trouble with them. Tonight had guard & pickets out on land for the first time, and it fell to my lot to be on the first detail.

Sunday, December 13, 1863. Rainy, at 6 ½ A.M. the boat started again, passed a timbered country, not much settled. Passed into the Ohio [River] about 11 A.M. and was a much broader stream than I had anticipated, and soon arrived at Cairo, and boat tied up. I went ashore at once & looked over the place. It was very muddy, built upon the point of land between the Miss & Ohio. Around the point and for some distance back both shores were built up quite high, the center not being filled, some buildings being down on the flat, the tops of the roofs being about on a level with the top of [the] bank. Some buildings were set up on long stilts as it were to bring them up with the level with [the] bank. All looked very curious & odd to me, but this being the terminus of the Ill Central R.R. makes it quite a busy point. It was well fortified and a good number of soldiers were quartered there. Saw several gunboats and the US Mortar boats, some 18 of them built for and used at Island No 10. Left here about 1 P.M., soon passed Mound City, Ill where we saw the US Navy Yard which seemed quite busy, and on we steamed up the beautiful Ohio, quite deep water and nearly straight along here until 11 P.M. when the boat tied up for the night at Paducah, Ky. I went ashore and for the first time trod the soil of a rebellious country, there being many Johnny Rebs living here, but kept quiet, because obliged to. Rather a dirty, dingy looking place, and rather dead to my notion.

Monday, December 14, 1863. Very windy. Some colder. Slept finely. Boat started again at 6 ½ A.M. Saw some fine looking country along the Ky. shore. Passed the mouth of the Tennessee River. Saw some of Uncle Sam's Navy here ready for duty when & where called, and to look out for the work up the Tenn. River, as there is yet a great work to do far up that river. About noon arrived at Smithland [Kentucky], a very small place, and only gains any notoriety by being at the mouth of the Cumberland River up whose stream we will shortly pass. Took on 500 bus[hels of] oats here, and then started on our way up the river, & then for fun, as we expect, as there are many guerrillas along its banks. It being a very narrow stream, though quite deep, there is no difficulty in firing into a boat from its banks anywhere, and many have been fired into and some have been actually taken by them. Went up the river a few miles, stopped by a gunboat, then the boat returned to Smithland to put off some private freight which had been overlooked on the way up. Was detailed for guard & the way I paced the deck and with such pride was a caution. At 6 P.M. got started again, with many passengers and some speed, also had aboard some soldiers who were returning to their commands near Nashville. Stopped for the night about 11 P.M. near the Gunboat. The boat ran into a tree, making one of the many short curves in the stream, and smashed into some extent the bow of the boat, and which for a time caused considerable excitement, many in the cabin thinking it an attack.

Tuesday, December 15, 1863. Beautiful sunshiny morning, got an early start and away we went again up the crooked river, rather pretty country on both sides, banks not very high, a gradual rise back from the river, except in a few places. About noon passed Canton [Kentucky] a small place, and about 4 P.M. came in sight of Ft. Donelson,[29] when all was excitement to see where the great battle of Grants was fought. Passed along under the works and had a fine view of the fort and earthworks, and had an explanation of the battle by the Captain. Saw some soldiers, the 83ᵈ Ill being on duty here. Saw two gunboats and quite a large village of huts, built by the Johnnies while the fort was in their hands for their quarters.

29. Located in Tennessee about eighty miles northwest of Nashville, on the Cumberland River, Ft. Donelson had been heavily fortified by the Confederates in order to protect access to the Tennessee River. In February 1862, Grant captured the fort.

Left here at 6 P.M. and soon passed the little town of Dover [Tennessee], on quite a hill & which lies above and overlooking the Ft. This was the rebel generals head quarters. Full guard out tonight & pickets.

Wednesday, December 16, 1863. Cloudy, rainy, at 2 A.M. the boat arrived at Clarksville [Tennessee], and tied up until daylight. Saw here the remains of the railroad bridge destroyed by the rebs. At 6 A.M. the boat started again up the river. Soon passed a camp of Union pickets, some eight of them & after saw other squads along the river banks. One trouble in carrying on a war in the rebels country is that not only does it require a great army to fight, but a large force to guard & keep up the lines of communication to the rear. About 7 A.M. we had a thunder shower with some lightning, to us it seems rather late in the season, but we are some degrees farther South, it was quite a warm shower. At 9 P.M. the whistle blew and the boat soon tied up at Nashville and our squad marched up to the H'd Qrs and reported, and were sent to the Zollikoffer House for quarters. It is a very large 5 story brick building, and at the commencement of the war was being erected for a Hotel, by one afterwards Rebel Gen'l Zollikoffer[30] who was killed at Battle of Mill Spring, Ky. It is now in an unfinished state, and here was where the Union soldiers had their quarters. We bunked down on the floor in our blankets.

Thursday, December 17, 1863. Cloudy, some cooler, got up early, got some breakfast at the mess here and went out for a tramp around the city, found it quite a large place. Some fine buildings, built upon several hills. Went to the Soldiers home, a very pleasant place, and quite a number of soldier boys there, then looked up & down the river, noticed that all the bridges were destroyed by the rebs when they evacuated the city.[31] Saw that there were a good many soldiers about here. Learned all about the battle of Chickamauga, where the rebs gained the day, and of the great victory by Grant over the Johnnies at Chattanooga, and there were many wounded soldiers here in hospital. In the evening got a pass to [illegible word] us from the Provost Guard and went to the Old Theatre, enjoyed myself finely. Sent a letter to mother, that she may know where I am.

30. Felix Zollicoffer (1812–1862) of Tennessee was a Confederate brigadier general who was killed on January 19, 1862, during the Battle of Mill Springs in Kentucky.
31. The Union captured Nashville on February 25, 1862, shortly after the Battle of Fort Donelson.

Friday, December 18, 1863. Quite cool, after mess took another tramp, this time went up to the market. Saw plenty soldiers here, some on guard mount, then went to the State House, a fine marble structure, the finest in the U.S. when built. Went all through the building, into the Senate chamber & Representatives Hall. Saw many taking the oath of allegiance to support the U.S., hundreds take it every day. Some desire to, but more are forced to, desiring to obtain provisions &c &c. Went up into the dome of the capitol and looked over the surrounding country, a very fine view. Saw many soldiers, and their many camps about the City. Saw the fortifications, and Fts Negley & College built by the rebels to protect the city from our forces, but they availed them very little. The state house was built about 11 years ago Wm Strickland, architect.[32] Nashville must have been a beautiful city before the war, and a thriving one, but all business is now suspended, except I might add the war business, and that seems to be quite extensive, as this is the base of operations for the great armies that are now pounding away in the vicinity of Atlanta. One of the bridges burned by the rebs I notice was a suspension bridge. The Columns of the State House were of marble, Number 28—4 feet in diameter, solid marble. Saw some guards patrolling the streets picking up the stray negroes, probably to use them in the ditches somewhere. Our boat nearly unloaded, we will not stay here much longer. Got a pass & went to the New Theatre.

Saturday, December 19, 1863. Much colder. I noticed some ice in my walk this A.M. Went and visited the homestead & tomb of Ex Pres't Polk, located on quite a hill near the Main Street. In a beautiful garden in square frame[33] with a common picket fence around, is situated the old fashioned, square frame dwelling with large fluted pine wood columns all around the same, his wife still living here.[34] In the yard is also seen his tomb or mausoleum about 12 feet square, built of marble, with a large column on each of the four corners and with a solid & substantial canopy

---

32. William Strickland (1788–1854) was a well-known architect who designed many buildings in Philadelphia and Nashville. He is buried in a crypt beneath the Tennessee State Capitol.

33. Buswell appears to have written "in square frame" here by accident when he copied the clean version of his diary. The entry should probably read, "in a beautiful garden with a common picket fence around." It is unclear, but he may have also intended to erase the word "around."

34. James K. Polk's home in Nashville, Polk Place, was demolished in 1901, a decade after the death of his widow, Sarah Childress Polk (1803–1891).

on top. Went from here over to the State House again. Saw many there taking the oath. Went into the State Library, found it quite extensive. The boat having unloaded and all being ready at 4 P.M. the whistle blew, the bell rung, and we started down the river. Had a few passengers, one a young soldier 1st Minn Cavl'y, who was wounded and discharged going to his home. Rather keen air this P.M., boat went down the river, and finally tied up on acc't of the fog at 5 P.M., and all was excitement on acc't of guerrillas, and pickets were put out on the bank near for the night.

Sunday, December 20, 1863. Pleasant morning. Cool, no disturbance though the pickets were kept out all night. Boat got ready and at 7 A.M. started down the river lively, much faster than on our upward trip. Passed Ft Donelson at 8, stopped at Canton and here took aboard 26 cavalrymen who had been scouring the country hunting guerrillas. They had bad luck, got into a scrimmage with them, captured none, but 5 of their numbers were taken prisoners. Poor boys may have to suffer if they have not already, with these guerrillas there is no quarter. Stopped at a wood yard for wood. Some of us went ashore and had a chicken hunt, captured & killed two. Passed Smithland at 6 P.M. and at midnight arrived at Cairo and went ashore. The Miss River being frozen up, we had orders to take Ill Central from Cairo to St Louis. Was quartered for the night in a building provided for that purpose.

Monday, December 21, 1863. Pleasant. Somewhat warmer, got breakfast and loitered around the town as the train did not leave here until noon, when aboard the cars we got, and away we went up through a very flat country. Passed the mining district of Du Quoin and arrived at Odin, Ill the Junction. Here we took the Ohio & Miss R.R. through to St Louis, arriving there at midnight, and went at once to barracks and to our bunks.

5
"Had a Talk with Some Prisoners"
Guard Duty and Promotion in St. Louis, December 22, 1863–June 1, 1864

○❋○

Buswell spent most of the next five months in St. Louis, a "flourishing metropolis" whose strategic location on the Mississippi River made it essential to the Union's control of the Ohio and Mississippi River Valleys. As the eighth largest city in the United States, and an urban center in a border slave state, St. Louis was politically divided. During the war, it became the home of thousands of political and military prisoners. Writes historian Louis S. Gerteis, "The St. Louis prisons differed from military prisons elsewhere in the country because they housed not only prisoners of war but also political prisoners, deserters from the Union army, and federal soldiers awaiting trial for crimes."[1]

For the first few months of 1864, Buswell guarded Confederate prisoners of war, guerrillas, political prisoners, and other "bad characters" at Schofield Barracks, the Gratiot Street Prison, the Provost Marshal General's Office on Fifth Street, the hospital at Fourth and Hickory Streets, and the Myrtle Street Prison. The largest of these facilities, the Gratiot Street Prison, had previously been the McDowell Medical College before it was confiscated by US authorities when its secessionist owner fled to

---

1. Louis S. Gerteis, *Civil War St. Louis* (Lawrence: University Press of Kansas, 2001), 1, 171; Mark E. Neely Jr., *The Fate of Liberty: Abraham Lincoln and Civil Liberties* (New York: Oxford University Press, 1991), 33–39, 128, 135. For an assessment of conditions at the various prisons in St. Louis, see Gerteis, *Civil War St. Louis*, 170–72, 186–201.

the South.² In September 1861, Union authorities had converted Bernard M. Lynch's slave pen into Myrtle Street Prison, a smaller facility than the Gratiot Street Prison. Over the course of the war, Myrtle Street Prison housed any number of people, including political prisoners such as the editor of the *St. Louis Christian Advocate,* guerrillas and their abettors, and Confederate prisoners of war. When one inmate—a Baptist minister who had been arrested for shouting, "Hurrah for Jeff Davis"—protested that he would have to "stay here all night,—it is a horrible place," an unsympathetic Unionist replied, "Yes, it is a slave-pen."³

While in St. Louis, Buswell applied to be an officer in a "colored" regiment, and he spent much of his time studying for the qualifying exams. After passing, he had to wait for quite a while until he was assigned to the 68th US Colored Infantry. He spent the latter half of the spring of 1864 reading and doing paperwork.

In St. Louis, the men of the 68th USCT did not receive the proper training to prepare them for combat. As historian Keith P. Wilson writes, an officer of the regiment, Daniel Densmore, "reported that his men appeared unprepared for fighting, so much so that he [Densmore] wanted combat duty omitted or delayed. He attributed their lack of combat readiness and their lack of manly pride to the fact that they had previously been the pet regiment of Brigadier General William Pile, commander of USCT troops at Benton Barracks, St. Louis. In this capacity they had been drilled for show, rather than to fight."⁴

While in St. Louis, Buswell took in the sites and sights of the wartime city, including the Grand Mississippi Valley Sanitary Fair, which was put on by the Western Sanitary Commission in May and June. Patrons—including Buswell and his men—enjoyed refreshments, activ-

---

2. Thomas F. Curran, *Women Making War: Female Confederate Prisoners and Union Military Justice* (Carbondale: Southern Illinois University Press, 2020), 20; Dennis K. Boman, *Lincoln and Citizens' Rights in Civil War Missouri: Balancing Security and Freedom* (Baton Rouge: Louisiana State University Press, 2011), 78, 121–22; Gerteis, *Civil War St. Louis,* 170.

3. Boman, *Lincoln and Citizens' Rights,* 95–96, 190, 250; O.R., ser. 2, vol. 8, p. 441; Galusha Anderson, *The Story of a Border City during the Civil War* (Boston: Little, Brown, and Co., 1908), 182–87, 191–93; John A. Wright, *Discovering African American St. Louis: A Guide to Historic Sites,* 2nd ed. (St. Louis: Missouri Historical Society Press, 2002), 11.

4. *Family War Stories,* 74.

ities, and entertainments at the fair, all in the name of raising money for soldiers and their families. Admission on opening day cost two dollars. On the second and third days of the fair, admission cost one dollar. For the remainder of the fair, admission was fifty cents. All told, the Grand Mississippi Valley Sanitary Fair brought in almost $620,000, more than $550,000 of which was profit that could be used for philanthropic purposes toward the war effort.[5]

Tuesday, December 22, 1863. Pleasant, though rather muddy here. Rec'd letters & papers from home & aunty, was glad to hear from the folks, ans^d them at once. Took a walk, went outside of guards, on to the river, where they were having gay times skating.

Wednesday, December 23, 1863. Pleasant, was detailed on guard at Schofield Barracks No 1, and attended to my regular business, being lord of all on that beat.

Thursday, December 24, 1863. Fine morning, got a pass and went out and up to the markets. Every body seemed to be busy preparing for Christmas, the bells are ringing, and all are interested in the preparation, one of the great days here, as well as in most of places in the South.

Friday, December 25, 1863. Pleasant. Christmas morning, the din was kept up all night, and very lively at midnight, ushering in the hallowed and joyful day. There were a great many processions today, guns firing, pistols, crackers, torpedoes and fireworks in the evening, puts a fellow in mind of 4th of July, but that day is no where here compared with Christmas. The darkeys have all got on their best calico & bandana, and ne'ery work today. It is a beautiful day, and here I am far away from home, and no one knows when I am to return, but I must make the best of it, a soldier should do his duty, and his whole duty, and today I was on guard. So did not enjoy the day here even as well.

Saturday, December 26, 1863. Rather rainy, muddy, had news from home, and that there was two feet of snow in Minn, rather wintry. Got a pass and went with some of the boys to the Theatre.

Sunday, December 27, 1863. Very muddy, drizzly day, though I went to meeting at the Union Methodist Church, heard a fine sermon, the people

5. Gerteis, *Civil War St. Louis*, 230–33; *Family War Stories*, 57–58.

of this Church are truly Union in sentiment, as well as name, and we the old soldiers are especially welcome, a beautiful church & quite large. After services went back to the barracks and found a letter from Mother. Sat down read and ans^d it at once.

Monday, December 28, 1863. Colder with some snow. Was on guard at Gratiot St Prison, and my post was near the circular dungeon, guarding the bad characters, spies & guerrillas, was as near being in prison as I want to be. While guarding here give[s] a person a chance to reflect, while those behind the gates also have their chance to reflect, me to keep out & they to get out if possible. There are some 700 rebels in this prison near my post, there were two Johnnies who had been making a disturbance and had been chained to a post. Among some of them the sentiment was very strong against the gov't, would almost gnash their teeth with rage at being guarded by miserable Yanks, while others were quite docile and would desert the reb army if they had an opportunity. Many such take the oath of allegiance to the U.S. and at once enlist in our army.

Tuesday, December 29, 1863. Warmer, more pleasant. River opened again, took a walk around the City, went into a monkey show, monkeys were trained to go through with many performances. Went into a gallery of paintings, remained there some time looking over the various works of art.

Wednesday, December 30, 1863. Rather rainy. Came off cold, froze, was on guard again at Gratiot St Prison, Post No 17. Had a talk with some prisoners who would take the oath if let out, they had no desire to go back to the Rebel Army. Went to the reb hospital, everything looks nice & clean, they are well cared for, much better, so they say, than our boys who have fallen into their hands.

Thursday, December 31, 1863. Very cold, disagreeable. Commenced snowing & blowing from the North, about 4 inches snow fell during the day, and growing cold fast. The old year is going out like a lion, the first real cold night of the season.

Friday, January 1, 1864. Another new years day, and the civil war is not ended, does it seem any nearer its close. During the year past many victories have been perched upon our banners, Vicksburg, Gettysburg, Port Hudson, and Chattanooga, and the Miss River has been opened to its very mouth. The Confederacy has been divided. Gen'l Grant the hero of Donelson & Vicksburg has been placed in command of the

Military Division of the Miss, which comprises all the country west of the Alleghanys. His name and his sayings are the watchwords, and the soldiers feel that he is the right man in the right place. At Chattanooga, it looked like defeat for our hemmed in army, but Grant went down there and snatched a victory from what seemed at best a certain defeat. The war for the Union is progressing, in my opinion, but how much longer. Many more hard fought battles. Many more brave boys will be sacrificed. Millions of money will be expended before the end is seen, but possibly never. France & England are appealed to by the Confederacy for recognition and they have thus far recognized them as belligerents.[6] All is mere speculation. Grant has now an important position, and with the prestige of his victories, and with Genl Meade, the hero of Gettysburgh, in Command of the Army of the Potomac, causes faith and renewed confidence that our army and cause will yet succeed. This morning we find the storm has passed away, and it is more clear & cold, the coldest day of the year, 24 below, and one of the coldest days ever known as far South as this, and snow nearly a foot deep. The river is closed partially up, navigation suspended. Was on guard at the rat holes, and pretty tedious to be tramping around on my beat, but had a good warm fire at Hd Qrs of the relief guard, and got well warmed up between reliefs. Saw Jim Pope, being near the quarters of Co C 10th Minn, went over & had a chat with Mrs Hayes. Our Capt Stevens gave a new years dinner to the Company, was sorry that I could not be present, very cold night. There will no doubt be a good deal of suffering in the City, and in other sections, and so cold here, what will it be away up in Minn.

Saturday, January 2, 1864. Very cold morning, Miss River frozen up & people crossing. A very cold night, about 20 below zero, and being out on guard part of the night, I had to tramp lively to keep warm, but had a good warm supper last night with Capt Hopsons Co. We were quartered near here in an old brick building near the levee. The telegraph gave us the news of the great storm, 30 to 50 below zero up North, big snow in many places, railroads all blockaded, no Eastern or Northern mail. Was relieved from duty, went to my quarters, glad to be relieved this time surely. In the P.M. went down into the City. Some warmer. Considerable

---

6. While England and France never recognized the Confederacy as a nation, in 1861 they did grant the Confederacy status as a belligerent which enabled them to conduct business with neutral nations and wage war on the high seas.

snow, good sleighing, and everybody that has a sleigh is out enjoying it this P.M. Horse cars were suspended today.

Sunday, January 3, 1864. Warmer, but cloudy, on guard again, this time at the Paymasters office. Teams crossed the river on ice, people are having great times skating on the river. Many booths were built where refreshments could be had, also fire, and a gala day for everybody that wanted fun, but here I am on guard, but near a store, and a pretty good post. I expected to go to the Union Methodist today, but my guard duty has prevented. Quite a scare, small pox has broken out in our regiment, one boy died today. The first time I was very near this terrible disease. All the precautions necessary are and will be taken to prevent its spreading, but it has got a start and no doubt more will be down with it. Another cold night.

Monday, January 4, 1864. Cold, cloudy, another sprinkle of snow. Relieved from guard at 10 A.M., paymaster is paying of [off?] clerks today, we will get ours soon. Beautiful sleighing, and the people are out enjoying it, as they may not see it here again this winter. Washed up and went down to the Young Mens Christian Ass[n] Rooms, changed my[7] book and looked over the late papers, a fine privilege for us soldier boys. Small pox broke out in Co's I, E & K of our Reg't, now three deaths, it is rather near, but no use running. Horse cars started up again today.

Tuesday, January 5, 1864. Cold, but pleasant. Detailed for guard again at Schofield No 1. It comes my turn about every other day. Today is the last day that the $400. bounty is paid, then for a draft. This forcing men to be soldiers, either by large bounties or by being drafted, does not make such soldiers as those who enlisted for the purpose of suppressing the rebellion. Considerable warmer this P.M., thawing in the sun, no mail yet from Minn. It must be a very bad blockade up there. Quite a small pox scare, a good many are now down sick, orders issued that all men be examined, and if considered necessary to be at once vaccinated. Several of the cases were taken to the Hospital on Blood Island down in the river. Having more faith in Dr Sheardown, Surg 10th Minn Infy, whom I knew in Minn, I got permission, and went to his office in the City, and he vaccinated me.

Wednesday, January 6, 1864. Quite cool, a good many sick and more coming down with the small pox. It may prove serious to our Reg't, not

---

7. Buswell appears to have written "my" over something else. He may have been returning a book to the YMCA and checking out a new one.

men enough to relieve us as guard and we remain on duty another 24 hours. No Minn mail yet. Spent part of my time in study, what for, or for what position military or civil I don't know. It is a good idea to learn something, at least so if I ever get out of the Army alive I may be prepared to take upon myself some more responsible position than a common menial.

Thursday, January 7, 1864. Pleasant & warmer. Relieved from guard at 9 ½ A.M. after two days service on same post. Boys having quite a time playing checkers. I spent part of the day in my studies. Rec'd news that the thermometer at Ft Snelling stood at 50 below zero morning of Jany 2^d, one of the coldest snaps known there, as well as here, no mail yet from Minn. I am still well and my arm is working nicely, not many new cases.

Friday, January 8, 1864. Pleasant day. Cool, on guard again at Schofield Bks No 1. Sun came out warm, felt good. Great fire last night between 3^d & 4th Streets, a wagon factory burned to the ground. The steam fire engines were out. Kept streams of water pouring upon the ruins all day. Rec'd a letter from Aunty, was welcome, but none from home.

Saturday, January 9, 1864. Very fine, warmer. A number of Colored Regts are to be formed in this Dept this spring, in accordance with a special order of the Secy of War authorizing the same, and they are to be officered by white soldiers, and at this City a Board of Examination has been established by order Sec'y of War, before whom all who desire a position shall apply. Quite a number of the boys, Lts, Sergts, Corporals & high privates even having applied for commissions, some have already been examined, passed, commissioned and assigned to duty at Benton Barracks, where these troops are organ[ized] under Brig Genl Wm A. Pile,[8] and while I know it is a very dangerous position as the Rebels are very bitter towards Colored Soldiers & their officers, but not

---

8. William A. Pile (1829–1889) was a Methodist minister who served as chaplain of the 1st Missouri Light Artillery from June 1861 to July 1862, when he became captain of Battery I. In September 1862 he was promoted to lieutenant colonel of the 33rd Missouri Infantry, then colonel in December. The following year, on December 26, 1863, he was promoted to brigadier general and was assigned command of the US Colored Troops at Benton Barracks in St. Louis. Following the war, he served in Congress as a Republican from Missouri who was known for advocating "death to all supporters of the South, past or present."

withstanding all this, I have made up my mind to apply to be examined for a Lieutenancy, and today having procured the proper blank, I filled out the same, signed it, and sent it to Adjt Genl Foster[9] of the U.S. Army. Quite a thaw, but I spent most of my time in studying tactics, regulations, History, Art & Science of War &c—Now I have something especial to study for. Was quite glad to get a letter from home, and answered it at once & sent one to Aunty.

Sunday, January 10, 1864. Beautiful day, warmer, on guard again at Schofield Bks No 1—It thawed a good deal today. Commissions all the talk now but it is not every person that can get one, as it is said the examination is very rigid. Several of boys, one Lt and one Serg't, were rejected. Wanted to go to meeting but could not, but took out my little Bible, a present from mother, and read in that. Our Reg't rec'd orders to move to the brick building in front of Gratiot St Prison, and the boys are packing.

Monday, January 11, 1864. Quite pleasant, & warmer—was relieved from duty in good season. After some study in the forenoon, then went down to the reading room, just in time to attend the day prayer meeting. Remained until it was over, found there was some union sentiment here, then read the news, and upon my trip back, I saw Tom Thumb's carriage & ponies, the same presented him by Queen Victoria.[10] He was riding inside and two boys outside, one as driver and the other as footman, both had on coachmans suits and silk hats, quite a sight and attracted a good deal of attention. Tom has a reception this evening at the Lindell. Bought me a history and arithmetic to brush up a little in these branches.

Tuesday, January 12, 1864. Beautiful day, warmer, on guard again at Schofield Bks. Paymaster came and paid us two mos pay up to Jany 1st. Our Regt moved to the buildings in front of Gratiot St Prison, better quarters, more convenient, but solid duty, I expect guarding the prisoners. Studied a good deal today, even while on guard, snow going off fast.

---

9. Charles W. Foster (1830–1904) of Massachusetts entered military service in 1846. In 1861 he was appointed assistant adjutant general of volunteers. He later organized the Bureau of Colored Troops.

10. Charles Sherwood Stratton (1838–1883), whom the *New York Herald* called "the wonderful dwarf" on December 25, 1842, attained international renown performing as "General Tom Thumb" in P. T. Barnum's shows and museums. He met Queen Victoria twice.

2^d Minn Battery arrived today at Illinois Town, opposite the City, could not come across on acc't of the ice.

Wednesday, January 13, 1864. Pleasant, very warm, rather too warm for health. The ice in river is weakening every day. After a good study, took a walk down to the river. Saw teams endeavoring to cross, found river open in many places, two teams went through and were drowned. Pinkham[11] & Lynn[12] bid us all good bye today, got their discharges and started for home. When I shall go is difficult to tell. Some are trying to get out, and I am now studying for the purpose of again enlisting for 3 years.

Thursday, January 14, 1864. Lowry. Smoky, warmer, was not on guard today, and a wonder it is. Took a good study, then a tramp around the city. Snow most gone, and rather muddy & wet. In the evening, for a change, got a pass for the night and went to the Varieties Theatre to hear Blue Beard, very beautiful scenery, and quite a play.

Friday, January 15, 1864. Pleasant, clear, warmer. Ice in the river getting weaker. Some horses & cattle were drowned today. Was on guard at Schofield Bks No 1. Study a good deal, though while tramping back and forth upon my beat, a good place for memorizing.

Saturday, January 16, 1864. Rather cloudy, looks like snow, was relieved from duty, in good season, and staid in Barracks nearly all day, studying. Rec'd letters from Mother & Lucy, glad to hear from them.

Sunday, January 17, 1864. Pleasant overhead, but quite muddy. On guard again, this time at a new place, the Provost Marshal Gen'ls Office on 5th St, a fine place. Wanted to go to church, but generally I am on duty Sundays. Wrote a letter to mother.

Monday, January 18, 1864. Beautiful day. Came off duty in good season. Did not go out today. Studied my history, tactics &c. Sent letter to mother.

Tuesday, January 19, 1864. Pleasant, was not [on] guard. Drying up fast. Took a good study in the morning, then took a walk about the City. Some

---

11. David A. Pinkham (1832–1917), a native of Maine, was a private of the 7th Minnesota Infantry, Co. B.

12. James Lynn (1837–1875), a native of New York, was a private in the 7th Minnesota Infantry, Co. B.

more of the boys have been examined, accepted & ordered to report to Gen'l Pile for assignment to duty. Expect every day to hear from my application.

Wednesday, January 20, 1864. Very pleasant, prospects of a fine day. Detailed on guard again at Schofield No 1. Studying & thinking up the work even while on duty. Rec'd my permit this day to appear before the Board of Examination of which Col Dan'l Houston, it came from the Adjts Office Washington D.C. and signed by C. W. Foster Asst Adjt Genl. Shall have to report soon.

Thursday, January 21, 1864. Quite cool, got relieved in good season & went to quarters, cleaned & washed up and put on my best duds, and went down to the Rooms of the Board and reported. Went into the waiting room and knocked, when the inner door opened saw that they were examining a candidate in Battalion drill. I was directed to report again tomorrow. Went back to Barracks at once and took up my studies again.

Friday, January 22, 1864. Pleasant and warm. Rec'd a letter from home, did not answer it at once, as time was now precious with me, in my studies. Went to the rooms again and reported, was invited into the Surgeons room, who gave me a thorough examination, and who endorsed my application favorably. This part was through, but the worst is yet to come, to appear before the Board of some 7 to 8 officers, alone, and to be required to answer such questions in the different branches, tactics, regulations &c as they may put to me, this I dread the worst, but I have started and I must now go through. Some of the boys have failed and two Sergts in our Reg't have failed, and if I, a high private in the ranks should fail, it will not be any great disgrace.

Saturday, January 23, 1864. Very pleasant, detailed for guard, this time in Gratiot St Prison, my post being in the tower among the worst of the Johnny Rebs, but they behaved quite well today, some ciphering, some reading, and one was painting, quite an artist. Rec'd a letter from Aunty.

Sunday, January 24, 1864. Beautiful & warm. Sun is out in all his glory. Relieved from duty at 9 A.M., went to quarters and washed up, then went to meeting at the Union Methodist & had a fine sermon. After church wrote some letters.

Monday, January 25, 1864. Very fine, got up at 5 A.M. and went to studying, warm day. The river is breaking up, the boats have got up steam, and ice is moving, quite a rejoicing in the City. Have rec'd news that Genl

Roscranz[13] and Genl Grant will be here tonight, Rosecranz to assume command of this Dept, and Grant to visit his old city & friends, here his old home. Shall want to see them, especially Gen'l Grant. Commenced taking the St Louis Democrat (Daily) by the week, nothing like knowing what is going on.

Tuesday, January 26, 1864. Very warm, thawing & muddy, the ice parted and moved out of the river and the ferry boats commenced running. Put on my best and went to the Board rooms and reported, and was ordered to report tomorrow. Studied a good deal, but upon learning that Grant was coming I laid aside all and went down into the city. A large force [of] troops was out to receive him. Saw him in the carriage drawn by four horses as he passed by, noticed that he was a rather short, thick set man, but not near enough to especially notice him.

Wednesday, January 27, 1864. Beautiful, rather warm day. Got up early, looked over my books again, the last time, then went and reported at Board Rooms at 9 A.M., was directed to report in the afternoon. Shall be glad when the suspense is over, but every delay I expect only prepares me for the effort. Got my dinner, ate a hearty one, and then went and reported again, and this time I was rec'd and appeared before the August[14] Board, and for several hours was subject to the many questions of these persons, first one & then another upon the common branches, everything except tactics, regulations &c which they would take up on the morrow. I was quite composed, after I got into the mill, did better than I had expected, and quite generally answered their many questions. Upon leaving I was satisfied from their pleasing countenances, more than what said,[15] that I had passed very well. Towards evening I took a tramp down to the river, all open & boats running lively. Gen'l Grant was serenaded to night at the Planters house, bonfires all over the City, and fireworks in many places.

Thursday, January 28, 1864. Very pleasant, quite hot for the season. Reported at 9 A.M., and the Board was ready for me and thoroughly ex-

---

13. William Starke Rosecrans (1819–1898), an 1842 graduate of the US Military Academy, was appointed major general of volunteers in 1862. In 1864 he commanded the Department of Missouri.

14. Buswell capitalized "August," but he clearly intended the word "august," meaning highly respected or impressive.

15. Buswell may have omitted the words "by" and "was" here. He likely meant, "more than by what was said."

amined me for some two hours in tactics, regulations, fortifications, and science of war, and after being through was told that I would hear their report within about a week, and I came away quite well satisfied, feeling that I had answered most of the questions correctly, and that I had my first war victory in the South. Being now relieved of my anxiety about the matter, I went to the Theatre, having first got a night pass, to hear Wallack & Davenport,[16] the great American Tragedians, and I enjoyed it finely.

Friday, January 29, 1864. Very fine, warm, looks like rain. Orders rec'd that our regiment report at Hd Qrs, Dept Mo, to join procession to receive Genl Roscranz, the new Dept Commander who is now enroute, & the Reg't reported. Procession formed and marched to the levee, and there rec'd the Gen'l with a present arms, he riding through the files of the different regiments who were at rear open order. He was escorted to Hd Qrs. He is rather a fine looking man, a good man I learn to his Command, but not much of a fighter. Had the pleasure of a finer, closer view of Grant, he was of medium height, a strong well made frame, rather careless of dress. We do not notice any pomposity or grandeur of air, as we soldiers have so often seen in lesser lights. He had his military hat, Kossuth pattern off, and noticed his hair was quite short, full brown color, rather blue eyes, a fine closed mouth indicating that grip & tenacity of purpose for which he was now so well noted, beard a reddish brown color, cut rather short and quite thick, and a square jaw & chin, and the inevitable cigar was in his mouth. He was the hero of the day, and this evening a great dinner was given by the citizens of St Louis at the Lindell to him & Rosecranz. Capt Stevens, our Capt, got a leave of absence and went home today.

Saturday, January 30, 1864. Cloudy, prospects of rainy weather. Was off duty today and learning of the great Union Meeting to take place at the Court House, I went down. Grant & Rosecranz were present, & many others of the army, and a perfect jam of people. Heard some good speaking & music.

Sunday, January 31, 1864. Rainy, was on duty, this time at the gunboat, quite a nasty day but staid under cover and learned something more about the make up of the craft. The turret was made of wrought iron,

---

16. James W. Wallack, Jr., (ca. 1794–1864), born in London, and Edward L. Davenport (1816–1877), born in Boston, were actors.

7 in thick, carried two heavy guns, and the turret revolved so that a shot could be fired in any direction, a great invention and took a long head to work it out, and a very powerful craft, capable of doing the Rebs very much damage. Boats making their regular trips now and the river raising fast. Recd a letter from home.

Monday, February 1, 1864. Very pleasant, on guard again at the Gratiot St Prison, a good place for Guard duty, and between reliefs slept in quarters, quite a luxury. Am hoping to have a report from the Board soon. Saw flags flying at half mast today, learned that it was on account of the death of Gov Gamble,[17] Gov of this State.

Tuesday, February 2, 1864. Very pleasant, warmer, drying up fast. Came off duty in good season, got a pass and hearing that the funeral of Gov Gamble was to take place today at the 2^d Presbyterian Church, I went down there, there was a very large gathering. After the Services I went up into [the] dome of Court House to see the procession, which was very lengthy & in the following order: Police, Band, Hearse & bearers, & guards, mourners, Gov's Staff, next the Militia, gen'l officers & their Staffs, and friends.

Wednesday, February 3, 1864. Pleasant, not on guard & nothing especial today. Got a night pass and went to the Varieties Theatre to see Mazeppa,[18] a great play where the chief character, being taken prisoner is tied to the back of a wild horse, and away the animal goes up & down over the mts [mountains] & through the valleys, jumping chasms, very exciting, fine scenery, and draws well. Saw Hopson & others there.

Thursday, February 4, 1864. Cloudy & cool, not on duty, and being a fine day, took a tramp down on Broadway, a great thoroughfare. Went into Hd Qrs Dept Mo to learn my destiny, but ascertained nothing. The papers are filled with the news of the return of Arkansas, by act of its Legislature, to the Union, which caused some excitement.[19]

17. Hamilton R. Gamble (1798–1864) was governor of Missouri from 1861 to 1864.
18. The play "Mazeppa" was based off a poem by Lord Byron which tells the story of Ivan Mazeppa, a Ukrainian military leader who had an affair with a married Polish countess.
19. The capture of Little Rock in September 1863 placed most of Arkansas under Union control. Following Lincoln's December 8, 1863, Proclamation of Amnesty and Reconstruction, which required ten percent of a state's 1860 voters

Friday, February 5, 1864. Cloudy, slight sprinkling of snow, on guard again at Schofield Barracks. It rained & hailed during the P.M., but I found a place of shelter near the beat. Z. Neal,[20] one of our Co "B," who having been a notorious drunkard, never fit for duty, having been sentenced by Regtl Court Martial several times to the guard house, for a number of days at a time, and not desisting from his habits, was finally brought before a Gen'l Court Martial, and upon trial was found guilty and sentenced to have one half of his head shaved and to be drummed out of the service, in public before the regiment. Rather rough, but he had warning, and several times being lightly punished and not heeding good counsel will now finally get it bad.[21] Norton[22] & Ward[23] came today from furlough.

Saturday, February 6, 1864. Cloudy, looks like a storm, came off guard in good season, no mail today for me. Learned that Pliny Putnam[24] from near home was in the City looking after his son Isaac, who went some years ago to Arkansas & there married a Southern girl. When the war

---

to take a loyalty oath, Union general Frederick Steele began working to establish a loyal state government. By January, ten percent of Arkansas voters had taken the oath, and a convention drafted a new state constitution that repudiated secession and declared slavery illegal. The convention also selected pro-Union state leaders. As Buswell noted in his March 21, 1864, entry, the loyal voters of Arkansas approved the new state constitution in March.

20. Zedekiah Neal (born ca. 1826 in England) was a private in the 7th Minnesota Infantry, Co. B.

21. Neal was charged with "habitual drunkenness to the prejudice of good order and military discipline." He was found guilty and sentenced to "have one-half of his head shaved and be drummed out of service in the presence of his regiment, forfeiting all pay, bounty, and allowances due him." In his defense, Neal claimed to suffer from "chronic pneumonia of the liver, and I have been taking stomach bitters ever since, which accounts for the smell of my breath; it was not liquor at all. I look upon this prosecution as all spite, and in consequence I desire and only ask that you will be as easy with me as possible." See Court-Martial Case File LL-1737.

22. Robert F. Norton (ca. 1836–1918), a native of Michigan, was a private in the 7th Minnesota Infantry, Co. B.

23. Levi Shanklin Ward (1833–1907), a native of Ohio, was a private in the 7th Minnesota Infantry, Co. B.

24. Pliny Leonard Putnam (1801–1887), a native of Massachusetts, had a son named Isaac (1837–1877) who served as assistant surgeon in the 15th Missouri Cavalry (Confederate). Isaac married Sarah Deguire (1841–1941) of Missouri.

broke out he joined the Rebel Army, but was taken prisoner, brought here & confined in Gratiot St Prison, and was among the prisoners I had guarded in the Tower, but is now at Camp Chase. His father came here, upon his call, to see him, and get him out if possible and he has the promise of release for him if he will take the oath of allegiance and renounce hereafter his rebellious friends. Shall go and see Uncle Pliny tomorrow.

Sunday, February 7, 1864. Beautiful day, warmer. On guard at Hickory St Hospital, the place where the diseased soldiers are kept, some 300 of them, and such terrible sights I never saw before. I should want and expect to die if I was in the condition of some of these men. Could not well go to meeting, but having the time between the reliefs, I got permission from Officer of the Guard and went to see Uncle Pliny. O. P. Light was at his room, the Chaplain of the 10th Min[n], had quite a pleasant chat with them. Uncle Pliny thought it was very doubtful that Isaac would renounce his rebellious friends to get released as he has strong Southern feelings, and his wife, it is said, such a red hot rebel, that she really compelled Isaac to go to war in the Rebel Army.

Monday, February 8, 1864. Pleasant, took a tramp this A.M. around the City, orders rec'd that Neal be drummed out at dress parade this P.M. At about 5 P.M. the regiment went out by Co's and formed in line on the colors for dress parade, and soon thereafter Neal was seen coming, in charge of a Corporal's guard, one corporal and eight men. He was taken to the head of the line, that is the right of line. At a given signal, two drummers & fifers who had been selected from the band, com'd to play the Rogues March, and started down the line in front of the Reg't, the Corporal in Command, four men in front of him and four in rear, with bayonets fixed and pointing towards him, his head had been one half cut with shears from front to rear, and his hair having been quite long, & the other side being clipped so short, made him look rather odd to say the least. The bayonets were bristling towards him, and almost close enough to prick him. Upon reaching the extreme left, the squad countermarched, and passed the regiment again, and the rogue was free, and a terrible disgrace, but how he felt about it we could not tell, because we never saw him after that, except we learned he started at once for a barber shop to get the balance of his head trimmed. He was free, but kicked out & drummed out, with that horrid tune of the Rogues March. In the evening I went to the Union Methodist, a very large attendance, and a good meeting. This is one church where they are not afraid to preach the war.

Tuesday, February 9, 1864. Pleasant, on guard again at Gratiot St Prison, this time was in the Tower again where the Reb officers are confined. Talked with some of them, others were so sulky that they would^{nt} talk except among themselves, and they were rampant Rebs.

Wednesday, February 10, 1864. Pleasant, cool, came off guard in good season. Got a pass and took a tramp around the City, went to the levee, business enough there, then went to the water works and shot tower. Saw how shot was made, quite interesting & something new, then went back by Grand Avenue & Broadway to quarters. In the evening got a night pass and went to the Theatre to see McClellans Spy,[25] an army piece and No 1, we all enjoyed it. The Monitor left today for down river, will probably hear from her before long.

Thursday, February 11, 1864. Fine weather, was not on guard duty today, but my standing guard is about ended, as I just rec'd my order from Dept Special Order No 40 from Dept Mo, Gen'l Rosecranz, Feby 10 1864, to report for duty as 2^d Lieut to Brig Genl Pile at Benton Barracks, Mo. So I was accepted & passed a satisfactory examination, and am told that but for my age I would have a 1st Lieutenancy, having passed a satisfactory examination for that position, but there are many boys who applied, among others Serg't MacDonald of our Co, that failed. So I washed up, put on some clean duds and after dinner took my order with me and rode on the horse cars & went to Benton Bks about 4 miles back of the City, and upon arriving reported at once at Gen'l Piles Head Quarters, and was directed to report again tomorrow. Then I took a tramp around the Barracks, found it a beautiful place, so many trees, many fine buildings, and quite extensive barracks. Saw that there was a good many soldiers here, white & black, regiments forming and soldiers drilling. Then returned to my Co quarters and wrote the news home, and spoke for some money $50. to purchase my new uniform.

Friday, February 12, 1864. Pleasant, after breakfast mess, fixed up the best I could and went out again to the barracks, and reported at Hd Qrs. Was directed to stay and was assigned to duty for the present in Gen'l

---

25. This play was probably based on the story of Pauline D'Estraye, a woman who dressed as a man to spy for the Union army. See Wesley Bradshaw [pseudonym], *Pauline of the Potomac, or General McClellan's Spy* (Philadelphia: Barclay, 1864).

Piles Office, and at once took up my abode in the room assigned to me just back of headquarters and then for new duties entirely, & no more standing out in the rain or cold on guard duty, that part I am glad of, but I may get something worse. It is hard to tell, as a soldier cannot tell what even a day may bring forth, but it looks to me as though I would not only have an easier, better time, but shall get considerable more pay than a[26] high private, and have more liberty. Saw the troops out on Co & Battalion drill.

Saturday, February 13, 1864. Very pleasant. Staid at Barracks in my new home for the night, slept finely. We have nurses here to take care of the rooms, and I have a very good bed, not hardly as it would be at home, but good for a soldier. Went down to Co "B," got my things, and left the boys for good, rather sorry to leave some of them, would like Alva Dearborn & All Bartlett[27] along with me. Shall have Corpl Harrison who has been accepted. Commenced my work today, was shown what it was by Adjt Gen'l Hemenway.[28] Met the Gen'l first time who seemed very friendly, appears like a fine man, and it is said that he is a Methodist preacher, a Missourian, a staunch Union man, and a great friend of the black race. The Adjt Gen'l also appears like a fine man. My first duty was to make out a list of the 1st Iowa Inf'y who left here today, which report has to be sent to Hd Qrs Dept Mo. I also took charge of all details in and around the Hd Qrs, (made out my ration return to draw rations for 17 days). Took my meals with Gen'l & Staff. Bought an officers military fatigue cap of Watson I Lamson,[29] paid him $1.50, this being the commencement of my uniform.

Sunday, February 14, 1864. Pleasant, no business. Saw troops on Inspection, went to the City. Saw Hayes & Hopson Co "C" 10th Minn who invited me to dinner, and I went with them to their quarters & had a good time, then went over to Co "B" 7th, had a good chat with the boys,

---

26. Buswell may have originally written "an" here. It is unclear if he intended the word to be "a" or "as."

27. Alfred Bartlett (1839–1925), a native of Maine, was a farmer who enlisted as a private in the 7th Minnesota Infantry, Co. B.

28. Edward Hemenway (1842–1866) was captain of 67th USCT, Co. I, before being promoted to assistant adjutant general on General Pile's staff. He had previously been a private in the 1st Iowa Infantry.

29. Watson I. Lampson (1844–1935), a native of Massachusetts, was a private in the 7th Minnesota Infantry, Co. B.

then returned to the Barracks about 4 P.M. & to my new home & though away from my old comrades, I enjoy it in my new sphere, though I would some better if Alva was here, but I now have from our Co Harrison & McFarland[30] and expect to have Bilbie[31] soon, and we will probably be together in the same regiment. Recd letter from Aunty.

Monday, February 15, 1864. Very pleasant, took charge of details, drew my 17 days rations from the Quarter Master of the Post and turned them over to the Cook in charge of the officers mess at Hd Qrs, with whom I am to eat for the present, and we have something a little better to eat than when messing in the old Co. I notice quite a material change. The Gen'l eats with us frequently, but his home is in the City, and is not with us all the time. Took a tramp around the grounds and spent the evening with Harrison & McFarland, who had been here some time before I came, and who gave me what information they had received about the Barracks and the organization of troops here.

Tuesday, February 16, 1864. Very cold, blustery, quite a change. Had considerable writing to do [to]day, not much stir around the Barracks, helped make out some descriptive rolls of men leaving here, worked until 10 P.M.

Wednesday, February 17, 1864. Pretty cold, not so blustery. Had a plenty of writing to do today. Rec'd a letter from home, they were glad to know of my success. Saw Jno Moulton[32] today, he is 2^d Lt 3^d Regt A.D.

Thursday, February 18, 1864. Pleasant but cold. The hydrants about here froze up last night. Took charge of details. Had plenty of work writing

---

30. James H. McFarland (born 1825), a native of New York, had been a wagoner in the 7th Minnesota Infantry, Co. B. In March 1864 he was promoted to first lieutenant in the 68th USCT, Co. C. He rose to the rank of captain.

31. Henry G. Bilbie (1836–1920), an immigrant from England, had been a corporal in the 7th Minnesota Infantry, Co. B. In April 1864 he became first lieutenant in the 68th USCT, Co. I.

32. John A. Moulton (1840–1864), a native of Maine, had been a sergeant in the 7th Minnesota Infantry, Co. F. He later served in the 3rd Missouri Infantry African Descent (later designated the 67th USCT). He was captured by the Confederates on May 15, 1864, at Mount Pleasant Landing, Louisiana, and, according to his pension file, was "killed by the enemy while a prisoner. Killed 12 hours after capture."

in the P.M., getting some warmer, wrote a letter for Jas Lewis[33] a black orderly. Very few of the black boys can write and not many can read. I begin to see the evil effects of that curse of an Institution, slavery, more than at any other time in my life. I see these black boys only a few months since the shackles of slavery taken off, and see the evil as near as I can ever see it. I see their ignorance and superstition, naturally religious and many the prayer meeting do they have here together, and pray & holler, with thanks to the Almighty and Father Abe for their release. How they love Old Abe, and are thoroughly Union in sentiment, and as a general thing obedient, and most of them are easily handled by a kind master, and it is believed they will make excellent soldiers. There has been some opposition to it by some, especially Democrats at Washington, but why should not they assist in carrying on the war, not only to save the Union, but because the war has been the means of striking off their shackles. The Johnny Rebs think it a horrible thing that their slaves are released from bondage and then furnished the musket to fight them, but I learn that the Rebel Congress have passed laws, and the rule is no quarter for a slave to [who?] goes over to the enemy and takes on the soldiers uniform, as well as to those who enticed the black into such position.

Friday, February 19, 1864. Pleasant, considerable warmer. Had charge of details this A.M. Then to City to Gen'l Rosecranz Hd Qrs as bearer of despatches, went there and walked in as big as a gen'l. Did not go to see the boys, as it was near noon, & very windy & dusty and returned at once to my headquarters at Barracks.

Saturday, February 20, 1864. Pleasant, warmer. Took charge of details. Not having much business on hand, I got out my books and commenced studying, as ere long I shall be called to put my knowledge into practice, and shall brush up every opportunity. In the evening had a pleasant visit with Harrison, who gave me more practical instruction of the ins & outs of this part of Army life and the work about the barracks.

Sunday, February 21, 1864. Pleasant day, and am at leisure. Saw 9th Iowa Cavlry on Inspection, also 2d & 3d Regts Mo A.D. Quite a stir today as the 13th Ill Cavalry Veterans came here today. Did not go to the City, but attended divine service in the chapel on the grounds. Was with Harrison part of the day.

---

33. We are unable to identify James Lewis.

Monday, February 22, 1864. Beautiful morning, nice as could be at this season. Had some business in office in A.M. Then after dinner went to the City with one Smith and reported him to Schofield Barracks. Boys were glad to see me. Washingtons birth day, a large number of troops are out in procession, flags flying, guns firing. Towards night returned to my quarters. The 7th Mo Infy Vets came in today.

Tuesday, February 23, 1864. Pleasant, attended to my regular details and morning work in office. Then went down to parade ground to see guards mounting here. It requires a large guard in & around the barracks, and took some notes, all troops on drill this P.M. Do not feel very well today.

Wednesday, February 24, 1864. Beautiful day, but I do not feel so, much pain in my head, backs & legs. Went into Dr Jordans[34] room near by and he gave me some pills, took them and kept quiet all day. Saw the 2d Mo A.D. on dress parade, and it was well done, and these are the persons that some say will not make good soldiers. I believe it was right to call them out, and they should assist the government in putting down the rebellion, and establishing their freedom. Father Abe issued the proclamation and let them have the musket and assist in maintaining it.

Thursday, February 25, 1864. Pleasant. Feel much better, plenty office business. Gen'l Rosecranz & staff were here today and viewed the barracks and troops, many recruits came in today. The 2d & 3d Mo A.D. are now full & soon will be drilled and ready for the work. Rec'd letter from Lucy.

Saturday, February 27, 1864. Pleasant, feel much better. Hope I will be all right again in a few days. Had quite a severe storm this P.M., commenced with hail and ended with a heavy rain, lasting fully an hour. A good many troops came in today. Rec'd a letter from Eddie Hodgkins, was real glad to hear from him. He has enlisted also in the 19th Mass Infy Vols.

Sunday, February 28, 1864. Very stormy. Some snow, more recruits, went over and visited Harrison and we went down to the prayer meeting by the blacks. Such zealous religious people it seemed to me I never saw. Came back & took supper with Harrison. Spent the day quite well, & with some profit.

---

34. Possibly Victor S. Jordan (1817–1897), a druggist and physician in St. Louis.

Monday, February 29, 1864. Better weather, though some snow on the ground. Had muster of all troops here on the parade grounds, and was quite a sight, 36 recruits came in. Did a good deal of office work. Rec'd $50. by Express from home, but no letter.

Tuesday, March 1, 1864. Pleasant, snow all gone, and somewhat muddy. Had more business than usual today. Troops out drilling on parade ground. Gen'l Pile left us today for Jefferson City for a few days. Rec'd two letters from home, good news, all well.

Wednesday, March 2, 1864. Beautiful morning, prospects to continue so. Went through usual routine of duty, 40 recruits came in today. Rec'd letter from Hatties folks, all well at Lynn.

Thursday, March 3, 1864. Pleasant. Alva Dearborn came up today, having got pass & permission to leave for the day, and I took real pleasure in introducing & showing him around. He staid to dinner with me, and I enjoyed his visit very much. A large number recruits came in today. Rec'd news that the bill before Congress making Grant a Lt Genl has passed and was signed by the President on the 2^d. He will take command of the entire armies soon. Sent a long letter to mother.

Friday, March 4, 1864. Cloudy, cooler, looks like rain. Usual business, nothing especial, a large no [number of] recruits came in. Lt Col Branson[35] of the 2^d A.D. came today, having seen Adjt Genl Thomas[36] at Cairo. Quite stormy in P.M. Snow & hail.

Saturday, March 5, 1864. Pleasant again. The storm passed over, but not enough hardly to lay the dust. Got my usual morning business out of the way, got a pass and went to the City, walked down, passed through the fortifications, and by the reservoir, went up in the shaft and looked around the country. Saw men plowing and making gardens.

Sunday, March 6, 1864. Beautiful, felt quite smart. Got my work done and went down to the City to the Union Methodist, heard an excellent sermon, and there was a big turnout, and many soldier boys were present.

---

35. Probably David Branson (1840–1916), lieutenant colonel of the 62nd USCT (previously designated as the 1st Missouri African Descent), and formerly a major in the 28th Illinois Infantry.

36. Lorenzo Thomas (1804–1875) served as adjutant general of the US army from 1861 to 1869.

After church took the horse cars back to Barracks, just in time for dinner. In the evening went to the chapel on the grounds, heard a good sermon by the chaplain of the 18th Mo Infy Vols, and it was quite lively among the darkies, who as a general thing are greatly interested in religious matters.

Monday, March 7, 1864. Pleasant weather, heard spring birds singing this A.M. Considerable business, quite a lively day. Two paymasters arrived today and all the soldier boys are quite jubilant. It being the first money that has been earned from the gov't, and the first really earned in many cases of those soldiers who have just recently been released from bondage, to become Uncle Sam's Soldiers. Being quite tired, went to bed early.

Tuesday, March 8, 1864. Most beautiful spring morning. Had a good deal of officer business today. The Rebel Gen'l Prices brother,[37] a slave holder, came into the barracks and had a talk with the black boys, & in rather a discouraging manner. He ought not to have been admitted & will not be again, but this is the way that the Johnny Rebs & their friends have tramped around through the North carrying their treason & rebellion with them, and it is done with impunity. The gov't should be more severe with these men, arrest them and incarcerate them in prison or send them over to the lines to their friends, as they did with Vallandigham[38] the traitor. Don't feel very well today.

Wednesday, March 9, 1864. Pleasant, but some cloudy. Saw bluebirds, considerable business, a rainy P.M. Orders rec'd that the 2d Reg Mo A.D. leave here tomorrow for the South. Rec'd letters from[39] about the great war meeting up there. They needed it bad enough certain, as there are several coppery-heads that ought to be drove at the point of the bayonet into the Army or across the lines, and the soldier boys would like nothing better than to do it, if an opportunity presented.

Thursday, March 10, 1864. Pleasant, heard blue birds singing, quite spring like. Had a plenty to do today. The orders to the 2d Mo A.D. were

---

37. Robert Pugh Price (1803–1873), brother of Confederate general Sterling Price (1809–1867), lived in Brunswick, Missouri. According to the 1860 US census slave schedule, he owned seven enslaved people ranging in age from three to forty-two.

38. Clement L. Vallandigham (1820–1871) was an Ohio congressman and Peace Democrat who was arrested for disloyal speech in 1863. Following his conviction by a military commission, Lincoln had him banished to the Confederacy.

39. Buswell omitted who sent the letters.

countermanded and they remain here to perfect the organization and drill. A large number of recruits came in.

Friday, March 11, 1864. Pleasant, plenty of business making out reports, something extra. The 2^d & 3^d Regts Mo A.D. got marching orders to leave tomorrow at 8 A.M., and this departure makes extra work at Hd Qrs, and for me especially. But that is what I am here for. Sent a letter to mother.

Saturday, March 12, 1864. Very pleasant day, all was excitement throughout the Barracks from an early hour. The 2^d & 3^d Regts making preparations, reveille being much earlier than usual, and at about 9 A.M. all was ready & they departed, with bands playing & flags flying, and away they went singing John Brown's Body, down through the City to the levee, and soon were about the boats and away to New Orleans. Don't know why I am kept here, as I ought to have been assigned to duty in one of these regiments, and now it will be some time, as the 4th is just filling up.

Sunday, March 13, 1864. Quite a cool morning, hailed & then rained, the birds will want to hide today. Went through my usual routine of business, made out some reports for the Dept Hd Qrs showing the statement of troops which left here.

Monday, March 14, 1864. Cool day. Had a good deal of business, was sent to the City as bearer of dispatches, delivered them at Dept Hd Qrs. Saw Dan Dana[40] there as clerk, we had quite a chat. From what I can learn it looks even doubtful that I may get into the 4th.

Tuesday, March 15, 1864. Ugly, nasty day, not much to do. Went to the City for the gen'l. Saw the 7th Ill Cavalry Vets drawn up in line in front of Hd Qrs. Genl Rosecrans came out and spoke to them very encouragingly, as to their reenlistment. Recd a letter from home, also from Mary C Waitt of Malden, Mass, a fine letter, and quite unexpected, also one from Hattie & Hatties picture.

Wednesday, March 16, 1864. Pleasanter, had more to do today. Father Abe has called for 300 000 more. With Grant at the helm, he has more and renewed confidence that the right man is in the right place, and more troops are called for to push the matter to a speedy close.

---

40. Daniel Dana (ca. 1844–1928), a native of Massachusetts, was a private in the 7th Minnesota Infantry, Co. B. After the war he was promoted to second lieutenant in the 5th US Infantry.

Thursday, March 17, 1864. Cloudy, but proves to be a pleasant day. Had my usual morning business, wrote some letters, one home, and one to Cousin Mary Waitt. Grant has issued his order dated Nashville taking command of all the Armies, as Lt Genl, Comd'g, Headquarters to be in the field on the Potomac. A general feeling throughout by the soldier boys that the rebellion will now be crushed out, and although there has heretofore been many doubts as to the result, the feeling is now that with Grant as our leader, who has had success in every field, who has never known failure, now all is enthusiasm with full confidence that success will finally be ours. Recd the glorious news that Louisiana, the first free state where slavery existed, has by her Legislature adopted resolutions asking to be restored to the Union.[41]

Friday, March 18, 1864. Cool morning, raw air, many recruits came in today. Business rather light, spent a part of time in studying, then went to the City. While there witnessed the arrival of the 11th Mo Infy Vets, their old flag looked all tattered & torn, as if it had seen active service, and we know it had.[42] Got back to Barracks about dark.

Saturday, March 19, 1864. Pleasant, my work light today. Went to the City with despatches from the Genl Comdg to Lt Col Orne,[43] found the Lt Col on board Steamer Empress bound for New Orleans. Having delivered the despatches I went up to the Museum, a place where many an hour might be profitably spent. Saw the wonderful Sea Lion, new to me, he was very large & powerful, the greatest wonder to me was, how do they move such a monster.[44] The 8th, 11th, 12th, & 15th Iowa Infy Vets came in today and reported at Hd Qrs.

Sunday, March 20, 1864. Pleasant but quite cool, had work in office steady all the A.M., made out the monthly report of troops &c at Bar-

---

41. In 1864, Louisiana adopted a new antislavery state constitution.

42. The 11th Missouri Infantry had previously been at Vicksburg, Mississippi, and Simmesport, Louisiana.

43. We are not confident that this says "Orne"; however, Buswell may have meant Lt. Col. Charles E. G. Horn of the 2nd Missouri African Descent (65th USCT).

44. Phineas T. Barnum's sea lion appears to have toured the Midwest in 1864. However, on August 26, 1864, the *Pittsburgh Daily Post* reported: "The famous sea lion, owned by P. T. Barnum, and valued at $20,000, which has been on exhibition for seven years, drew his last breath in Cincinnati on Friday morning."

racks, for Hd Qrs Dept Mo. This is always quite a job, but it don't come very often.

Monday, March 21, 1864. Pleasant, rather cold, made out my reports and had considerable other business on hand. More glorious news, Arkansas has followed Louisiana and applied to our Congress to be once more restored to the Union, and little by little the Confederacy gives away.

Tuesday, March 22, 1864. Pleasant but cool, was at the office most of the day, quite busy, commenced work on the monthly Returns, no prospects of my commission yet. I don't believe it is right to keep me here all this time on duty as an officer, and drawing only privates pay.

Wednesday, March 23, 1864. Pleasant, quite warm, plenty of work, worked at the monthly and made a copy of Tri-monthly for Adj Genl Thomas U.S.A.

Thursday, March 24, 1864. Pleasant, had a good deal to do. The veterans are coming in every day, and more recruits. Rec'd news of Genl Grants arrival at Washington, and his reception,[45] now to reorganize the Army of the Potomac & then *On to Richmond*. He has full control, without interference from any body, he is fully trusted. Soldiers & citizens look to him as the great leader, to take the great army through to Richmond and to victory, and generally have confidence in his fidelity to the Union and his ability to command so great an army.

Friday, March 25, 1864. Quite a Spring morning, warmer, birds singing, some sprinkly during the day. Worked quite hard, worked on Monthly returns.

Saturday, March 26, 1864. Very pleasant, quite like Spring, birds singing. 15th Mo Infy Vets left here today for the front, they went down through the City singing old John Brown.

---

45. In February 1864, Congress passed a law reviving the rank of lieutenant general, and Lincoln soon thereafter nominated Grant for that rank. On March 8, Grant met with Lincoln at the White House to discuss military strategy. At the commissioning ceremony on March 9, Lincoln told Grant, "With this high honor devolves upon you also a corresponding responsibility. As the country herein trusts you, so under God it will sustain you. I scarcely need to add that with what I here speak for the nation goes my own hearty personal concurrence." Grant stumbled through his reply with a few gracious remarks that he could barely read because he'd scribbled them down so quickly.

Sunday, March 27, 1864. Beautiful day, got work done early, got a pass to be gone until 6 P.M. Walked to the City, went out of Barracks, first over to view Fremonts fort, built at the commencement of the war when the Rebs were advancing upon St Louis, with intent to take it. Then went up to the reservoir & went to the top of [the] shaft, had a fine view of city & surrounding country. Quite warm, grass begins to show quite green.

Monday, March 28, 1864. Rainy morning, blustry, march wind. Had considerable work today, worked on Monthly returns. Colder towards night.

Tuesday, March 29, 1864. Cold. Stormy day. Don't look as much like Spring. Friend Dearborn came up to tell me to go down to the Co to sign pay rolls, got permission & a pass and went at once down with him. Signed the pay rolls, was kindly rec'd by the boys. Found quite an addition to the Co, new recruits. Heard from Aunty. She speaks glowingly of the prospects.

Wednesday, March 30, 1864. Quite cold. Rec'd news of a copperhead fight over in Ill,[46] no more than I expected as there is a bad crowd living over there. The 4th Mo A.D. is now called 68th USCI. All colored troops are made by special order War Dept US Troops, instead of state troops, as they are formed independent of states and by order of the War Dept. The 68th Officers are arriving, H G Bilbie of Co "B" 7th Minn reported today, having been recommended for a 1st Lieutenancy by the Board. Rev Munger[47] got app't as Chaplain 62nd USCI, now at Port Hudson, La. Spent the evening with the officers of the 68th getting acquainted.

Thursday, March 31, 1864. Some warmer, quite busy on reports. Rec'd more news of the trouble in Ill, would like to be over there to help quell it. There is a bad element down in Egypt. Adjt Clendening[48] mustered in today as Lt Col 68th USCI.

---

46. Violence erupted in Charleston, Illinois, on March 28, 1864, when Democrats clashed with Union troops, leaving six soldiers, one local Republican, and two Democrats dead. Although Buswell describes this as being in "Egypt" in his March 31 entry, the riot actually took place in Coles County in central Illinois.

47. Enos Munger (1825–1873), a native of Massachusetts, had served as a private in the 7th Minnesota Infantry, Co. C, and later served as chaplain of the 62nd USCT.

48. James H. Clendening (1834–1898), a native of New York, was a first lieutenant in the 30th Iowa Infantry before becoming lieutenant colonel of the 68th

Friday, April 1, 1864. Cool, was quite busy all day, made out returns and drew forage for the Hd Qrs, & worked on the monthly returns. Recruits coming in lively.

Saturday, April 2, 1864. Weather about the same, unsettled. Quite busy on monthlys and finished them. Quite a job. Spent the evening with the officers of 68th.

Sunday, April 3, 1864. Rainy day, staid at my office all day. After morning work was done, sat down & looked over the news, then read some. It being so wet, did not go to church.

Monday, April 4, 1864. Rainy, had little to do except my regular duty. Staid at office most of the day, reading. In the afternoon went to the Provost Marshals Office in City in charge of two prisoners, which were committed to Myrtle St Prison. Got my receipt for them and returned at once to Barracks.

Tuesday, April 5, 1864. Cleared away in the night and turned out to be a beautiful day. Not much to do, went to the Library in the City and got a book. Saw Ed Starr of Co "C" 10th Minn. He says that the boys of his Co are getting along nicely. 34 recruits came in today.

Wednesday, April 6, 1864. Pleasant, more recruits this A.M., beautiful day, not very busy. Read a good deal. Saw 13th Ill & 12th Mo Cavalry on dress parade—they did very [well] I thought. In evening went down to 68th Quarters and had a good time with the officers.

Thursday, April 7, 1864. Beautiful. Sun out & feels good, not much business, do not feel very well. The buds on the trees begin to show and the grass is quite green.

Friday, April 8, 1864. Rainy again, quite muddy. Kept in office most of the day, and after work was over, looked over tactics battn drill.

Saturday, April 9, 1864. Rather stormy day. Had arrangements to go to the City, but it being so stormy, I remained at H'd Qrs and read my books, and wrote letters home & to Aunty.

USCT. Daniel Densmore considered Clendening a "flunky" and "a regular blowspout!" See Daniel Densmore to brother, August 1, 1864, and September 6, 1864, Densmore Papers. See also *Family War Stories*, 84–85, 119–21.

Sunday, April 10, 1864. Very pleasant, got my morning work done, and went to the City with despatches from the Ag't Genl of Barracks to the Genl Comdg who was at his residence on 14th St in the City. Was invited in, delivered them and with a good morning left. Saw some Co "C" 10th Boys, who informed me that Mrs Hopson & Hayes had come.

Monday, April 11, 1864. Pleasant, birds singing. Considerable to do in office. Gen'l Inspection at Barracks of all troops, by Col Marcy USA, Inspector Genl, and the troops made quite a display, and a very respectable one, I being with Genl Pile & Staff who accompanied Col Marcy. Rec'd some papers from Lynn.

Tuesday, April 12, 1864. Quite pleasant, business at a stand. Heard quite an excitement down behind the Barracks, every body running, and I went down too. Found the bakery was burning down & pretty much in ruins, now we will suffer for bread unless it is brought from the City. Rec'd news today of the terrible massacre at Ft Pillow by Forrest & Chalmers forces.[49] The fort was garrisoned by Colored troops and troops organized in Tenn & Ky, and the cry of the Rebs was "no quarter," kill the "Southern Yanks," and about 400 out of some 684 were killed & missing, many being killed after the surrender, and while the flags of truce was flying. Guerrilla warfare, and our gov't should retaliate and learn the Johnnies something. Great excitement in Congress over the expulsion of Long.[50]

Wednesday, April 13, 1864. Pleasant. Had some extra work. Starr came up, brought me a letter from Lucy, through the kindness of Mrs Hayes. I must go & see them the first chance.

Thursday, April 14, 1864. Pleasant. Had very little to do today. Was introduced to some ladies from the City of the Sanitary Commission who are to hold an entertainment here at the Chapel, and at the request of the

---

49. On April 12, 1864, Confederate forces under Nathan Bedford Forrest (1821–1877) and James R. Chalmers (1831–1898) captured Fort Pillow on the Tennessee River and massacred the black Union soldiers who occupied the fort when they tried to surrender.

50. Alexander Long (1816–1886) was a Peace Democrat from Ohio who served in the US House of Representatives from 1863–1865. Republicans mounted an unsuccessful movement to expel him from Congress in April 1864 following a speech he gave on April 8 with anti-emancipation and antiwar sentiments. While Congress could not muster the votes to expel Long, it did succeed in censuring him for "treasonable utterances."

Gen'l I went with them to assist in arranging the stage & scenic effects. Then bought a ticket but finally concluded to go to the City to Mercantile Library Hall where another & larger entertainment was given for the benefit of Sanitary Fair. Had a fine time. Saw Dearborn, Starr & others.

Friday, April 15, 1864. Rather pleasant with April showers. It having been determined to hold another entertainment at the Chapel tonight, I went and helped the ladies about rearranging the stage and had things in better shape, then went to the performance in the evening. It consisted principally of tableaux, singing, recitations, was well attended, and quite an interest manifested.

Saturday, April 16, 1864. Pleasant, not much to do, went to the City at noon with a 24 hour pass. Bought a few necessary articles, then went to see the old company boys, and then down and had a splendid visit with Mrs Hayes & Hopson. They were glad to see me and I equally as glad to see them. Some one just from home, they had a good word from the folks at home, learned all that was going on, had a fine chat, and finally towards night tore myself away & went back to Co and staid with Alva all night, and I might add that I ordered a new suit of officers dress uniform.

Sunday, April 17, 1864. Very pleasant, took breakfast with the boys, then fixed up and went with Dearborn and All Bartlett to the Union Methodist Church & Sabbath School, a large, fine school, and all seemed pleased to have us come. Then went down to Qrs, got my things, and those sent me from home, and returned to Barracks very much pleased with my trip. Rec'd letter from Father & Mother, was glad to hear from them. Had my descriptive roll sent me from Adj's Office 7th Minn, so I can now draw my pay here.

Monday, April 18, 1864. Pleasant, not much to do. Roster of officers at Hd Qrs made out and sent to Dept Mo Hd Qrs. Recruits came in lively today. 9th Iowa Cavalry Vets ordered to Dixie today. Recd news that the 7th & 10th Minn are ordered to move at a moments warning, to the South it is supposed, to intercept Forrest.

Tuesday, April 19, 1864. Pleasant but some cool. Have a stye on my right eye, which bothers me some, otherwise feel pretty well. Did not have much to do, was sent to the City with despatches. The Minn Regts had not gone. Some veterans came in tonight and new recruits.

Wednesday, April 20, 1864. Pleasant, quite warm, two veteran regts came today, and some recruits. War seems to be all the go now, every loyal person it seems is fully awake to the great task of putting down the rebellion, and they are coming continually, meetings are held, men enlist & soldiers reenlist, all are interested, and business in many places to a great extent suspended.

Thursday, April 21, 1864. Pleasant, not much to do, and put in the time this A.M. in study and reading the news. Bad news from Banks[51] Red River Expedition, great losses to the Union forces, and nothing gained, our army on the retreat down the river, and it is thought by many that the army would have been entirely destroyed but for Genl A. J. Smith[52] & the 16th Army Corps. They were fighters, not white glove-paper collared-dress-parade soldiers. Spent the evening with officers 68th, pleasant time.

Friday, April 22, 1864. Rainy, nasty day, not much business in office. Kept up my reading. The 68th is nearly formed, and the men are drilling, but where is my commission? Rec'd letters from Aunty & Willie, ans'd them.

Saturday, April 23, 1864. Continues to rain, very nasty & muddy, not very good weather for field duty, more recruits came in. Recd letter from Mother & Flora,[53] pleased to hear from them, and they are ever watchful and prayerful for their dear ones in the army, fighting for their Country.

Sunday, April 24, 1864. Cloudy, but no rain, 21 recruits came in early. Staid at my room most of the day studying, reading the Bible and the news, and writing letters, and in the evening went to the Chapel and heard the Rev Mr Canada Com' of Freedmens Institute in the City preach, and it was a very able discourse.

Monday, April 25, 1864. Cleared away, quite warm again. Did not have any extra work. Some lady friends of the Genl and his daughter came

---

51. Nathaniel P. Banks (1816–1894), a former speaker of the US House of Representatives and governor of Massachusetts, served as a Union general during the Civil War. In the spring of 1864, he led an offensive in northwest Louisiana intended to prevent Confederates from using the port at Shreveport. Although Banks's forces vastly outnumbered the Confederates, the Red River campaign ended in Union defeat.

52. Andrew Jackson Smith (1815–1897), a graduate of the US Military Academy and a veteran of the Mexican American War, commanded a division of 7,500 men of the Sixteenth Corps during the Red River Campaign. For an account of his actions, see the official report of the 8th Wisconsin Infantry in *Mineral Point Weekly Tribune*, June 22, 1864.

53. Flora Buswell Richardson (1853–1935) was Buswell's sister.

up today, came to H'd Qrs, and the Genl introduced me. They were on a mission to sell tickets for the Tableaux to be given at the Chapel for the benefit of the Freedmen's Aid Society, and I went with them around the grounds and assisted in the Cause in which they were engaged.

Tuesday, April 26, 1864. Beautiful. Quite warm, quite a change. The 13th Ill Cavalry & 35th Wis Infty left here today for the South, drums beating & flags flying. I went down to City, the State Militia were being called out, for what purpose I did not learn, possibly for the practice. In the evening I went to the Chapel and assisted the ladies about the entertainment, introduced to several others, and they had me all rigged up to represent an Indian in one of the tableaux. I had seen the Indians, had some experience with them, and it was said I represented the Chief in good shape. Enjoyed it hugely.

Wednesday, April 27, 1864. Rainy day, nearly all day. Went to the City with despatches for the Gen'l, while there bought some books and got my pants fixed over. Sent letter to Mother.

Thursday, April 28, 1864. Stormy day, not much work, but staid in office and read most of the day.

Friday, April 29, 1864. Stormy again, muddy, no extra work but instead of idling my time away, I profitably spent it in going over my tactics & regulations, becoming more thorough.

Saturday, April 30, 1864. Stormy again, quite rough day, read considerable and commenced work on the monthly returns.

Sunday, May 1, 1864. Cleared up in the night, and came out pleasant. Went to the Sabbath School in the Chapel, acted the part of a teacher, and had quite a large class. Then went with J. D. Rogers,[54] recently appointed 1st Lt and assigned to Co "K" 68th U.S.C.I., to his Quarters and took dinner. He was a member of the 8th Minn Infy, and while stationed at Ft Abercrombie in Minn, he applied to the Secy of War for permission to appear before the Board of Examination at St Louis, Mo. His app'n was accepted, was ordered to report, which he did at his own expense,

---

54. Jacob D. Rogers, Jr. (born ca. 1841), a native of Illinois, enlisted in the 8th Minnesota Infantry in August 1862. He was discharged in April 1864 to accept an appointment as first lieutenant of the 68th USCT, Co. K. In October 1865, he was promoted to captain.

was examined & passed, and at once assigned to duty in the 68th. I hope I may be assigned to the same Co, have spoken to the Gen'l about it, and if he can possibly grant the request, he will. After dinner we took quite a walk out into the Country, behind the Barracks, vegetation was quite well advanced. Saw apple trees in bloom, had a pleasant time.

Monday, May 2, 1864. Pleasant day. Business not very lively, but studied a good deal. Rec'd letter from home, and news of Lucy's marriage to Geo G. Knowles. Don't know what to say about it, but looks as if she had done better than to marry that worthless scamp of a Jim Pope. I never could think of her marrying him. Rec'd news that the soldiers wages are raised, privates to $16–per month, rather late to do me much good. $16–is not much for a fellow to run the risk of his life. It is not the money, at least the wages, that holds men, bounty might do it, but they are patriotic with the idea of beating the Johnny Rebs.[55]

Tuesday, May 3, 1864. Pleasant, studying tactics & regulations. Upon orders of Genl Pile Comd'g, the 68th moved into Block No 10 which has recently been repaired, quite a warm day. Starr came up and ate dinner with me. J H Baker, Col 10th Minn his regiment, is the Comdr Post of St Louis, and the 10th are now the Provost Guard.[56] Showed Starr around the camps & Barracks. Heard a rumor that Forrest has sent a flag of truce into Paduca, Ky, and desires an exchange of prisoners. The scoundrel guerrilla ought to be shot. Many ladies came up from the City with the genls family, was introduced to them. Saw dress parade of that part of the 68th which is organized. It will soon be full, then for Dixie.

Wednesday, May 4, 1864. Sprinkled rain, but soon cleared up. Had very little to do today, but kept up my studies. Drew forage for Hd Qrs.

Thursday, May 5, 1864. Pleasant day, rather dull and quiet, read my books, took a walk about the grounds and down to officers quarters 68th, had a pleasant visit with them.

Friday, May 6, 1864. Beautiful morning, worked on returns, birds singing, grass growing very fast. Rec'd news that Grant gave orders, and the

---

55. On June 20, 1864, Congress increased the pay of enlisted men from $13/month to $16/month.

56. On October 23, 1863, Baker was appointed commanding officer of the post of St. Louis. See *Minnesota in Wars*, 461.

great Army of the Potomac moved on Tuesday the 3ᵈ inst, enroute to Richmond. We hope and pray for success, though many brave boys must fall before it is accomplished. The Rebs although are cornered, will not yield until I might say, nearly, if not quite annihilated. The fight and grit is in them not to yield. No one can say that they are cowards, as they have already demonstrated that fighting ability on many a bloody battle field. They live on hopes, and so do we.

Saturday, May 7, 1864. Pleasant, worked quite hard making out returns and other documents. In the afternoon went to the City with despatches for Gen'l Hd Qrs.

Sunday, May 8, 1864. Pleasant, got up early, washed all over, dressed up in my best and went to Church at the Chapel. After dinner went down to see officers of the 68ᵗʰ, spent most of my time with Lt Rogers & Co K, had a pleasant visit. Got a letter from Aunty.

Monday, May 9, 1864. Pleasant but threatens rain, finished up the returns today and sent them by mail to Dept Hd Qrs. Letter from home.

Tuesday, May 10, 1864. Rainy day, towards evening it cleared up. The long looked for appointment as 2ᵈ Lieut 68ᵗʰ came today. Most of the officers have had their commissions for some time and mine was only issued by Adjt Genl Thomas USA, April 28ᵗʰ/64. I can't see why mine did not come before, and why it was not dated with the rest of them. Here I have been on duty nearly three months as an officer, awaiting commission, but it has finally come, am glad to receive it even at this late day, but justice is justice. I shall now be mustered in as 2ᵈ Lt as soon as an order from Dept Mo is issued, authorizing my discharge from Co "B" 7ᵗʰ Minn, which the gen'l has this day requested.

Wednesday, May 11, 1864. Beautiful day, not having much to do, I took a good study in tactics and then made out my muster-in-roll as 2ᵈ Lt 68ᵗʰ U.S.C.I. Think I am pretty well prepared to assume the responsibility of a commissioned officer. I have taken all the practical lessons I could since I have been here. I have the tactics in School [of the] Soldier and Co nearly all at my tongues end, as Capt John Curtiss wrote in my Book of Tactics on that memorable Feby 16ᵗʰ 1863, "Study its Contents" when the book was presented to me. I have studied its contents and now I am getting my reward, and I have quite a knowledge of battalion drill also.

Thursday, May 12, 1864. Pleasant as usual, nothing especial on hand in office. Rec'd Special Order No 130 Hd Qrs Dept Mo, dated March 11ᵗʰ

1864, signed by Genl Rosecranz, by O. D. Greene[57] Asst Adj Genl, discharging me from Co "B" to accept promotion as 2ᵈ Lieut in 68ᵗʰ U.S.C.I., and I at once made out my discharge and final statements, and they will be signed by Gen'l Pile when the mustering officer comes, which will be in a day or two. Rec'd news of Grants six days battle in the wilderness, that he was pushing Lee though no very decided advantage, and of Grants famous order congratulating his forces, cheering them on and in which he winds up with those words which already form the head lines to the leading papers, and is upon the tongue of everyone, soldier & citizen, "We will fight it out on this line if it takes all Summer," watch words which show, indicate to the most doubting that Grant has the true metal.

Friday, May 13, 1864. Pleasant, not much on hand now, except to wait for the mustering officer. So kept up my studies, and spent a part of my time with the reg't getting better acquainted.

Saturday, May 14, 1864. Pleasant day, the mustering officer came and Gen'l Pile signed my discharge and final statements to date May 11ᵗʰ 1864, and the officer then mustered me in as 2ᵈ Lieut to date from May 12ᵗʰ 1864, for 3 years or during the war. I was then relieved from duty at H'd Qrs, and assigned to duty as 2ᵈ Lieut Co "K" with Lt Rogers as I had requested, and at once moved my things to the H'd Qrs Co "K." Was well received by Lt Rogers and the boys of the Company, and trust we will get along together in peace & harmony. Put on my new uniform, sword & sash and appeared for the first time in them on dress parade. Now I shall have still another experience while at Hd Qrs. I was not subject to Reveille, nor any special discipline, but now I have got to come to it again. Military discipline, reveille, roll-call, &c &c.

Sunday, May 15, 1864. Pleasant day, got up early, washed up, slept first rate in my bunk. Remained at my quarters all day making things convenient and getting acquainted with the company, a good many names to learn, and some of them very peculiar. Several Geo Washingtons and Thos Jeffersons so that they had to be called in roll-call 2ᵈ & 3ᵈ. Had quite a chat with our Col J. Blackburn Jones,[58] a young but fine dashing looking

---

57. Oliver Davis Green (1833–1904) was assistant adjutant general in the Department of the Missouri.

58. J. Blackburn Jones (1840–1896) was in his final year at Chicago Law School in 1861 when he raised a company of men and became a captain in the 15th Illinois Infantry. In 1864 he was appointed colonel of the 68th USCT. Jones

man, and a stirring brave man I believe, he might be a rash man in battle, an Illinois gent and formerly a member of the 15th Ill. Also met Lt Col Clendening, a man I cannot bear, a great big pompous chap, more pomp & style than force. Then our Major Daniel Densmore, who was formerly a capt in the 8th Minn Infy, think he is a fine man and steady.[59] The Adjt Enoch Root,[60] a Chicago boy, a short, sharp, well educated fellow, and a good voice, which is requisite for that position. And now comes our Chaplain, and I greet him, A. C. McDonald[61] a very fine gentleman. The regiment has not its full complement of officers, is not fully organized, no doubt will be ere long, & then we will be off to Dixie, and adventure. In the evening took a walk with Lt Rogers down to Hyde Park, a fine place, and a great Sunday resort on pleasant days. When I returned a telegram was handed me, it was from Gen'l Pile and directed me to report with a corporals squad at his house in the City at 5 ½ A.M. tomorrow. What for was a puzzler, but it makes no difference, orders must be obeyed, and before going to bunk I notified the Sergeant of the guard to have me awake at 3 A.M.

Monday, May 16, 1864. Pleasant. At 3 A.M. some one rapped, I was called, and soon recollected that I had a trip on hand. Up I jumped, dressed, and with my men was soon off for the City, and reported, nearly on time at the Genls residence, & from him rec'd instructions to take the

---

was wounded several times during the war and rose to the rank of brevet brigadier general in October 1865. Three days after Jones was appointed colonel of the 68th, Daniel Densmore called him "a grand prize" for the regiment who was "young, stirring, vigorous, & frank, and has backbone enough to take the charge of the regiment upon his own shoulders." Later, Densmore added that Jones was "one of these indefatigable workers who have no mercy on themselves, and kick in their coffins." Jones died by suicide in the Hudson River near Yonkers, New York. Daniel Densmore to brother, July 1, 1864, and Densmore to friends at home, October 12, 1864, Densmore Papers. See also *Family War Stories*.

59. Daniel Densmore (1833–1915), a native of New York, had been a lieutenant in the 7th Minnesota Infantry, Co. G, before being promoted to major of the 68th USCT. Buswell listed the wrong regiment in his diary.

60. Enoch Root (1838–1915) served as a first lieutenant and as the adjutant for the 68th USCT. He was later promoted to the rank of captain for Co. H. Prior to his time in the 68th, Root served in the 2nd Colorado Cavalry and the 3rd Colorado Infantry.

61. A. C. McDonald (1828–1877) was chaplain for the 68th USCT. For an incident involving McDonald, see *Family War Stories*, 115–16.

Col. J. Blackburn Jones. (Collection of Jonathan W. White)

Iron Mt R.R., go out about 40 miles to Tunnel Station and get some cedar or evergreens for the Sanitary Fair, soon to be opened in the City, and he gave me passes, and we started for the depot. Went to the point, cut the evergreens, hauled them to the station, and when the train came they were put aboard the cars, and we ret^d to the City, getting back to Barracks—about 10 P.M., quite tired. The country passed through was quite barren, cedar & pines, and we went far enough South to see Iron Mt & Pilot Knob in the distance.

Tuesday, May 17, 1864. Pleasant. Today being set for the opening or Inauguration day of the Great Sanitary Fair, which the citizens of the City and others have [been] preparing for some time under the auspices of the Western Sanitary Commission, head Quarters at this City, and there is to be a general military display and procession, our regiment rec'd orders to be present, and to report at Hd Qrs Dept Mo at 9 A.M. So this morning reveille was earlier than usual, and at 6 A.M. the regiment was in line & started on the march for the City, where procession was formed, and marched around the City, thence to Fair. It was a long procession, several bands, Artillery, Infantry, and Cavalry, gen'ls and their staffs, Mayor & City Council, &c &c, a huge affair, and a tremendous crowd of people.

Having arrived at the fair grounds the procession broke and our Reg't started enroute for the Barracks, arriving there about 3 P.M., being out all day with out a mouthful to eat and quite tired. So much for style.

Wednesday, May 18, 1864. Pleasant. Discharged my regular duties, then had company drill for about three hours, and battalion drill in the P.M., and dress parade in the evening. My first experience in drilling men, did well, made only a few mistakes, but there is always a chance for improvement. Expect to go to City to visit the fair tomorrow.

Thursday, May 19, 1864. Pleasant. Rec'd orders to report at H'd Qrs, and was then directed to report with a detail of 15 men at the Sanitary Fair in the City to assist in the preparations. Took charge of my men, took the horse cars to City, and at once reported at the office of the fair. Rec'd instructions and set the men at work where directed, and I looked around. Found it was very extensive, the most magnificent display that I ever saw. Met some ladies, to whom I had on a former occasion been introduced by the Genl, and they invited me to partake dinner with them in the cave, it being an artificial one, with fountain, brook &c, and I accepted of course, and had a splendid time, and got back to the Barracks in good season well pleased with my duty.

Friday, May 20, 1864. Cloudy, cool, looks like snow. Tried my hand as a drill master in Company movements in the A.M. Had Batt^n drill & dress parade in P.M.

Saturday, May 21, 1864. Very pleasant, no drill today. The Regt was paid off today, but I did not get any, next pay day I will draw. Rec'd some money from Lt Rogers which had been loaned to him. Quite a warm day, had a good clean up and washed all over. Employed a servant, a colored boy about 16 yrs old—Jack, to attend to my wants, and it is necessary to have one, to draw the pay from government. Had my washing done outside. I have got done washing my own clothes.

Sunday, May 22, 1864. Beautiful, got up early, washed up and shaved, and got ready for inspection and at 8 A.M. the bugle blew, the drums beat, and the Co's fell in and inspection was held. Found things in very good shape, especially for raw recruits, though some of them, it seemed difficult for them to understand that it was necessary to keep their guns & clothes perfectly clean, but when we consider that these boys are just from the bonds of slavery, we gave them suitable praise and showed them just what was necessary. They seemed anxious to learn and generally obedient, and very quick to imitate. Some have thought they would not make soldiers, but that idea is being exploded, as they have already proved good fighters. Went to the chapel in the evening.

Monday, May 23, 1864. Pleasant, but rainy towards night. Lt Rogers was Officer of the Day, and this left me in charge of the Company. Took the boys out and gave them a good drilling, then took them on dress parade, and discharged my duty as commander in my best style. Serg't Turner[62] & some others were reprimanded on dress parade for being absent without leave. Took up a subscription to purchase a sword for Genl Pile Comd'g and succeeded admirably.

Tuesday, May 24, 1864. Rather cloudy, pleasant towards night. On guard as officer of the Guard for the first time. Went on guard mount, and the guard was turned over to me, marched them to the guard house, formed reliefs and the old guard was relieved from duty. Had considerable to look after and considerable more responsibility than when I used to stand guard. Then I was responsible only for myself, now I am responsible for the entire guard, but one thing certain, I am not obliged to stand out, rain or shine, cold or hot. I parade around, inspect the guard and posts, teach them how to salute, as it is necessary you know for a guard to salute every officer, great or small, who approaches near the guard, and the officer salutes in return. The Sergts & Corporals have to look out for the calls of the guard, and [it is] necessary for them to be near the guard all the time. I as officer of the guard am permitted to sleep at my Co quarters. Raised nearly $50. among the boys of Co "K" for the Sanitary Fair, and some more for the genl's present. The Sanitary Fair is especially for the benefit of the soldiers, and the Gen'l is a great friend of them, especially of the black race, yet a Missourian, but he was a minister of the Gospel.

Wednesday, May 25, 1864. Pleasant, relieved from guard about 9 A.M. everything being quiet in the night, and my first trial as Officer of the Guard, not only satisfactory to myself, but to my superiors. Lt Rogers went to the City in charge of a detail, and I am in command of the Company. Took them out and drilled A.M. & P.M. Also dress parade. Rec'd a call from the Corkhill girls, friends of the gen'l, who are greatly interested in the Sanitary Fair. Got our money together and bought the gen'ls sword, a fine one. Sent letters to Hattie.

---

62. William Turner (ca. 1832–1924), a native of Albemarle, Virginia, enlisted as a private in the 68th USCT, Co. F, and rose to the rank of sergeant. He had previously been enslaved in Pike County, Missouri.

Thursday, May 26, 1864. Pleasant. The 68th was given permission to visit the Sanitary Fair today, and at about 8 A.M. the drums beat the assembly and the regiment fell into line and marched to the City, and went direct to the fair. No admission fee was required, the reg't marched in, and broke ranks, with orders to meet at a given point at noon, then the sights were seen, and there were many of them. At noon, the Reg't collected together and returned to the Barracks. I then got a pass from the Gen'l and went back again, especially to go into the fair, went into the Curiosity Shop. Saw the Washington relics, Dan'l Boones rifle, and many others. Met Miss Anderson and other ladies—whom I had before met at Barracks, and escorted them around, and had a good time, generally, got back to Barracks about 11 P.M.

Friday, May 27, 1864. Pleasant, very warm. Had a drill in A.M. and at 2 P.M. orders given to fall in, and the regiment was soon in line, and the beautiful sword was presented by our Col to Genl Pile, for and in behalf of the Reg't, when he in a very few appreciative remarks, accepted the same. Two colored gents from N.Y. made short speeches, which were quite interesting, and pleased the boys very much.

Saturday, May 28, 1864. Pleasant, not much to do, no drill, so as to allow the regiment to wash their clothing and clean quarters. In the evening had dress parade. Rec'd letter from home and papers from Aunty, which were very welcome.

Sunday, May 29, 1864. Pleasant day. Had usual morning inspection including knapsacks. They begin to handle their guns well, but slinging and unslinging knapsacks is quite difficult. I look back to the time our old company was practicing, what a time they had in learning this particular feat. To do it properly & in time, a great deal of practice is required, and all for the purpose principally of making a grand show on gen'l Inspection. Went to church. Dress parade in the evening.

Monday, May 30, 1864. Still pleasant, had Co Drill in A.M. In P.M. got a pass and went to the City, had some pictures taken to send home, went into fair again for a few hours, then back to Barracks, and dress parade.

Tuesday, May 31, 1864. Pleasant but quite dusty. Reg't about full, though not quite officered, and getting well drilled. Rec'd orders to be ready to march at a moments warning, and everything is hurly-burly, as things are being packed to tramp. Wrote letters to Mother & Aunty and sent each pictures of myself, told them of the order to leave here, but where we go,

I could not tell, at some point South no doubt. All we have to do is to obey orders, go where we are sent. A soldier that obeys orders is a true soldier, even though he never sees an engagement, obey orders is the true discipline.

Wednesday, June 1, 1864. Pleasant, everything is in a bustle, orders recd to leave here at 1 ½ P.M. and everything in readiness. At the appointed hour the bugles blew, the drums beat, and we were soon into line, and on the march bidding Good bye to the old Barracks, and I especially to friends at Hd Qrs, for the levee in city. Lt Rogers officer of the day, and I in command of Company. Marched through principal streets, cheered on the way, and the Reg't answering with a cheer, and singing old John Brown, to the foot of Morgan St where [we] got aboard the boat, and about 9 P.M. the band played, and the boat started down the stream for Dixies land, which was played by the Band, with renewed energy, and amid the cheers of the boys. All felt well, though I did not, got a bunk early & went to bed.

6

"A Close Shave"

Duty in Memphis and the Battle of Tupelo, June 2–July 23, 1864

On June 1, Buswell boarded a boat for Memphis. As he headed south on the Mississippi River, he took note of several important sites of the war. A few days later, on June 4, he arrived at the Bluff City. By 1860 Memphis had emerged as the South's sixth largest city and one of the region's most important railroad hubs and port towns. At the intersection of four railroad lines, and with docks on the Mississippi River, Memphis was a center of both the cotton trade and the slave trade. But the Confederate stronghold had fallen into Union hands in June 1862, and Northern soldiers, missionaries, nurses, and businessmen had flooded into the city. Buswell and the men of the 68th USCT encountered a magnificent riverside town with beautiful homes, yards, and gardens. Over the previous decades, as the amount of wealth in the city increased, the size of homes had grown larger. By the time of the Civil War, brick houses predominated, and commercial buildings reached five stories.[1]

From Memphis, Buswell reported on the military situation in the

---

1. Hannah Rosen, *Terror in the Heart of Freedom: Citizenship, Sexual Violence, and the Meaning of Race in the Postemancipation South* (Chapel Hill: University of North Carolina Press, 2009), 27–28; Andrew L. Slap, "African American Veterans, the Memphis Region, and the Urbanization of the Postwar South," in Andrew L. Slap and Frank Towers, eds., *Confederate Cities: The Urban South during the Civil War Era* (Chicago: University of Chicago Press, 2015), 172; Gerald M. Capers, Jr., *The Biography of a River Town: Memphis: Its Heroic Age* (Chapel Hill: University of North Carolina Press, 1939), 118–134.

Western Theater. During the summer of 1864, the Union army engaged Confederate cavalryman Nathan Bedford Forrest in several battles in Mississippi in order to stop him from attacking the railroad line that supplied William T. Sherman's army outside of Atlanta. In May, Confederate general Stephen D. Lee ordered Forrest to destroy the Nashville and Chattanooga Railroad. On June 1, Forrest took 2,000 cavalrymen and a battery of artillery to Tupelo, Mississippi, and then into Alabama on his way to middle Tennessee. That same day, Union general Samuel D. Sturgis left Memphis with 4,800 infantrymen, 3,300 cavalrymen, and 400 artillerymen with 22 cannons in pursuit of Forrest. His mission, in the words of historian Herman Hattaway, was "to find and destroy Forrest and his men." Aware of the Federal advance, Forrest returned to Mississippi. He knew that the Union army "greatly outnumber the troops I have at hand," but he also knew they would make "slow progress" over the muddy roads. If he acted quickly, he could strike a devastating blow. "It is going to be as hot as hell," he said, "and coming on a run for five or six miles over such roads, their infantry will be so tired out we will ride right over them."[2]

The Federals under Sturgis first skirmished with the Confederates at Ripley on June 7. Although Forrest was about eighteen miles away, he pushed his men toward Brices Cross Roads, and on June 10, he routed the Union army there (which Buswell refers to as the Guntown Raid). While Sturgis's men had taken ten days to march from Memphis to the site of the battle, they retreated to Memphis in a mere sixty-four hours. Union casualties numbered 2,612, while Forrest reported only 493. Hattaway writes, "The amazing reality is . . . that Forrest was correct in assessing that his own men could travel more than twice the distance that the Federals would cover and still be fit to fight." Despite the humiliating defeat, Buswell noted that the men of the 55th and 59th US Colored Infantries "though suffering dreadfully kept together and fought like madmen, and

---

2. Edwin C. Bearss, *Protecting Sherman's Lifeline: The Battles of Brices Cross Roads and Tupelo 1864* (Washington, D.C.: National Park Service, 1972), [14]; Herman Hattaway, *Shades of Blue and Gray: An Introductory Military History of the Civil War* (Columbia: University of Missouri Press, 1997), 200–205. For an account of other Minnesotans in the battle, see John B. Lundstrom, *One Drop in a Sea of Blue: The Liberators of the Ninth Minnesota* (St. Paul: Minnesota Historical Society Press, 2012), chaps. 7–10.

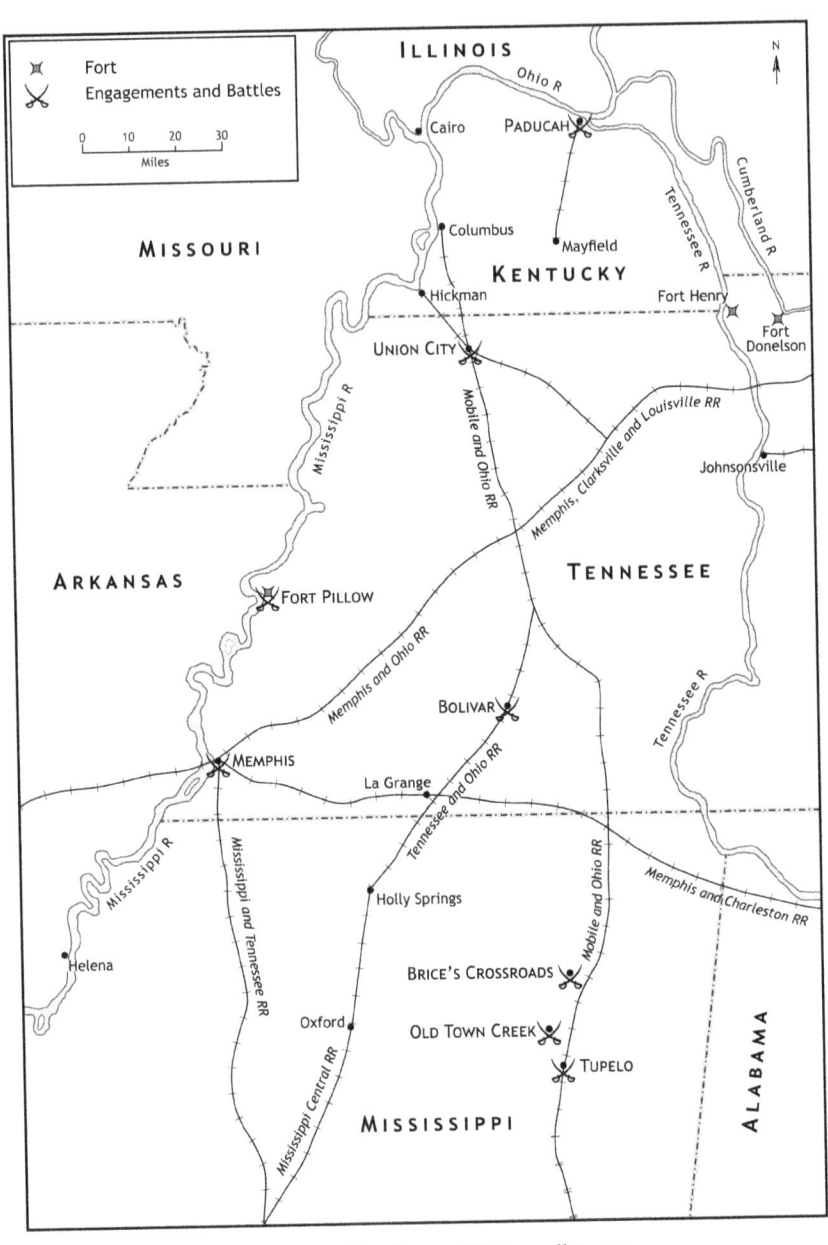

Map 3. Battles and cities mentioned by George W. Buswell in 1864

kept the enemy at bay." Tragically, though, some of the black soldiers captured by Forrest's men were sold back into slavery.[3]

When William T. Sherman learned of the Union defeat at Brices Cross Roads, he worried that Forrest would now be able to ride into middle Tennessee and destroy the railroads that supplied his troops. Sherman informed Secretary of War Edwin M. Stanton that he wanted the Union commanders in Memphis "to make up a force and go out to follow Forrest to the death, if it cost 10,000 lives and breaks the Treasury. There will never be peace in Tennessee till Forrest is dead."[4] Sherman ordered Maj. Gen. Andrew Jackson Smith on a diversionary raid into northern Mississippi to attack Forrest. After weeks of serving as officer of the guard, Buswell was pleased to learn that he would be joining the forces sent out to face Forrest.

Smith's men—Buswell among them—departed Memphis on July 5. As they marched south, Smith used diversionary tactics to hide his true intentions from the Confederates. Forrest and Lee had prepared to ambush Smith on the road to Okolona, Mississippi, but the ambush failed because Smith took the route to Tupelo, a railroad crossing where Union forces could both destroy the Mobile & Ohio Railroad and engage Forrest from a strong position. As historian Thomas E. Parson writes, Smith's "enemy was never sure where he was going." One officer on Smith's staff observed that "it was apparent that Forrest knew he now had a general to fight, of whom, he must be, to say the least, very wary" because in Smith the Confederates had "an antagonist worthy of their own commander."[5]

The armies met near Tupelo on July 14 (the 68th USCT occupied a position toward the rear on the left of the Union line), and over the course of several days' fighting, the Federals repulsed the Confederate attacks. Although Smith returned to Memphis after the fighting ceased

---

3. Diary entries for June 12, 13, 14, 1864; Hattaway, *Shades of Blue and Gray*, 201; Robert K. D. Colby, *An Unholy Traffic: Slave Trading in the Civil War South* (New York: Oxford University Press, 2024), 160–61.

4. William T. Sherman to Edwin M. Stanton, June 15, 1864, O.R., ser. 1, vol. 39, part 2, p. 121.

5. Thomas E. Parson, *Work for Giants: The Campaign and Battle of Tupelo/Harrisburg, Mississippi, June—July 1864* (Kent, Ohio: Kent State University Press, 2014), 66, 104, 117, 121–22, 274; Edwin C. Bearss, *Outwitting Forrest: The Tupelo Campaign in Mississippi, June 22—July 23, 1864*, ed. David A. Powell (El Dorado Hills, Calif.: Savas Beattie, 2024), 47–49.

(causing some Confederates to claim victory), the battle was a both tactical and strategic victory for the Union. As Parson concludes, "Sherman's supply line remained intact and the Confederates in Mississippi had been dealt a harsh defeat.... The combat effectiveness of Forrest's corps was destroyed in the period of July 13–15 . . . never again would his corps be able to stand and fight Union infantry." Moreover, the courageous service of the black soldiers—including the 68th USCT—influenced how men of color were viewed by at least some whites. "I am free to confess that their action has removed from my mind a prejudice of twenty years' standing," observed General Smith.[6]

Thursday, June 2, 1864. Pleasant. Slept very well, got up, felt better. Learned that the boat tied up in the night, but about 5 A.M. she started again, arriving at Cairo about 8 P.M. & tied up here for the night. Many of the officers went ashore and looked around for an hour or two, but I not feeling tip top went to bed.

Friday, June 3, 1864. Pleasant, but some cloudy. Slept quite well, got up, found some late papers from St Louis, Chicago & Cincinnati, and had a good read, the boat starting again at 7 A.M. Good news from Grant, he is crowding Lee towards Richmond, little by little, though many hard fought battles have been fought & many more lives will be lost before he gets there. Sherman is near Atlanta, the Rebs are being hemmed in, but they are tenacious and will not yield until their Armies are completely wiped out and the leaders either killed or captured. Passed Belmont where Grant had his first battle.[7] Also Columbus, Miss [Kentucky], which had been strongly fortified by the Rebs. Saw the forts, but now unoccupied, they looked almost impregnable. Soon passed Island No 10, the scene of many a hard fought battle by our mortar & gunboats. The boat kept running and at 11 P.M. went to bunk.

Saturday, June 4, 1864. Quite warm, but cloudy, got up, washed & found that the boat had been running all night. Passed by a very rough looking Country, partially timbered, settled by a poor class, corn crackers,

---

6. Parson, *Work for Giants*, 160, 177–97, 240, 274; *Family War Stories*, 81.

7. The Battle of Belmont was fought in Mississippi County, Missouri, on November 7, 1861. Both sides claimed victory—the Confederates because Union forces retreated to Paducah, Kentucky, after the fight; the Union because the Confederates stopped detaching forces from Columbus, Kentucky.

or butternuts, and some of them bushwhackers, as along here is where boats have been fired into, but we passed without difficulty. About 2 P.M. passed Ft Pillow, the scene of that terrible massacre, not much of a fort—simply embankments on the two sides and rear, and in front at the waters edge, the Union forces less than 700 in all was overpowered by the Confed forces under Forrest & Chalmers. It was garrisoned at this date by only a few men. That is one great difficulty in carrying on the war. It not only requires a large army to confront the enemy in his own Country, but no end of men to fortify & hold the many strategic points, and keep up the line to the base of operations, and in many such places the force is necessarily small and a band of raiders like Forrests, Gordons[8] or Morgans,[9] pass to the rear, and not only cut the lines, but take these different garrisons prisoners. But in this slaughter Forrest did not take them prisoners, carried on a guerrilla warfare, hoisted flags of truce, then advanced their lines under cover of them, and finally effecting an entrance into the Union works, charged down the hill, and notwithstanding the surrender, shot & cut right and left, killing about 400 out of the number with cries of No quarter, kill the d—d Southern Yanks, meaning the troops organized in Tenn. About 200 were taken prisoners here, but they were nearly all killed, or murdered.[10] Passed two gunboats lying near in the river. About 9 P.M. the whistle blew, and the boat arrived at Memphis, Tenn, and tied up, and learned that we get off here, but remain on the boat until morning. Went to bed at 11 P.M.

Sunday, June 5, 1864. Very warm, got up early, and we got everything in readiness to move when the order is given, and about 8 A.M. the Reg't

---

8. Col. Anderson Gordon (1820–1893) was a cavalry commander in Arkansas who participated in Sterling Price's raid into Missouri in 1864.

9. Brig. Gen. John Hunt Morgan (1825–1864) invaded Indiana and Ohio in July 1863. He was killed in Tennessee in September 1864.

10. About a half mile below the fort, Daniel Densmore saw "a group of children playing, all as unconcerned as though their *forefathers*, even, had forgotten long ago the fiendish 'massacre of Fort Pillow.' I felt that every brat there deserved powder & lead. Had they not sympathized with the murderers, would they now be enjoying that sunny spot, where the cries of the victims & the smell of freemen's blood filled the whole air? The motto of the 68th is,—'Remember Fort Pillow'—and from the grim faces that gazed so intently today, upon that silent bluff, and the fierce threats that were passed around, I *know* that Fort Pillow will be held in remembrance when the 68th come to show mercy." Daniel Densmore to friends at home, June 4, 1864, Densmore Papers.

left the boat, went up through the City. Looked like a fine place, some fine buildings and plenty trees, and marched to a point about 2 miles north of City, and camped in a beautiful grove, right among the fine residences, a beautiful place for camp, just rolling enough. The tents were unpacked and soon placed in their proper places, though not as quick as might be, as this was the first time tents had been used by the Reg't. Ate supper with some officers of the 61st USCI, who were encamped near by, and was informed by them that a force of some 8000 men, under Com'd of Genl Sturgiss,[11] had gone on a raid East into Miss. Learned also that the 9th Minn Infy were on this expedition. Saw dress parade 61st, they did well in the manual.

Monday, June 6, 1864. Pleasant, feel pretty well. Was detailed as Officer of the Guard, put in most of the time instructing the guard. Made arrangements to board out near here at $5. per week for meals, having found one family about here with some Union sentiment, but had hardly commenced boarding before an order was issued that the officers must mess in camp.

Tuesday, June 7, 1864. Pleasant, very warm. Do not feel extra well. Lts Talbot,[12] Taisey,[13] Rogers & myself established a mess, employed a cook and got things together to cook with, and rations. Rec'd quite a treat, a letter from home, all is well.

Wednesday, June 8, 1864. Very pleasant, with occasional showers. Orders rec'd Brig Genl Buckland[14] Comd'g Dept Memphis, that no soldier

---

11. Brig. Gen. Samuel D. Sturgis (1822–1889), an 1846 graduate of the US Military Academy and a veteran of the Mexican War, was transferred to the Western Theater with the Ninth Corps in 1863. Following his defeat by Forrest at the Battle of Brices Cross Roads in June 1864, his Civil War service was effectively over.

12. Edward R. R. Talbot (ca. 1844–1865), a native of Canada, was a first lieutenant in the 68th USCT, Co. E. He previously served as a private in the 7th Minnesota Infantry, Co. K.

13. Albert H. Taisey (1837–1920) was a second lieutenant in the 68th USCT, Co. G. He would later be promoted to first lieutenant. He previously served as a corporal in the 8th Minnesota Infantry.

14. Brig. Gen. Ralph P. Buckland (1812–1892) entered the service as colonel of the 72nd Ohio Infantry in 1862. After commanding a brigade under William T. Sherman at Shiloh, he was promoted to brigadier general and placed in

[is] permitted to pass the lines in any direction except for drill or picket duty, which caused quite a gloom to come over the visages of many officers, as we expected the privilege of going down into the City on passes. But we are not in St Louis now, we are very near, if not in the enemies country, this whole city being guarded around by a picket and guard with orders for the strictest vigilance. We have learned that frequently the guerrillas attack the lines, and the people as a gen'l thing are unrepentant Rebs, except the black race, which are almost universally loyal, a black rebel would be a curiosity surely, that there are now several thousand soldiers in and around this City, and more coming. Heard that the 7th & 10th Minn would be here soon. Have got quite a cough, do not feel well, water is very bad here, quite slippery, learn that the water generally about the City is bad. Lincoln was nominated at Baltimore on the 7th inst.[15] He will be reelected.

Thursday, June 9, 1864. Very pleasant, thunder showers during the day. Duty is quite heavy here, detailed for Officer of Picket to report tomorrow morning at Brigade Hd Qrs. Lt Talbot was arrested rather rough, I should say, when carrying out the Col's orders, but active duty we find is different from City or garrison duty. Comd'g officers are more vigilant & strict. The Col made a mistake, and in order to save himself had Talbot arrested. Find him rather rash as I had judged him on first acquaintance, yet I think he is kind.

Friday, June 10, 1864. Pleasant, got my breakfast at 5 A.M. and at once reported at Adjutants tent. When our detail was ready, the Adjt reported us to the Brigade Hd Qrs, where we had brigade guard mount, each soldiers cartridge box was well filled with [missing word]. The guard was divided, a portion under my charge, and I went to my station some two miles from camp, on to one of the main roads leading out of the City, on the Picket line, divided my men into reliefs, relieved old pickets, stationed

---

command of the Fifteenth Corps during the Vicksburg Campaign. He assumed command of the District of Memphis in January 1864, a position he held for a year until he resigned from the army to take a seat in Congress.

15. The Republican Party nominated Lincoln for a second term as president at their national convention in Baltimore. They replaced Lincoln's vice president, Hannibal Hamlin of Maine, with a Unionist Democrat, Andrew Johnson of Tennessee, and rebranded their party identification that year as the Union Party.

my men, and gave each the instructions. Here is a new duty, not only to look after the guard & see that they do their duty, but to examine all persons that pass out, none being allowed to pass out without passes from Hd Qrs. I learn something new nearly every day. I now learn that the Gov't is helping to feed and cure up the sick in the Confederacy, and I might add Army, as a system has been established, and a very pernicious one, by which people can come through the lines, every body being allowed to come in, except of course those in a hostile attitude. Some of these people live hundreds of miles away, being destitute of clothing, dry goods, groceries, medicine, [and] Quinine which is worth its weight in gold down in the Confederacy. These people come in, go to the Provost Marshals Office, then apply for a permit to take the goods mentioned in the permit out of the lines. They are first required to take oath of allegiance, then the permit is signed and a pass given authorizing them to go out of the lines with their goods. The travel is on about 3 main roads, and where they cross the picket line there is an army tent, and two officers at each road to inspect, not only the goods, examine the permits, but the people themselves, who are directed to the tent and are examined even to stripping them if necessary, and if thought a suspicious character, as many a bottle of quinine has been carried out the lines secreted under their clothing, we frequently have a woman inspector to examine the lady rebs who desire to pass out, and they frequently find quinine & other contraband goods hanging to their crinoline or secreted in their bosoms. When unpermitted goods are found, if of a trifling nature, they are taken from them, but if important, the goods are taken & the parties are arrested and sent to Hd Qrs under guard, and notwithstanding the most extreme vigilance, many contraband goods are passed out, and away they go to the Confederate Army. I learn that there are parties, regular smugglers who have contracts to furnish the Confed Army with certain goods. Then the permitted goods, clothing, dry goods, groceries, &c no doubt many of them find their way to the Reb Army and are sold by some [of] these parties at exorbitant prices again, as the officers of the picket can testify that very few, if any of these people have experienced any change in their sentiment, they are good Lord here and good Devil over the line. A forced oath as they call it, is nothing but form. And the Gov't permits this for humanity sake, but the gen'l opinion here is that if the Gov't had adopted a policy to starve them out, and destroy their property, the gov't would not have to fight over the country from whence these people come, some 3 to 4 times. This was quite a busy day and I got quite initiated in the Inspection business. Experience on a picket line at night is quite interesting, as we don't know at what minute we may be attacked as Dick Davis[16] the notorious guerrilla, the terror of this section, and his band stay around within a few miles of the lines and frequently attack the picket at night. Three soldiers having been convicted by Gen'l Court Martial for leaving their post while on picket and committing robbery & rape were this day executed within the walls of Ft Pickering. Our regiment and many other troops were present at the execution.[17]

Saturday, June 11, 1864. Pleasant, was relieved from picket, and felt quite sick. Went to bed soon as I arrived at camp, and remained there nearly all day, had quite a fever, did not have a wink of sleep last night, nothing alarming on the line during the night. Learned all about the execution. I never saw one and don't know as I want to. The troops were formed in nearly 3 sides of a square, in the center were placed the three coffins, the three soldiers were then marched out, each blindfolded, and caused to sit on his coffin, his hands tied and also his feet, then the corporals guard with all guns loaded but one with blank cartridge, marched up to a reasonable distance in front of them. At a given signal the guard fired—all at once, and they fell back dead upon their coffins, and the guards— neither of them could testify that his gun caused their death. Talbot was rearrested today by the Col, for attempting to seek redress, and there will no doubt be a Court Martial.[18] Talbot says he was not to blame, that he was arrested without cause, then released with [without?] any inquiry, and he did not propose to give it up in that way, and desired his case to be carried up to the Brig Gen'l Comdg the District, and the Col then again arrested him. Considerable talk and dissatisfaction among the officers of the Reg't at the Col's rash act.

16. Dick Davis (ca. 1843–1864) of Kentucky fought under Confederate cavalryman John Hunt Morgan before becoming a Confederate guerrilla in the vicinity of Memphis. He was described by one Union soldier as a "blood-thirsty human monster" who ambushed soldiers, murdered his prisoners, and "inspired more fear than Forrest himself." See Thomas Sydenham Cogley, *History of the Seventh Indiana Cavalry Volunteers* (LaPorte, Ind.: Herald, 1876), v, 129–30.

17. John Callaghan (18), Thomas Johnson (22), and John Snover (40), all members of the 2nd New Jersey Cavalry, were shot to death on June 10, 1864. See Robert I. Alotta, *Civil War Justice: Union Army Executions under Lincoln* (Shippensburg, Pa.: White Mane, 1989), 114.

18. Talbot was released from arrest on July 28, 1864. Nothing in Talbot's CMSR indicates that he was ever court-martialed. He died on April 5, 1865, from wounds received at Blakely, Alabama, on April 2.

Sunday, June 12, 1864. Pleasant, but cooler. Lay in bed most all day, feel a little better. Our tents are all open, and the wind blows through them, and the rain wets our clothes, and the bad water has caused many in the Reg't to have the Pneumonia, and several have already died. Had preaching in the open air by our chaplain. Did not go out, but could hear him from my tent. Rec'd a report today that Sturgiss and his army of 8000 men are now on the retreat towards this City, that they met Forrest at Guntown, Miss, on the 9th inst, that our forces were defeated, and are now on the retreat. Scouts came in and a force of some 5000 soldiers were sent out under Gen'l A. J. Smith to reinforce Sturgiss. All was excitement in and around the City.

Monday, June 13, 1864. Pleasant morning. Reveille beat at 2 ½ A.M., what for I could not learn. Do not feel well at all, quite weak and slow fever, back troubles me. Sent a letter to Aunty and one home. Gen'l Sturgiss and his staff came in today and his command was left behind scattered in every direction, from Guntown 135 miles to this place. It is reported that Sturgiss was drunk, that his men were put into the fight with Forrest by detail, and having suffered a succession of defeats, a panic ensued, and the army completely routed, and every man for himself, many regiments being cut all to pieces. The 9th Minn Infy, having went out nearly 1000 strong, came back all cut up about ½ destroyed, and worse than all the rest our force were mostly Infantry, and Forrests men mounted, one can imagine a route under such a condition of affairs, and old Sturgiss deserted his command and fled to save himself, and left his army to take care of itself as best it could.

Tuesday, June 14, 1864. Very pleasant. Many more soldiers from the raid came in during the night, and the condition of affairs is worse than reported. Old Sturgiss deserted his men and has now left the City and gone up the river, the men threatened to shoot him, and he is wise in getting out of danger. The army is badly demoralized, many soldiers were killed, wounded, & taken prisoners, and more were driven into the swamps to hide, many never got out. Some of the boys in order to run with ease, wiped their guns around trees,[19] & threw them & the cartridge boxes into the swamp. Forrests cavalry were close upon them, but there was

---

19. The word we have rendered as "wiped" may be a misspelled version of "whipped" or "wrapped." A soldier in the 9th Minnesota recalled that he "knocked [a gun] against a tree to make it useless and threw it away with his 60 rounds of ammunition." See Lundstrom, *One Drop in a Sea of Blue*, 164.

one brave man who assumed command and got together all the soldiers possible, and although on the retreat, occasionally made a brilliant stand, and kept the Enemy at bay, this Col Wilkin, of the 9th Minn, a little man in size, but not very little in bravery.[20] The two negro regiments though suffering dreadfully kept together and fought like madmen, and kept the enemy at bay until relieved by Gen'l Smith. The colored boys were praised by every soldier for their valor & bravery. In this fight colored soldiers were taken prisoners and paroled, same as others. But Old Sturgiss has left. Lucky for him, as the boys swear they will shoot him if they can get a sight at the coward or drunkard, as he was certainly one or the other. The Gen'l will not meet [sic] out Justice unless this mans straps are not shorn, & that speedily. Men straggled in a few at a time all day. Several died in our camp today of Pneumonia.

Wednesday, June 15, 1864. Pleasant. I have quite a cough this morning. Heard that more of the boys of the Sturgiss raid came in during the night, nothing much worse for an army than a dastardly running retreat. I always thought it must be terrible, but now I see its effects, and know it so.

Thursday, June 16, 1864. Pleasant, got up rather late. Lt Rogers went on picket. Coughed considerable and do not feel well, no appetite, but I had to get out and look after the Co as Lt was away. About 3 P.M. the wind blew almost a hurricane, blowing down many tents, then it commenced to rain & poured in torrents. I got back into my tent. More of the soldiers from the Guntown Expedition came in today, having dodged around from place to place, their only friends being the blacks, who fed them. It is estimated that more than ½ of the 8000 in that army have been killed, wounded & missing, and many that returned came without arms or anything but themselves, a great disaster, and a great deal of property to account for and to charge to the acc't of old Sturgiss. It will take several Boards of Survey to settle up this affair.[21]

---

20. Historian Thomas E. Parson describes Col. Alexander Wilkin as a "pugnacious colonel, just over five feet tall and barely a hundred pounds with his uniform on.... A Yale lawyer and president of the St. Paul Fire and Marine Insurance Company, Wilkin was an outstanding soldier. He was a captain in the Mexican War and one of the first sons of Minnesota to volunteer after Fort Sumter fell." See Parson, *Work for Giants*, 159.

21. A court of inquiry investigated the "disaster" at the Battle of Brices Cross Roads, and whether or not Sturgis was intoxicated while he was in command. Sturgis never faced any charges, but he spent the remainder of the war "awaiting

Friday, June 17, 1864. Pleasant. Got up, but did not feel much better, cough worse, and I reported to the Doctor. Today this Reg't recd orders to be ready to move tomorrow A.M. with three days rations in knapsacks.[22] No transportation, no knapsacks. I am directed by the Surgeon to remain at camp. I wanted to go but it was thought best that I remain. So I accepted the situation & wrote a letter to mother.

Saturday, June 18, 1864. Very warm, feel no better. The 68th, about 600 strong, left to join A. J. Smiths command against Forrest, it is supposed. Rec'd good news from Grant again. His forces are now at the James River, Lee having drawn in his lines from time to time to that point, and Morgan has been severely whipped in Kentucky.[23] Took a walk out of camp. Saw the 50th Ill Cavalry on dress parade, rather poor show, I thought, especially for veterans.[24] Sent some papers to mother.

Sunday, June 19, 1864. Pleasant, very warm. Slept quite well. Am anxious to hear from the Reg't. Was on duty as Officer of the Guard, as well as the Camp, got quite tired out. Our Chaplain had a meeting & I attended, not many present, but had a fine sermon. Was at the Surgeons tent and had an opportunity to see his record. Noticed my name and opposite the word Pneumonia, it rather started me. The Dr had not told me what ailed me, and no doubt it was best, as there is quite a scare about that disease, so many have died with it.

Monday, June 20, 1864. Rather cloudy, looks like a shower. Heard from the Reg't, they are mending and guarding the Memphis & Charleston R.R., about 30 miles out. Recd news that the 10th Minn Infy came in today but where they camped is the next question. Shall hunt them up.

Tuesday, June 21, 1864. Pleasant, warm, felt considerable better and started out in search of the 10th boys, went some distance, saw some Reg'ts,

---

orders." See Edwin C. Bearss, *Protecting Sherman's Lifeline: The Battles of Brices Cross Roads and Tupelo 1864* (Washington, D.C.: National Park Service, 1971).

22. Buswell appears to have written "haversacks" and "knapsacks" over top of each other.

23. The news out of Virginia was not as good as Buswell believed. During the Overland Campaign, which took place in May and June 1864, Ulysses S. Grant lost nearly sixty thousand men killed, wounded, and missing. In Kentucky, however, Confederate general John Hunt Morgan was soundly defeated by Union forces at the Second Battle of Cynthiana in June 1864.

24. There was no 50th Illinois Cavalry; this was probably the 3rd Illinois Cavalry.

but not finding any account of their whereabouts gave up the hunt. Took supper with Q.M. Serg't at Col's tent. Rec'd despatch that the payrolls, must be as the paymaster was coming, good enough.[25] I need some funds bad. Had quite a chat with the Surgeon and his wife who had just arrived. One of the boys was taken and died in 24 hours with the Pneumonia, he was opened and I saw his lungs, they were all soft.

Wednesday, June 22, 1864. Cloudy, cooler, looks like rain. No news from the front today. Heard that the 7th Minn Infy had arrived in City and went out to hunt them up, but learned that they had gone to the front, & I came back to Camp. Rather lonesome here. Only a few of us here with the Camp.

Thursday, June 23, 1864. Pleasant & warm. Feel some better, am gaining fast. Heard from the front, the boys were mostly well, they had built huts out of boards & shakes & are guarding the R.R. Troops are coming in and going out on the R.R. to the front now, nearly every day, concentrating near La Fayette. Something is certainly going on. Another raid I guess. Was glad to hear from home.

Friday, June 24, 1864. Warm. Rec'd news that the train that went to the front yesterday was fired into and four soldiers killed and ten wounded, and six of our boys captured while on picket. One got away to tell the story, that the other five were murdered by the Rebs after they had surrendered. Sent out a bundle to Lt Rogers.

Saturday, June 25, 1864. Very warm, feel much better. Was in Command of Camp today, quite an honor to be sure though I would prefer to be with the Reg't. During last night the guerrillas attacked the picket lines and they had quite a skirmish, and the guerrillas were driven with a loss, one of their party dead, certain, good, and two of our boys wounded. The whole pack of guerrillas ought to be caught and shot, they are no good anywhere, though sesesh in sentiment, they dodge their army and kill all they can on the Union side. It is plunder only that they are after, & seldom take prisoners, and if taken are cruelly maltreated and killed.

Sunday, June 26, 1864. Still warm. Was again Commander in Chief of the Camp, ordered out guards and made the countersign, and gave it out with all the pomp & splendor of a Brigadier Gen'l. Feel much better, got acquainted with a citizen near here named Benjamin, went over to see

---

25. Buswell appears to have accidentally omitted some words in this sentence.

his garden, plenty of apples, plums, cherries, pear and fig trees, and some of them loaded with fruit. He is a fine man and has the true blue Union sentiment, but such men are a novelty here.

Monday, June 27, 1864. Pleasant, quite hot. Two of our men buried today, died of Pneumonia. Heard news that we were to have a new Col of our Reg't. Q.M. Chase[26] and Adjt Root came into Camp today with orders to take all men able for field service back to the regiment.

Tuesday, June 28, 1864. Very pleasant, warm. Feel quite smart. Am anxious to go. Learned that the troops moved to La Grange, Tenn, and are now encamped there.

Wednesday, June 29, 1864. Pleasant, warm. Lt Col & Major came in from Reg't, and today 80 men fit for duty were sent to the reg't. Feeling quite well again, I shall go too. Rec'd letter from home with their pictures enclosed, glad to hear from them as it will no doubt be the last for some time. Ans'd it and told the folks that I should start to go with the command under A. J. Smith in a day or two.

Thursday, June 30, 1864. Pleasant, very hot. Was relieved from duty here, & ordered to join the Reg't, which is all satisfactory to me, and I started for the depot, upon arriving there, found that no train went out today, and then returned to camp. All the disabled & sick remain here. The Lt Col reports a large force concentrated at La Grange, Tenn, supposed to be preparing another expedition into the enemies country. Trust it may not turn out like the Sturgiss raid, but I dont think there is any fear as we have got one of the best fighters, Genl A. J. Smith, for a commander.

Friday, July 1, 1864. Pleasant, got breakfast and started early for the depot. Found the train was going, a train of freight cars, jumped aboard and the cars soon started, quite a good many soldiers on board, and we soon passed out of the lines. Saw pickets & troops at several points along the road, passed a number of villages, or where they had been, but now pretty much in ruins, the terrible horror of war. About noon arrived at La Grange, Tenn, found a large force here. The officers of our Regt & the boys generally were glad to see me, and I equally as glad to again be with them. After dinner hunted up the 7th Regt and after tramping around

---

26. Nulan M. Chase (1832–1899), a native of Maine, was the quartermaster and a lieutenant in the 68th USCT from 1864 to 1866. He had previously served in the 7th Minnesota Infantry, Co. C.

Maj. Gen. Andrew Jackson Smith. (Library of Congress)

some time found them, had a very pleasant chat with them. La Grange, Tenn, the point of concentration of this Army, is on the Memphis to Charleston R.R., about 50 miles from Memphis, is an old town, partially destroyed by the war, and what is left is rather old & dilapidated. It lies also on the Wolf River. Towards evening I went down to the river and had a good bathe, river about 40 ft wide, rather deep, crooked, and rather sluggish at present, well skirted with timber.

Saturday, July 2, 1864. Pleasant though slight showers in P.M. There is now quite an army encamped here, and yet I might not say encamped, as there is not a tent in the entire command, except a few flys for Hd Qrs of the command and each regiment and the Commissary Dept. The men rolling up in their rubber blankets and lying upon the ground with no other cover than the canopy of heaven. It is certainly fighting trim throughout, no luggage of any description, except the men have their haversacks & canteens and a rubber blanket, not even a change of under-clothing. The 59th USCI came today all mounted, they had been in the country foraging. They report the R.R. cut between here & Collinsville. Looked around some among the camps and down by the river. Saw several faro banks[27] in full blast, and many of the boys loosing their hard earned earnings in this foolish game of chance. Recd letter from Aunty.

Sunday, July 3, 1864. Cloudy, muggy & warm, a gen'l Inspection of all the troops was held this A.M., then I went to Wolf River to bathe, a very good place and many improved the opportunity. After dinner went up to see the 7th boys, took supper with Dearborn and All Bartlett, then went back to my camp and found that the Col had arrived.

Monday, July 4, 1864. Rather cloudy, cooler, and a little stormy. Our National day, but not a very pleasant one. No especial doings, except to fire a national salute. This is no time or place to celebrate, we can only talk and think of the times up North. Went up into La Grange, got dinner and bought a few things at the Commissary for our mess. The entire force rec'd orders to be ready to march tomorrow morning, for what point we have yet to learn. Saw the 10th boys, had quite a pleasant time with them, then went to the 9th near by. The regiment looks quite small, owing to recent disaster at Guntown. Country around here quite well timbered, good water. Soil rather sandy. Before we leave we receive the good news of the engagement on the Coast of France between the U.S. Man of War Kearsa[r]ge under Capt Winslow, and the Rebel-English Privateer Alabama under Commander Semmes of the Confederacy, and after a hot contest for a few hours, the rebel privateer was sunk, a great naval victory.[28] Glorious news and gives our troops an impetus for victory.

Tuesday, July 5, 1864. Cloudy, feel first rate and am ready for the march. Reveille early, and the command under Brig Genl A. J. Smith of about 12000 men, and with Brig Genl Grierson[29] in command of the Cavalry, with 12000, including all troops, Infantry, Artillery, and cavalry, with a small wagon train, and a drove of cattle for beef, broke camp, and started

---

27. Faro was a popular card game for gambling in nineteenth-century America.

28. At the Battle of Cherbourg, off the coast of France, the USS *Kearsarge*, commanded by Capt. John Winslow, defeated the CSS *Alabama*, commanded by Capt. Raphael Semmes, on June 19, 1864. This naval victory held great meaning for the Union as the *Alabama* had been a successful commerce raider destroying Union merchant vessels on the high seas.

29. Benjamin Grierson (1826–1911) rose through the ranks from colonel of the 6th Illinois Cavalry to brigadier general because of his successful raid through

in the direction of Ripley, Miss. A portion the 7th & 10th included left in the forenoon, and about 5 P.M. our brigade and balance of the force marched about 8 miles through a heavily timbered country and camped in a field near Wolf River, a full picket out tonight.

Wednesday, July 6, 1864. Pleasant morning. R at 3 A.M., got our breakfast and started again at 6. Crossed the Miss Central R.R. at 8, the 59th U.S.[C.]I., who were on the Sturgiss raid, had orders to burn public property, and a railroad bridge and a great many buildings were burned. All buildings where the owners had deserted them were as [in?] general put to the torch, and surely in all cases where the then occupants during the Sturgiss raid had fired upon our retreating soldiers, their property had to suffer. The 59th also done a great deal of foraging. Marched until 2 P.M. and rested & we took a lunch of hard tack, then started on again and marched until 6 P.M. 12 miles today, and camped on the Coldwater branch of the Tombigbee River in the bushes. We found the roads rather rough, quite heavily timbered, passed a few plantations. Had a fine supper, potatoes, geese, chickens, sheep and pigs, the fat of the land, or what there is left of it. Feel first rate. Stand it well.

Thursday, July 7, 1864. Pleasant. R at 2 A.M. Start at 7, passed over a very rough country heavily timbered with Oak, Ash, Cypress, Chestnut, Beech and quite a plenty of blackberries. Plantations generally deserted, buildings burned, went through one fine looking mansion. It was evident that the occupants had quite recently fled, as the household furniture was all there, but saw the work of the invading forces, a fine piano was quite generally smashed and a very large full length mirror was knocked into pieces, and after the command passed, upon looking back saw the building in flames. While crossing a stream, the cattle were permitted to stop & drink. The troops had quite generally passed when some guerrillas appeared and upon firing upon the droviers [drovers], they fled, leaving the stock in the enemys hands, but a portion of the command returned and recovered the cattle. Marched 14 miles and camped on a beautiful stream at 7 P.M. We rec'd the news that the enemy are ahead [and] that Gen'l Grierson had a skirmish with them. Quite an excitement in camp.

Louisiana. In 1864 he commanded a cavalry unit in the Army of the Mississippi. See Bruce J. Dinges and Shirley A. Leckie, eds., *A Just and Righteous Cause: Benjamin H. Grierson's Civil War Memoir* (Carbondale: Southern Illinois University Press, 2008).

Friday, July 8, 1864. Cloudy, cooler. R at 3 A.M., got breakfast early & started again at 6. Soon passed through Ripley, a county seat, and a town of about 800 to 1000 inhabitants before the war, and the command having passed through, the 59th and the Kansas Jayhawkers[30] as they are called, burned the entire town except three buildings, the occupants of which were friendly to our wounded boys on the Guntown raid. Here was where the old rebs, the young rebs, and the woman rebs fired guns [and] pistols out of the windows of their houses as the soldiers on the Guntown raid were retreating through that place, and how much good it done those boys who were on that raid. Revenge is sweet and the occupants of those 3 houses where our boys were cared for had their reward.

Saturday, July 9, 1864. Pleasant. R at 3 A.M. Started at 7, passed over a very rough country, but many fine plantations, all deserted, where we got plenty of fruit and what forage could be found about the premises. Left the Guntown road & kept towards the South, a very hot day, found plenty good water. Some fine springs. Marched 15 miles & camped on the Tallahatchie River, near the ruins of the late town of New Albany, which was burned by Grants forces some two years ago. This is a very flat valley, and the bridge having been destroyed we had to ford the river. Am feeling first rate, but my feet are getting some sore.

Sunday, July 10, 1864. Pleasant day. R at 2 ½ A.M. Start at 6. Our Company was rear guard, passed over quite a level country, good well water, though wells quite deep. The plantations generally deserted, and very little crop, and plenty of fruit. Quite a number [of] cotton gins and some cotton burned. Marched 12 miles and camped at a creek, fine water. The cavalry had a skirmish with Forrests men near the R.R. whipping them and capturing 120 prisoners. They were brought in and were the usual butternut kind.

Monday, July 11, 1864. Very pleasant. R at 3 A.M., got breakfast early & start at 6, orders given to keep the command closed up and ready to act at any moment, as a general engagement was expected. Passed over quite a hilly, rough country, and Forrest will either to have to fight or retreat and he can pick his own ground as we are the invaders and acting on the offensive. Cavalry had skirmishing in front most of the day, and quite a running fight through the town of Pontotoc, quite a number killed and

---

30. Buswell later added "9th Kansas Cavalry" in pencil. Jayhawkers were Unionist guerrillas in Kansas.

wounded on both sides. We passed through the town and camped near it, having marched 8 miles, on a beautiful spring creek, and the town, quite a large place, was burned. Had a shower in the night and we got quite wet.

Tuesday, July 12, 1864. Cloudy, rather wet, rather bad business while sleeping on the ground without tents, but we rolled up in our rubber blankets and let it pelt. No marching for the Infantry today. The cavalry were sent out to reconnoiter and feel of the enemy, about 2 miles out they encountered them in considerable force with a loss of 7 killed & 10 wounded. I went over to see the 7th boys, had quite a chat. Some Johnnies were seen towards night lurking around the Camp, just outside the picket, and our company was ordered out to scatter them, which we did on the double quick, and finally started them off. The first scrimmage for us.

Wednesday, July 13, 1864. Pleasant. R at 3 A.M., orders to start at 6. Our company and two others detailed for rear guard, a Lt Col in command. The Gen'l Comd'g having thrown out his feelers and learned that Forrest was prepared, entrenched on the main road South, on which we [were] then marching, with the calculation to come[31] the same tactics on Genl Smith as he did on Sturgiss. A flank movement was ordered by our Commander, to the East, for Tupelo, which rather upset Forrests calculations and left him and his force in our rear. They soon discovered the movement, and pursued commencing the attack upon our rear, with shot & shell, from their Artillery, and they kept it up all day. Sometimes they came up very near, on the double quick, wheel, plant their cannon, and shell us as long as could reach us, then limber up, and after us again, their horses on the gallop, their batteries were well supported by Forrests cavalry, and the fight was kept up all day. The different regiments took turns in forming lines in the rear, our regiment having formed line 3 times, but the enemy were not near enough in the first part of the day to even shoot, except by our rear guard, and was most wholly a battle between the Artillery, ours was placed in position on every knoll. I being with the rear guard was in the most dangerous position as the shells from the enemys guns reached and passed over us most of the time, & once the whole rear guard came very near being captured.

---

31. This word is likely "come," meaning to bring about; however, it may be "cause," meaning to cause Forrest to use the same tactics against Smith as he had against Sturgis.

The Lt Col comd'g the same had orders to remain at a certain creek we had just crossed to check the enemy, until orders were rec'd to come forward. The creek was in a valley, skirted with timber up & down the same. We heard the enemy coming along on top of the hill, close behind us, their Artillery firing and the clash of their small arms. All at once, the firing ceased, the timber being so thick we could not see up the hill. Our column, or the rear reg't, was quite a distance ahead, and no orders rec'd to fall back, every minute seemed an hour to us all, as we then had thoughts of Meridian, Andersonville or Salsbury.[32] All seemed anxious, officers as well as the men, they consulted in whispers. The Col was being urged to leave the valley, but he had to await orders. Many were terror stricken, but finally orders came & hastily, almost upon a run, we got out from that cover, but we had not been out long before the enemys were seen coming, closing in from both directions, having made a double flank movement to close in upon their enemy, which it was evident they had suspected were yet at the crossing. Had we been there even 3 minutes longer it would have been certain capture or death, a very close call.

Then again at points along the road, where there were clearings, the Rebs would take a part of their batteries, ahead by some road, & plant them in the timber on our flanks, some times on one flank, then on the other, and in one place on both flanks, and as we passed these clearings, they kept up a continual fire of shot & shell, enfilading our lines, which we were marching lively, sometimes at a double quick, to gain a position, which Gen'l Smith had chosen near Tupelo. It got so lively, was doing our forces so much damage, shooting our men out of the ranks as they passed along, Geo Blackwell[33] Co B 7th having had a leg taken off by a cannon ball & left in the enemys hands, and many others killed & wounded, that finally orders were given for certain regts to form line of battle, and charge them on the flank. The fire in the rear being kept up as well, which order was obeyed with some damage, and the Johnnies were compelled to limber up and get away from that point, to plant them again in some other favorable position. They harassed us in this manner all the way to Tupelo. It having been a running fight for about 20 miles, with considerable loss to our forces, and without much loss to the enemy, I finally got to Tupelo, found it a small town, a station on the Mobile & Ohio R.R.,

32. Meridian, Mississippi, Andersonville, Georgia, and Salisbury, North Carolina, were notorious Confederate prisoner of war camps.

33. George Blackwell (ca. 1840–1864), a native of Ireland, served as a private in the 7th Minnesota Infantry, Co. B. He died on August 6 at Mobile, Alabama.

the[34] gen'l having already selected his position for the camp, and from which to give Forrest battle, and everything was being put in readiness for the expected engagement. The batteries were planted on convenient eminences overlooking the camp, (which was in a sort of basin,) and the adjacent country. A double picket was placed out tonight. Felt quite tired out, but thankful for even my present condition.

Thursday, July 14, 1864. Pleasant. Some cooler. R at 2 A.M., routed out early to get everything and everybody ready as it was expected that an attack would be made and the ball open by sunrise. About 7 A.M. skirmishing was heard along the line at the West, and the troops were soon at the different points as designated by our commander. On the West side of the camp, just along our lines was a stone wall along the flat, and a Virginia rail fence, at the South end of same running up the hill. In front of the stone wall was a clearing in the timber about ¾s by a mile in extent, being an old cotton field. It was ascertained that the enemy [was] advancing from that direction and a force was ordered, two lines deep, running from the extreme right of the line in the timber to the extreme left up the hill, though a side hill, yet this was a clearing also. The troops were ordered to keep close down and keep quiet behind this stone wall and fence. In front of the wall in the clearing was placed six batteries, six guns each, about 40 rods apart.

Soon the rebs were seen coming through the timber the other side of the clearing, and the batteries commenced firing, with shot & often with shell. My reg't was just to the left of this clearing, and though not in the thickest of the fight, being on the side hill, I had a fine opportunity to see the rebels charge, and it was a brilliant one too. They came out into the clearing 3 divisions, 3 lines deep, dismounted, their leader, who we learned was Chalmers, riding back & forth behind their ranks on a noble white charger, his hat in one hand and sword swinging in the other, cheering on his men calling out "take their batteries." They had not as yet fired a gun, the batteries fairly stowed with shot & shell, enfilading their ranks and the effects could be plainly seen, as their ranks were mown[35] through & through, but they charged and charged, until nearly up to the cannon, when orders were given to our forces to fire, when we arose from behind the wall & fence and met them face to face. It was desperate, they came on with many a cheer and occasionally a rebel yell, their losses were tremen-

---

34. Buswell appears to have written "the" over "and" here.
35. This word may be "worn."

dous. Finally one of the commanders, who proved to be Genl Forrests brother,[36] fell mortally wounded. Their ranks swayed back & forth, and great holes could be seen through them. They were intent on the guns and victory. No braver men could be, but they were finally compelled to give way, and back they fell across this field.

For 2 to 3 hours the battle had raged, the rebs loosing heavily, some 2000 killed, wounded & prisoners. In some places on the field they lay so thick that one could not step without stepping upon them. The loss on our side was very light, though one of the bravest and best Commanders, Col Wilkin of the 9th Minn, Comd'g Brigade, was shot while setting upon his horse in the rear of the lines. He continually cautioned the men to keep down behind the wall while the Rebs were charging, but he continued to set upon his horse, a brave man, a true hero, and a great loss to us.[37] With great losses to the enemy they retired for the balance of the day, arrangements were made to bury the dead, and the wounded were taken care of. The troops as a gen'l thing remained in line of battle all day, and orders were rec'd to remain so all night, our coffee & hard tack being brought to us on the lines.

After dark the lines all around the camp were quietly contracted to prevent any break, as I learn, should they attack us in the night. Our brigade was withdrawn from their lines on the hill and formed at the base thereof. The pickets were strengthened, and we lay on our arms in line of battle for the night. Some time about midnight, the Johnnies opened on us from the top of the hill, direct in our front, without any previous notice of their whereabouts, and shelled our camp, quite lively, and accompanied with rifle shots indicating that their troops were supporting the batteries. The enemy not knowing our true position, or if they did

---

36. Buswell's information here was not accurate. This may have been Forrest, who was badly wounded on July 14, or his son, Capt. William Montgomery Forrest (1846–1908), who was thrown from his horse when a shell exploded nearby. Forrest had lost two brothers earlier in 1864, Jeffrey Edward Forrest on February 22, and Aaron H. Forrest on April 19.

37. Historian Thomas E. Parson writes that Wilkin "had gone with his two regiments to place them in their new position. When all was well he turned his horse and while he rode back to the brigade, he was struck by a bullet that passed through his body from the left side to the right. The diminutive colonel slid out of the saddle and fell lightly to the ground. He died a few minutes later in the arms of one of his soldiers." He was the highest-ranking Union officer to be killed in the battle. See Parson, *Work for Giants*, 195, 265.

know it, failed to lower the muzzles of their guns sufficiently to do us any special harm, though we were quite near them, near enough to distinctly hear the commands of their officers. Orders were whispered along our line to keep perfectly quiet. It was a very dark night and the fire from cannon and their lines of musketry created a lurid glow along the lines. The roaring of the cannon, the bursting of the shells, the crack of their rifles, and the whizzing of the bullets, as they went over us, was a sight terrible to behold. Such a one I never saw, and never want to again.

Up to this time very little damage was done our line, quiet was maintained, not a shot on our side, except from distant batteries, while the rebs were advancing down the slope. When they got sufficiently near, so that they could be distinguished in the glow of the cannon, orders were sent along our lines to commence firing rapidly and at the same time to advance. Our lines were quite close, and the contest for a time was hot, when the rebs fell back, we following and firing, until they went down the hill the other side, into the timber, and ceased firing, with what losses we know not, but there must have been a considerable one. Our loss was not very severe, one captain in our regt was killed[38] and several men, and two officers, one a captain, the other the Lt Col showed the white feather.[39] Such a night, it never can be forgotten.

Friday, July 15, 1864. Very warm. R at 3 A.M., troops remained in line of battle, (rations brought to them by cooks & special detail,) expecting another attack. Remained in line until 9 A.M. when orders were rec'd to break camp, and after the railroad for a few miles above & below Tupelo had been torn up, the ties burned and the rails burned & bent, also burning all public property, cotton gins, cotton &c, the advance started out of camp. Our brigade was assigned to the rear. Soon after the advance started the Johnnies were seen approaching from the rear, the troops left, were soon in line of battle, our Co out as skirmishers, and an engagement was carried on for about two hours. I stood on the line and used my Navy revolver, continually shooting it at the Johnnies, and came very near paying dear for my service, as a bullet passed through my hair, a close shave, and a spent bullet struck my foot, which I stooped down and picked up.

The enemy were driven back with much loss, and ours not very severe. Orders were then rec'd to march, and keep well closed up, and we went about 6 miles, when the enemy again attacked us. The train was corralled

---

38. Buswell wrote "killed" in pencil over the word "shot."
39. Showing the "white feather" indicates cowardice or surrender.

in the flat of old Town Creek—which is in quite a deep valley, with heavy timber on the hills. The troops were nearly famished for water, and upon arriving at the creek were considerably out of order in their efforts to get water, when suddenly the enemy opened upon us from the top of the hill with several guns, one a large gun. Our troops, Infantry, Cavalry, Artillery, Mules &c were quite generally mixed up, and there was quite a flurry for a time. The Genl came along, and the troops yelled out "3 cheers for Old A. J." The gen'l, a big fighter, yet with a kind heart, lifted his hat at the response. He at once gave orders to park the batteries, the train was hurriedly taken ahead, the troops got to their respective regts and soon in line when our batteries opened upon the rebs batteries, an artillery fight for a time. When it was ascertained that the big gun, a 20 pounder, of the rebs was silenced, then orders were given to charge up the hill, and up they went, and soon met the rebels in force. It was a hotly contested fight, the rebs being repulsed and obliged to fall back, leaving 3 guns, and many prisoners in our hands, and heavy losses in killed & wounded, our force loosing 30 killed and more than 100 wounded. I saw Starr, All Bartlett, and Dearborn, they are safe yet, but poor Poly[40] was shot. Marched about 8 miles, and camped, the troops laying in line, on our arms all night, a strong picket was out. Forrest has learned by this time that they have not got Old Sturgiss in[41] their front this time.

Saturday, July 16, 1864. Very pleasant. R at 3 A.M., no disturbance during the night. Broke camp at 6. Our brigade towards the front, guarding the wagon train, no rebs front or rear seen this A.M., though they are looked for at some point on the road. Passed through a better country, plenty forage. Camped on the Tallahatchie River at 3 P.M., having marched 15 miles. After arriving in camp heard heavy cannonading in the rear, but the Johnnies did not make much of a fight. They had been badly defeated, with heavy losses, and Forrest, though he likes a good fight, had got more than he bargained for this time. There is no Guntown raid about this. The expedition has accomplished all that it was organized for. The cutting of the Mobile & Ohio R.R., the defeat of Forrests Army, which we learn was about 14000 strong, and ours 12000, and the destruction of a

40. Possibly Lt. Col. James W. Polleys (1826–1896) of the 14th Wisconsin Infantry, who was wounded at the battle. Polleys lived in La Crosse, Wisconsin, which bordered southeast Minnesota—not far from where Buswell lived.

41. Buswell appears to have written "in" over "to."

large amount rebel property, and now victoriously returns to its base of operations.

Sunday, July 17, 1864. Pleasant. R at 2 A.M. Start at 4, was on train guard. Passed over a very rough country, rather few plantations, and those uncultivated this season. Feel first rate, have got through thus far all safe & sound, and have stood it well. One of my sergeants, when we started, rather laughed at the idea that I could out tramp him, but the laugh is on him, I am still on the tramp, while he is laid up for repairs. Passed New Albany our old camp ground and camped on the Hatchie, having marched 16 miles and no appearance of the enemy.

Monday, July 18, 1864. Very pleasant. R at 2 A.M. Start at 4 as train guard again. Passed over a rather rough country, heavily timbered with fine springs of water, thinly settled, in fact none at present. Marched 22 miles & camped on a branch of Wolf River, not molested by the enemy in any shape today, rather poor foraging, our Company on picket tonight.

Tuesday, July 19, 1864. Pleasant. R at 2 A.M. Start at 4, as train guard again. Passed very rough country. Crossed Wolf River at 11 A.M., very heavy timber, thinly settled, poor foraging. Cavalry while out after forage captured a few guerrillas. Marched 18 miles and camped near the once town of Salem, it having been burned in /62.

Wednesday, July 20, 1864. Very pleasant. R at 3 A.M. Start at 6. Passed better country, though scarcity of water mostly drop wells, plantations lying idle, got plenty apples and blackberries. Arrived at Davis Mill[42] on the Miss Central R.R. at 3 P.M., rested for a time, then marched to La Grange, 18 miles today, arriving there about sunset, and now back again at the old stamping ground, safe & sound, but very tired.

Thursday, July 21, 1864. Pleasant. R at 6 A.M. Feel first rate, am now ready to go to Memphis. Heard the welcome whistle of the train coming in at an early hour this A.M., and a portion of the command got aboard and went to Memphis. The town was full of boys to buy eatables as rations and forage are short. I went down to Wolf River and had a good wash. The mail came and I had letters from home & Hattie, was very glad

---

42. Located about a mile south of the Tennessee line and now known as Michigan City, Mississippi, Davis' Mill was the site of a skirmish that took place on December 21, 1862.

to hear from them, and no doubt they will be very glad to hear from me & that I got through the campaign all safe.

Friday, July 22, 1864. Continues very pleasant. Rec'd orders that our Brigade be in readiness to move at 1 P.M. and there was a general hurrah throughout the command, and while singing "John Brown" and "We'er going home," we marched to the depot and stacked arms. The train came but could not take the whole brigade, and the right wing being designated, we remained here until the next train. Got hold of a Memphis paper and greedily devoured the news, every item. Saw an account of our expedition, called a great success.

Saturday, July 23, 1864. Fine weather. Took it easy, a late breakfast, am getting anxious for some clean clothes, not a rag of anything clean since we left Memphis the 1st inst. The train came & the left wing got aboard and at 12 M. the whistle blew, and away we went for Memphis, arriving there at 4 P.M., very shortly we were in our old camp.

7

"Remained Out in the Wet"

From Memphis to the Tallahatchie Swamps, July 24–August 29, 1864

WILLIAM T. SHERMAN was disappointed that A. J. Smith had not completely destroyed Nathan Bedford Forrest's command at Tupelo. Writing from the field outside Atlanta, Sherman informed Maj. Gen. Cadwallader C. Washburn that he and Grant had wanted Smith "after his fight to pursue and continue to follow Forrest." Writing from Memphis, Washburn informed Sherman in late July that "I have ordered General Smith to put his command in order to again move against Forrest. He will so move as soon as he can get ready."[1]

Meanwhile, Forrest's new commander, Gen. Dabney H. Maury, told Forrest, "I intrust to you the operations against the enemy threatening an invasion of North Mississippi." Maury informed his cavalryman that he would not "interfere with your plan for conducting these operations" but would "confine myself to the duty of sending you the means, as far as I can, of accomplishing the successful results it has been your good fortune to achieve." Forrest replied that he would "do all that can be done to drive the enemy back." But he added, "At the same time I have not the force to risk a general engagement, but will resort to other means in my power to harass, annoy and force the enemy back." Not knowing exactly what Smith was planning, Forrest ordered his subordinates to various places

---

1. Brian Steel Wills, *The Confederacy's Greatest Cavalryman: Nathan Bedford Forrest* (1982; reprint, Lawrence: University Press of Kansas, 1998), 231–32; C. C. Washburn to Sherman, July 23, 1864, O.R., ser. 1, vol. 39, pt. 2, p. 201; Sherman to Washburn, July 25, 1864, in ibid., 204.

in Mississippi, including Okolona, Pontotoc, Grenada, and the crossings of the Tallahatchie River.[2]

As A. J. Smith's men moved southward (Buswell among them), Forrest ordered Gen. James R. Chalmers to "contest every inch of ground." But, as historian Brian Steel Wills writes, "the Union forces outflanked or forced him out of each defensive position he took." By August 10, the Union soldiers had made it as far south as Oxford, although they only occupied the university town for a day. According to Wills, "Forrest became justifiably concerned that he would do no better against the Union's advance than Chalmers had done earlier. . . . Smith was slow and cautious, but there appeared to be no way to stop him from pushing ever southward." As a consequence, Forrest came to believe that his best option would be to get around Smith and cut off his supply line, thus forcing Smith to retreat. Forrest formed a raiding party of some two thousand men and a battery of artillery. After several days of riding in rain and mud, Forrest reached Memphis about 4 A.M. on August 21. Among other things, he hoped to capture Gen. Stephen A. Hurlbut at the Gayoso House Hotel and General Washburn at his Union Street residence. While Forrest did not capture the two generals, he did seize about six hundred prisoners (although he could not feed and clothe most of them, so soon thereafter he released many of them on a pledge not to fight against the Confederacy until they had been officially exchanged). Within five hours the raid was over and Forrest was heading back into Mississippi.[3]

Meanwhile, back in Mississippi, Chalmers engaged some of Smith's men in battle (although Buswell was not part of this fighting) before Smith finally returned to Memphis. The consequence of Forrest's raid was to stop Smith's invasion of Mississippi.[4]

☙

Sunday, July 24, 1864. Very pleasant. I wanted to go to the City to church, but felt tired, had a good rest, a good wash up and some clean clothes. Had the pleasure of meeting the Capt of our Company, recently appointed Capt Jas G. Thompson[5] late of Co "E" 9th Minn Infy. He was

---

2. Wills, *Confederacy's Greatest Cavalryman*, 232–33.
3. Wills, *Confederacy's Greatest Cavalryman*, 237–44.
4. Wills, *Confederacy's Greatest Cavalryman*, 244–46.
5. James G. Thompson (1833–1899), a native of Vermont, had been a private and corporal in the 9th Minnesota Infantry before being promoted to captain of the 68th USCT, Co. K.

on the Guntown raid. The Co went out nearly a 100 strong with its full complement of Com^d & non-Com^d officers, and he as Corporal came back to Memphis in Command of what was then left of the Co, 14 men, all the officers being either killed, wounded or missing, except himself. He ought to have a Captaincy, and Lt Rogers, the Co and myself welcomed him. Appears like a fine man, but it seemed to me on first appearance that he had only a very limited education. Wrote letters, one of 10 pages to mother, giving her full particulars of the campaign.

Monday, July 25, 1864. Continues very pleasant. Felt pretty well. Worked quite hard over company records & looking on company matters, as a change will now be made from Lt Rogers Comdg Co to the new Capt. The Capt orders and dictates and don't know much about either. Learned of a peace movement by Horace Greely and C. C. Clay and other rebs at Niagara Falls, propositions made by them through Greeley, and Uncle Abe answers that on no other condition will peace be restored than a full & complete restoration of the states and the endorsement by them of the principals [sic] of the Emancipation Proclamation.[6] Old Abe is sound. Regt had dress parade.

Tuesday, July 26, 1864. Pleasant day, worked hard most of the day on books and receipts, &c. Do not feel tip top, back troubles me again. The Company drew and issued clothing today, the men needed it bad enough.

Wednesday, July 27, 1864. Still pleasant, feel some better, good cool breeze, got our company business closed up today. Lt Rogers relieved

---

6. In July 1864, *New-York Tribune* editor Horace Greeley informed Lincoln that there were Confederate officials in Canada, including Clement C. Clay, who were willing to negotiate for peace. While Lincoln doubted that they had any official authority from Jefferson Davis, he permitted Greeley to go to Niagara to meet with them. In Canada, Greeley purposefully neglected to tell the Confederates that Lincoln required "abandonment of slavery" in the Confederacy as a stipulation for peace negotiations. Eventually, on July 18, Greeley admitted to Lincoln that the Confederates were not actually "empowered" to negotiate. In response, Lincoln published a public letter "To whom it may concern," informing the Confederate emissaries that he would entertain "Any proposition which embraces the restoration of peace, the integrity of the whole Union, and the abandonment of slavery, and which comes by and with an authority that can control the armies now at war against the United States." When the Confederates now learned about the prerequisite that Greeley had withheld from them, they wrongly concluded that Lincoln had been duplicitous.

from the Co responsibility & the new Capt now assumed it. We are now ready for another raid, but it is hard for a soldier to tell what the next day will bring forth. Wrote some letters.

Thursday, July 28, 1864. Pleasant, quite warm. Had considerable duty about camp. Got hold of a late paper, learned that Sherman was near Atlanta driving Hood,[7] he having superseded Johnston, and Maj Genl McPherson had been killed.[8] I trust the rebellion is on its last legs. Sometimes I think so, and then I have my doubts. Had skirmish drill, the men did very well on first trial.

Friday, July 29, 1864. Pleasant, worked hard today. Rec'd orders to issue what necessary clothing is needed and be ready to march next Monday or Tuesday, for what point we know not.

Saturday, July 30, 1864. Quite pleasant, no special duty except to issue the clothing. In afternoon had skirmish drill.

Sunday, July 31, 1864. Still pleasant, weather quite warm, had Morning Company Inspection, found things in very good shape considering the recent raid. Attended divine service by the Chaplain on the camp grounds, a fine sermon and a large attendance.

Monday, August 1, 1864. Pleasant day. I was requested by the Col to assist the Adjt about his reports, and I at once reported to the Adjt for duty and worked hard most of the day.

Tuesday, August 2, 1864. Continues pleasant. Got a pass and went to the City on business, my first trip since I came here. Reported at Gen'l Bucklands Hd Qrs in quest of the paymaster in order that I might get a final settlement with the gov't on my discharge from Co "B" and final statements, but not finding him, I took a look around the City. Went into the park, a whole square in the center of business, enclosed with an iron and stone fence, densely covered with beautiful trees, and many hundreds of squirrels, jumping and running around the grounds & trees, and which were very tame.[9] In the center of the square is a Monument, erected to the

---

7. On July 18, 1864, Confederate general John Bell Hood (1831–1879) superseded Joseph E. Johnston (1807–1891) as commander of the Army of Tennessee.

8. Union general James B. McPherson (1828–1864) was killed at the Battle of Atlanta on July 22.

9. Many Union soldiers commented on the tame squirrels at Court Square. See, for example, George N. Compton, diary entry for June 18, 1863, and Benja-

"Jackson's Monument at Memphis, Tennessee, Defaced by the Rebels," *Harper's Weekly*, July 5, 1862. (Lincoln Financial Foundation Collection)

memory of Jackson, the base of which having had thereon those immortal words from his lips "The Federal Union must and shall be preserved" but the hand of the vandal rebel was plainly seen, the word "Federal" which gave them such great annoyance being chiseled or cut out of the same. Gen'l Jackson though a great patron saint of the Democracy, yet he was not a disunionist.[10] Went over to the Irving Prison, quite a large 5 to 6 story building, and there were several hundreds of rebs confined there. Then went down to the Gayoso House, the leading hotel in the City, got dinner, a good square meal, then getting my fill of ice cream, melons &c at a restaurant, I then returned to camp.

Wednesday, August 3, 1864. Pleasant. Got a pass and went again to the City. Saw the paymaster and got settled up on old matters, and having received my pay, started back to Camp, getting there about 3 P.M. and found that the regiment had left about two hours before. Got my things

---

min R. Hieronymus diary entry for January 3, 1863, both at the Abraham Lincoln Presidential Library and Museum, Springfield, Illinois; Silas W. Haven to Jane, January 3, 1863, in Brian Craig Miller, ed., *"A Punishment on the Nation": An Iowa Soldier Endures the Civil War* (Kent, Ohio: Kent State University Press, 2012), 36; *Daily Milwaukee News*, March 29, 1863.

10. Andrew Jackson had helped found Memphis in 1819. As president in the early 1830s he took a strong stand against South Carolinians who threatened to leave the Union over the federal tariff, declaring, "Our Federal Union, it must be preserved." The statue of Jackson, which had been dedicated in 1859 and defaced sometime in the first year of the war, was repaired in 1908 and is now inside the courthouse in Memphis.

together hastily and packed them away, then started after the command across lots, and at about 6 P.M. I reached their camp in an old cotton field about 10 miles out. There were some 3 to 4 [of] our troops in the command, and were headed in a southeasterly direction but for what point or what purpose I have not learned.

Thursday, August 4, 1864. Pleasant. Some cooler. Had quite a shower during the night, and we got somewhat wet. R at 2 A.M. Start at 3 ½. Passed over a fine country, considerably settled, plantations under very good state of improvement, plenty of fruit and vegetables, at one place found about a half acre of melons, great luscious, fine ones. We stopped & went into the patch, the old man came out & sought to drive us off, but the officers first ascertained who he was & learning that he was an unrepentant Johnny, we had no mercy on him or his melons, and soon cleaned the patch. A large party of Cavalry were sent out on the flanks to forage, as only a limited amount of supplies were taken along, the intention of Gen'l Smith Comd'g being to feed more or less upon the enemy and the enemies country. The foragers had good success and brought in cattle, sheep, & hogs, burned several cotton gins and quite a quantity of cotton. Marched 20 miles and camped.

Friday, August 5, 1864. Pleasant. R at 3 A.M. Very heavy shower in the night with high wind, we rolled up in our rubber blankets and kept as dry as possible. Had plenty forage, fruit [and] vegetables, but not sufficient of breadstuffs, went to the Commissary and got a limited supply of hardtack. The country the best I have seen, and some fine residences, as they were generally occupied they were not interfered with. Country rather hilly, some timber and fine water, passed through Holly Springs [Mississippi] about sunset and camped just over the railroad near the place. This must have been a beautiful town before the war, but now somewhat dilapidated, the railroad building, machine shops, the rebel armory, and many other buildings having been burned by Grants forces nearly two years before. Some fine store buildings, windows smashed & empty, the Court-House looked as if it had been badly used, and very few people were left in the place. March[ed] 22 miles today. About night was truly glad to hear the welcome whistle of the locomotive, and a train of supplies and soldiers from Memphis.

Saturday, August 6, 1864. Pleasant. R at 5 A.M., no marching today. About 9 A.M. Capt & Lt went foraging, in charge of 50 men. They had a fine time, captured & drove in 25 head of cattle, some sheep, got some honey, molasses, meal flour, &c which looks like a fat living. At 3 P.M. had battalion drill. Rec'd orders assigning me to duty with Co "H."

Sunday, August 7, 1864. Very pleasant. Was detailed with Co "H" for picket duty, and at 9 A.M. we went on duty a short distance from camp. Fine picket duty, as no enemy was in sight or our knowledge. The Col, Q.M., Ass't Surgeon and many others with an armed squad went out foraging. They reported a fine time, having captured and brought in a drove of mules & horses, also a buggy and considerable forage. Was glad to receive a letter from Lucy this far from our base, and ans^d it at once.

Monday, August 8, 1864. Continues pleasant, quite warm, was relieved from duty at 9 A.M. and orders were rec'd to be ready to march at 30 minutes notice, which got up quite a flurry. Three trains came in loaded down with soldiers—3^d Div 16th Army Corps. Flying reports in regard to a fight at the front. Orders again rec'd to move tomorrow morning without fail, and the camp was spread out again for the night.

Tuesday, August 9, 1864. Pleasant. R at 3 A.M. Start at 7. Bid good bye to the Springs and away we went for the front, and South. Marched 8 miles through a very good country, though thinly settled, good water, rather light crops, and camped at Waterford near the railroad.[11] Learned that the 1st Div had a fight at Tallahatchie River. Saw Lt Rice, Beach[12] & others. Was quite surprised to see two trains come into camp, a good ways [from] the base into the enemys country.

Wednesday, August 10, 1864. Cool, foggy. R and long roll at 4 A.M. and the troops fell into line in their proper places. A fight was anticipated but soon the scare was over, and the ranks broke. Co "K" went on picket

---

11. As the regiment was preparing to depart Holly Springs, Daniel Densmore noted that Lt. Col. Clendening would be left "behind under arrest, it being much too monstrous a bore to have him along." According to Densmore, "He knows nothing of it yet, & will there not be a mad gent, when the light breaks upon him? It will probably hurt him much more than to be dishonest." Densmore noted that Clendening sent Colonel Jones two letters "filled with piteous appeals to be allowed to go with the expedition, anything only to be allowed that privilege. Col remarked something about 'a driveling whine,' & lit his cigar with the letters." Daniel Densmore to brother, August 1, 1864, and August 11, 1864, Densmore Papers. Clendening would be court-martialed later in the year.

12. Jacob C. Beach (1829–1914), a native of New Jersey, was a private in the 7th Minnesota Infantry, Co. B.

today, and the bal[ance] of the reg't had permission to go to the river to wash. No news from the front of importance. 3^d Brig, 3^d Div 16th Army Corps came marching in today from Holly Springs. A company of Heavy Artillery came with them bringing two 24 pounder siege guns—they came to the Springs by rail, the road being washed out this side of that point, they marched.

Thursday, August 11, 1864. Very warm night, no marching today. The 3^d Brig, 3^d Div went to the front this A.M. and a train came through from Memphis with more troops and supplies, a mail came but none for me. A great foraging party went out, they got several wagon loads of corn, some potatoes and several contrabands came in with them, fleeing from slavery and their masters to their freedom. They had heard of Massa Lincoln and his proclamation of freedom. Had Co drill, skirmish drill for an hour, boys are improving very much.

Friday, August 12, 1864. Cloudy looks like rain this A.M., no marching orders yet. The Col, Q.M. and quite a party went foraging, they got quite a drove of cattle & sheep. Lt Rogers took twenty men and went out in the afternoon, they got plenty apples and peaches, which were very fine, besides plenty forage.

Saturday, August 13, 1864. Cloudy, no marching yet, was detailed with Co C, D & E to go foraging. Start at 6 A.M., went about 10 miles near Chalahoma [Chulahoma, Mississippi], found rather rich foraging—got 3 wagon loads corn, which we found in pens hid in the brush, the reliable contraband giving us the required information. Also found & drove in 30 sheep, got some apples, peaches, melons a plenty and returned to camp about night with our plunder, without encountering the enemy or any difficulty. About sundown, heard heavy cannonading at the front, all are anxious to know what it means, and all are excited.

Sunday, August 14, 1864. Cloudy, foggy but before noon it cleared up, quite hot, no marching. Rec'd an invitation to go to Hd Qrs & eat peaches, and of course I attended, and we had a plenty of such luscious ones. I never saw better and I never ate so many at once. Heard firing again at the front, report that the rebs are in force near Abbeyville [Abbeville, Mississippi], just beyond our front. Had services in the evening.

Monday, August 15, 1864. Pleasant, very warm, no orders for our brigade, though quite a force of Infantry & Cavalry went forward to the front. Was on guard—guarding the cattle, horses, and forage, and had a good swim in the creek. What we remain here so long for we cannot imagine but we must live & learn.

Tuesday, August 16, 1864. Very hot, two trains came today from Memphis, one of them by our camp to the front. Learned particulars about the fight Saturday, 42 of our men killed and wounded and 80 rebs. Lt Spencer[13] Brigade Q.M. was shot by one of the Union soldiers.

Wednesday, August 17, 1864. Very pleasant. Another train came today loaded with soldiers, and the entire command rec'd orders to march at 11 A.M. The camp was torn down, the tents packed and all other articles that were difficult to carry, & were returned to Memphis. The command now numbered about 10000 men, Infantry, Cavalry & Artillery, a company of heavy artillery with two siege guns, a small wagon train and a drove of cattle, under command of Brig Genl A. J. Smith. All luggage of every description, extra clothing &c was packed on the train and ret^d, each soldiers having only his haversack & canteen, and a rubber blanket. The Army was stripped for fighting, and a forced march if necessary. At 1 P.M. the assembly blew from Div & Brig & Regt Hd Qrs and the command soon fell in & started, roads quite muddy. Arrived at the Camp of the advance at the Tallahatchie River, being in a large cotton field, very flat, near the river, very misty and rainy at night. Found out where the 7th Regt was and went & saw them, had a pleasant chat with Alva, All, Capt Stevens & Dr Ames. Saw some 9th Minn boys also 10th boys.

Thursday, August 18, 1864. Very misty, foggy, had a drizzly rain all night. I not having any tent and there not being one in our regiment except a fly for Hd Qrs, took two rubber blankets and some stakes and made a kind of tent, and crawled under, though my head or feet, one or the other, remained out in the wet. I slept some, though a good deal of noise, as the boys being rolled up in their blanket on the wet ground, or sitting around the fires with smouldering embers, did not sleep much and were quite noisy. Got out early, got a cup of coffee & hard tack, then went up to the 7th camp, they were on higher ground and somewhat out of the mud. Co "K" on guard. Genl Smith came in from Waterford, and we expect to march.

---

13. John F. Spence (ca. 1841–1864), first lieutenant of the 61st USCT, Co. K, was "accidentally killed" on August 16, 1864, "near Waterford, Miss.," according to his CMSR. He had previously been a private in the 2nd Iowa Cavalry, and was detailed as acting assistant quartermaster of the brigade in April 1864.

Friday, August 19, 1864. Very rainy weather, rained all night. I slept very well, being rolled up in my blankets, the boys having bro't in a large number of rails from the fences near by, and I took two, laid them near together in the mud and then stretched out on them, rolled up in my blanket. How's that for a comfortable lodging. I have heard of sleeping upon the broadside of a barn, but on the broadside of a rail was new to me and to us all, as many had this very comfortable bed. It was certainly comfortable, though a little hard to a fellows back, it kept us up out of the mud, and I slept and the rain pelted upon me, my head resting upon a canteen for a pillow. Many of the boys sit around the smouldering fires all night, and if they slept, they did it in a sitting posture, but I have learned that when a man is real tired he will sleep in most any position. Orders were rec'd to march at 6 ½ A.M. About this time it rained very hard, camp broke, but the command or any part thereof did not go far, the train and the cannon were stuck in the mud. Our brigade did not move at all, at 9 A.M. orders rec'd that we do not march, and here we are in the Tallahatchie Swamps. I had heard of them but had never seen and felt them before. The Artillery had sunk into the black mud up to the hubs and the wagons though unloaded had to be left in the ruts. The river was rising rapidly, and has already commenced to overflow the flats so that some of the troops were obliged to retire to a higher position, and here we were, no tents, no cover except our rubber blankets, and though we could not move the army, yet if occasion required, we would have given the Johnnies a warm reception, if they attacked us in our position, but they did not molest the general command and only showed fight at the front with the Cavalry outposts.

Saturday, August 20, 1864. Still rainy, having kept up most of the night. Slept some on my bed of rails, which barely kept me up out of the water, as by this time the flats where we were [were] covered with water an inch or two deep. Got out and warmed up the best I could at the smouldering rail fires, got a tin of coffee and some hard tack and took my morning repast, and this is what they call soldiering. Very few of the people up country, who are snugly ensconced around their warm fires during such cold rainy weather can realize what [we] have to endure here. The bridge washed away, the train & cannon sinking deeper in the mud, and water more or less all over the flat. About 2 P.M. the rain ceased, the clouds broke, and we rejoiced at a ray of sunshine. I went up to see the 7th boys, who had a much better, a higher place for camp, and had a fine time.

Was invited to supper with Lts Eastman & Hoag[14] and very thankfully accepted, it being the first square meal I had rec'd for two to three days. About this time we began to be troubled by a tiny little varmint called "jiggers," a species of tick, red color, and very small, so small that we did not notice them until they had burrowed into our legs and we felt them, and if not taken out or killed they make a quite large and troublesome sore. They have to be dug or scraped out with a sharp knife. It was said by some one that salt grease would keep them off, so I covered myself with it, taking a good bathe as it were, in salt grease, after having quite a dig for the varmints. Laid down upon my soft bed of rails again for the night, rolled up in my blanket, and was soon in the arms of Morpheus.

Sunday, August 21, 1864. R at daylight. Got up, it was pleasant. Rec'd orders to march at 8 A.M., got our frugal meal and at 9 A.M. a heavy detail having been sent to assist the train out of the mud, the troops fell in and made a start, but did not go far, as the train seemed bound to the elastic mud. The men lifted and pushed, the mules did their best and the train & artillery were finally extricated from their bounden condition, and the command moved on, but slowly, only marching 7 miles and camped at Hurricane Creek at 3 P.M., the place of the fight on last Saturday. Nothing whatever today to indicate that it was Sunday, but I thought of the folks at home, the church services, and the many prayers this day uttered for the success of our Army.

Monday, August 22, 1864. Foggy morning, though the sun penetrated the fog and it was clear by noon. R at 3, start at 6, passed Abbyville on the railroad at 7, it was all ablaze. Went over rather a rough country, mostly oak timber, and about noon arrived at Oxford, Miss. Quite a large place, the seat of Oxford University and the home of one of the South's prominent men L. Q. C. Lamar.[15] He[re] we remained for some [time] apparently resting, but [what] it meant, we could not learn, & finally orders were rec'd to countermarch. The reason we ascertained was that the en-

---

14. Loel B. Hoag (1830–1883), a native of Vermont, eventually rose to the rank of captain of the 7th Minnesota Infantry, Co. A.

15. Lucius Quintus Cincinnatus Lamar (1825–1893) of Mississippi had served in the US House of Representatives from 1857 until Mississippi's secession in January 1861. He had a brief military career in 1861–1862. After the war he served in the US Senate, as secretary of the interior, and as an associate justice on the US Supreme Court.

emy had dodged us, not desiring to again encounter Old A. J. and his forces, and a portion of the rebs under Forrest had put to our rear and gone through the lines into Memphis. We did not know much about it, and all was excitement and much speculation as to the effect of Forrests raid.[16] The Cavalry went through Oxford and 4 miles beyond, and on their return through the place set fire to many of the buildings. We went back to our old ground at Hurricane Creek and camped. I was detailed on picket duty for the night.

Tuesday, August 23, 1864. Pleasant. R at 1 ½, picket relieved at 2 ½ A.M., got breakfast and start at 4 A.M. Took the back track and soon arrived at the Tallahatchie river, the bridge having partially gone out in the flood, was put in repair by the pioneers, and a team started across, when down went the bridge into the torrents below, all the mules being drowned and the driver only escaped. The entire command was then ordered into Camp in the swampy valley as before, and the pioneers went at work to build a bridge. Meanwhile firing was heard in the rear, the long roll beat & the troops fell in, it was quite exciting. We could not march out on the line of march, but we could fight out at the rear. Our brigade were marched to the rear, and there we had quite a heated skirmish, a considerable loss on both sides, besides we took several hundred prisoners. Towards night the lines were drawn in, and we returned to our old camp in the bog. Further news rec'd that Forrest entered Memphis with 3 to 4000 men all mounted, and was whipped with some loss by Gen'l Hurlbut's troops.[17] A heavy picket out tonight.

Wednesday, August 24, 1864. Pleasant. R quite early, pioneers had labored hard and with an extra detail, but the bridge was not complete & no prospects of moving today, and no signs of an immediate engagement, but the Gen'l was cautious considering our situation and some of the force including our brigade laid in line of battle all day, the enemy being reported near Hurricane Creek. My Co was on guard. The bridge progressed finely today. We hope to get out of this place soon as possible. A foraging party was sent out and they brought in about 50 head of cattle.

16. As noted in the chapter introduction, Confederate general Nathan Bedford Forrest attacked Memphis with two thousand cavalrymen on August 21, 1864.

17. Stephen A. Hurlbut (1815–1882) commanded the Union army's Sixteenth Corps and was headquartered at Memphis. The rumor that he had whipped Forrest was unfounded.

More rumors about Forrests raid on Memphis, it being reported that Gen'l Buckland and several other officers were taken prisoners, and that Forrests army crossed the Hatchie above us today, about 20 miles. Quite warm, murky this P.M. I hope we will get out of this swamp before it rains again.

Thursday, August 25, 1864. Rather cool morning, owing very much to the dampness in this swampy valley. Learned that there was prospects of our moving today. At 8 ½ A.M., there being no enemy that would stand fight, and the bridge being complete, the command was ordered to march, and three times three, the cheers went up. Went across the new bridge, which was quite substantial, and over the same road and camped on a stream near Waterford. My back troubles me again, the damp & cold of the night having brought on my old trouble. After camping, I went upon a hill near and had a fine view of the Camp and the surrounding country.

Friday, August 26, 1864. Cloudy, but cleared off pleasant by noon. R at daylight, and soon were ready to march. Orders issued that the expedition break up and all the Infantry but the brigade of Colored troops [and] the 7th & 9th Minn were ordered to proceed at once to Memphis, and from there to Sherman's Army, so it is reported. Our brigade, the 7th & 9th, two regiments of cavalry, the siege guns & a battery of artillery, & the supply train moved over to Waterford and camped on the old camp ground, for what purpose or how long we remain here, we cannot learn. There are *some* things we know and *many* that we do not. The cavalry were sent out foraging & returned with some corn and plenty of apples and peaches, and we again had a feast. The fattest country I have seen in Dixie is about here, a good place to soldier, as long as it lasts.

Saturday, August 27, 1864. Very pleasant. Took it easy, did not get out until sunrise, got rested and my back felt better. The supply train unloaded near the railroad, and a train is soon expected. Am getting anxious to learn the news, also to get a letter from home. It seems like an age since we have heard anything. Rec'd orders to march and everything had to be loaded up again, and soon broke camp enroute for Holly Springs, arriving there about noon, and went into camp on the old ground. My back ached and I was quite tired.

Sunday, August 28, 1864. Very pleasant, quite hot. Rec'd orders to march, packed up and started, the 3d Div & Colored Brigade for Memphis, the 1st Div to La Grange, Tenn, and with a "good bye" to each other and to the tune of old "John Brown" and "Johnny Comes Marching home," we separated, each on its journey. We took the old back, the foragers took in a drove of cattle & aplenty apples, and we having marched 23 miles camped on the Cold Water near our old camp. I was quite tired, my back ached, and glad to camp.

Monday, August 29, 1864. Pleasant. R early, broke camp at daylight, our brigade ahead, my Co as rear guard. Passed over the old road, foraged all the cattle that could be found, stopped for rest and hard tack at a small stream of fair water, and then hurrah for Memphis, arriving there after a tedious tiresome march about 10 P.M., and soon were in our tents and to bunk, thinking there is no place like home.

8

"A Change Is What the Soldiers Like"

Memphis and Fort Pickering, August 30–December 31, 1864

While performing guard and garrison duty in Memphis in the fall of 1864, Buswell turned much of his attention to national politics. Although he had been an antebellum Democrat who supported Sen. Stephen A. Douglas of Illinois in the four-way presidential contest of 1860, by 1864 Buswell had become a Republican. The war had clearly radicalized him on the slavery issue, and his experiences leading men of color in battle had changed his perspectives on African Americans. Like many other antebellum Democrats in the army, Buswell had also become disgusted with the Democratic Party because it appeared to verge on disloyalty. At their national convention in Chicago in late August, the Democrats nominated George B. McClellan, the popular Union general, as their presidential nominee. However, to balance their ticket they placed McClellan on an antiwar platform that called the war a "failure." To make matters worse, the Democrats selected George H. Pendleton, a Peace Democrat from Ohio, as McClellan's running mate. This divided ticket proved to be a major misstep as it disappointed both the Peace and War factions of the party. Moreover, after the fall of Atlanta in early September, the war no longer looked like a "failure," and the Democratic Party simply appeared disloyal to many voters. On November 8, Lincoln sailed into reelection, carrying 55 percent of the popular vote and winning 212 electoral votes to McClellan's 21.[1]

---

1. On the election of 1864, see Jonathan W. White, *Emancipation, the Union Army, and the Reelection of Abraham Lincoln* (Baton Rouge: Louisiana State University Press, 2014).

"Forrest's Raid into Memphis" past Irving Block Prison, sketched by George H. Ellsbury of the 7th Minnesota Infantry, *Harper's Weekly*, September 10, 1864. (Lincoln Financial Foundation Collection)

Tuesday, August 30, 1864. Pleasant, got out at sunrise, got breakfast, a good square meal once more, having had a good rest & sleep in my bunk, got the particulars of Forrests raid. He came in through the lines on the 18th inst, with about 4000 men all mounted, suddenly passed through the picket lines and before the alarm was given and the troops could assemble—there being about 6000 men under Gen'l Hurlbut in & around the City—Forrest & his force went down through the City, direct to the Gayoso House, for the purpose of capturing Genls Buckland, Hurlbut & other officers, a portion going to Irving Prison to release the reb prisoners, but failed in both attempts. He finally got his force together, after creating a great deal of excitement and scare among many of the people, and started out of the City. In the meantime, Genl Buckland had got his force together and met Forrest near the picket lines and gave him battle, and there was a considerable loss on both sides, Forrest taking away some prisoners and loosing about 200 prisoners. His raid did not accomplish anything except to suffer a loss. I was relieved from duty with Co "H" and I was glad of it. Lt Rogers went down to city to get a fresh supply for our mess, bought about $15–worth of rations of the Commissary, while I worked on the muster rolls of our Co, getting ready for the paymaster. Rec'd news about the Democratic Convention at Chicago held yesterday.

McClellan nominated upon a peace platform, am sorry for M^c, too good a man to be sacrificed by those *peace* Democrats.

Wednesday, August 31, 1864. Pleasant. I was requested to assist the Adjt in his duties, and cheerfully complied, and worked hard all day. Took dinner at Hd Qrs. Rec'd the glorious news that Forts Gaines & Morgan at the entrance of Mobile Bay are now both in our hands and Grant is yet hammering away at the gates of Petersburg. Glory! Glory!! Glory!!!

Thursday, September 1, 1864. Pleasant, worked hard in adjts office, was glad to receive a letter from Mother, & that they are all well. She will soon [receive] my letter and [hear] of my safe return to this City. Rec'd more particulars about the great Dem-Peace Convention at Chicago. Old Vallandigham the banished traitor was there and cheered by the Convention. How disgraceful, martial law ought to be declared and such work stopped, those cheers give aid and comfort to Jeff Davis & his cohorts and will cost many more thousands of precious lives. Gen'l Tom Price[2] recently from the rebel army was also present, and many other rebels or copperheads, and they called it a peace convention. No doubt Old Jeff had his representatives and Confederates there, the same as he has had at Washington. Such an assembly in time of war in a foreign country would be dispersed at the point of the bayonet and the leaders arrested and cast into prison. I say all honor to the Douglas democrats[3] who have laid aside their party views and come out boldly to the support of the administration in its efforts to quench this mighty rebellion.

Friday, September 2, 1864. Continues pleasant, worked quite hard most of the day assisting the Adjt, and yet I don't get any extra pay, nothing except the bare honor and the experience, but sometime it may count. Officers call at 6 P.M. today and the officers of the regiment all repaired to the Col's tent where we were agreeably surprised in finding a collation

---

2. Thomas L. Price (1809–1870), a Democrat from Missouri, had been a brigadier general in the Union army in 1861 and 1862 until he resigned to take a seat in the US House of Representatives. Buswell was incorrect to say that he had been in the Confederate army.

3. Douglas Democrats had supported Sen. Stephen A. Douglas of Illinois in the presidential election of 1860. During the secession crisis, Douglas publicly supported Lincoln and the Union, and encouraged his supporters to do likewise.

all in readiness by Maj Meatyard.[4] Then we ate heartily, had a good chat, after a few toasts and speeches, singing and music on the banjos by the boys, we parting at the late hour of 11 P.M. and each to his quarters.

Saturday, September 3, 1864. Pleasant, was detailed by Special Order No 10 on duty at Hd Qrs, though no extra pay, but I accepted the situation and reported for duty and worked quite hard all day. There is a good deal of work in and about an Adjts office, more than one would suppose and help is needed.

Sunday, September 4, 1864. Pleasant, got up, had a good wash, a change of clothes, put on my dress suit and went to meeting in the grove, quite a large attendance. After I attended to some necessary work at Hd Qrs, and rested the balance of the day, reading, also wrote some letters. The Adjt was taken sick which will give me more work and more responsibility.

Monday, September 5, 1864. Very warm, pleasant. Was detailed by Gen'l Order No 10 as Acting Adjt, order signed by the Col Comd'g, and I assumed the full charge of Adjts Dept, & think myself capable for it, having already got quite an idea as to its duties.

Tuesday, September 6, 1864. Pleasant. Had guard mount first time as Adjt, had quite a shower in the P.M. The tents of the Command being only shelter tents, except those of the officers, they afforded poor protection from a driving shower, they answer very well to guard against a dew. Worked in the office all day.

Wednesday, September 7, 1864. Very warm, about noon quite hot, & in P.M. had another shower which laid out the dust and wet up things considerably.

Thursday, September 8, 1864. Warm though pleasant, got up early and discharged what work I could, then had guard mount, and during the heat of day took it easy.

Friday, September 9, 1864. Pleasant and warm, did considerable work. 100 guns were fired today by Gen'l Order Dist Memphis in honor of the recent victories at Atlanta and Mobile, a gen'l rejoicing by a good many

---

4. Edward B. Meatyard (1836–1889) was major of the 64th USCT. Earlier in the year he had been first lieutenant in the 68th USCT, Co. D, and before that he had been an officer in the 27th Illinois Infantry.

people, and especially by the soldiers. Had guard mount as usual and acted as Adjt the first time on Dress parade, and was quite well satisfied with my effort, and was complimented.

Saturday, September 10, 1864. Pleasant day, labored quite hard. Find there is a good deal when I have to do it all, but attended to it to my best ability, and I learn the Col is quite well satisfied. Camp was moved today to higher ground. The regiment is now furnishing a detail for picket, and they speak of having fine times going through the Johnny rebs and their goods on the lines, this fun I am loosing. The City was illuminated and fireworks this evening, rejoicing over the recent union victories, hooray! tiger!!

Sunday, September 11, 1864. Pleasant. Attended preaching by the Chaplain in the grove. Today is a special Thanksgiving day, set by the President to return thanks to God for the recent victories, and the day was quite well observed here. Did nothing more than actually necessary. Had guard mount and Dress parade.

Monday, September 12, 1864. Very pleasant, warm day, nights rather cool. Our Reg't in very fair health, attended to my regular duties and did considerable work in the A.M. After dinner took it easy, read the late news. McClellan accepts the nomination and says he is in favor of the restoration of the Union, that he is in favor of peace, but in favor of fighting for it, rather sits down upon the peace platform of the so called peace democrats, or Copperheads, who seemed to be in the majority in that convention. McClellan rebukes them. Bully for Little Mac. He would not be a bad man if elected but his constituency in these times would be a bad one. I have studied the parties quite well and though my tendencies in the past election had I been old enough were for Douglas, yet now I am thoroughly determined to cast my first presidential vote for the success of the Republican party and the reelection of Abe Lincoln. He is prosecuting the war to the best of his ability, and as he once said "It wont do to change horses while crossing a stream."[5]

---

5. A day after receiving the Republican nomination for president in June 1864, Lincoln told a delegation from the National Union League, "I have not permitted myself, gentlemen, to conclude that I am the best man in the country; but I am reminded, in this connection, of a story of an old Dutch farmer, who remarked to a companion once that 'it was not best to swap horses when crossing

Tuesday, September 13, 1864. Pleasant. This work in office is rather confining and I begin to feel it, though discharged my regular duty today. This P.M. we heard a terrible noise and racket in the direction of the City, and learned soon after that it was the explosion of a magazine in Ft Pickering, killing 3 men.[6]

Wednesday, September 14, 1864. Continues pleasant, had considerable to do today, wanted to go to the City, but so much work on hand, could not.

Thursday, September 15, 1864. Pleasant. After attending to my regular duty I got a pass and went to the City, had to walk a short distance when I took a horse car, got some ice cream and some things for camp, went over to Ft Pickering. Saw a good deal to amuse me, quite an extensive permanent work. The 3^d U.S.C. H'y Artillery Col Kapner[7] comd'g is quartered here, and the fort is well manned with cannon, most of them 64 & 100 pd'rs, barbet[te] guns, or large Columbiads on swinging gun carriages. Saw them drilling with the big guns, quite interesting to me and a new service. Then went to the Old Miss River and went in bathing, and then for camp, getting back just in time to form the reg't for genl Inspection. The men, guns &c looked very well under the circumstances.

Friday, September 16, 1864. Beautiful morning though quite a cool night. Staid in office and finished up considerable work today.

Saturday, September 17, 1864. Beautiful, worked hard today, made out several appointments for Non-Com^d officers, recently appointed. More

---

streams.'" See Roy P. Basler, et al., eds., *The Collected Works of Abraham Lincoln*, 9 vols. (New Brunswick, N.J.: Rutgers University Press, 1953), 7:383. These views were common among Democrats in the army. See White, *Emancipation, the Union Army, and the Reelection of Abraham Lincoln*, 112–17.

6. The explosion at Fort Pickering was caused by the accidental igniting of 110 shells by sparks from the Steamer *Neill*. Two African American soldiers and one Irish laborer were killed. See *New York Times*, September 18, 1864.

7. Ignatz Kappner (1827–1891), an immigrant from Austria, was colonel of the 3rd US Colored Heavy Artillery and the officer in command of Fort Pickering. Despite its designation as an artillery unit, the 3rd never saw combat and performed garrison duty at Fort Pickering in Memphis as an infantry unit. See Stephen V. Ash, *A Massacre in Memphis: The Race Riot That Shook the Nation One Year after the Civil War* (New York: Hill and Wang, 2013), 76. Daniel Densmore resented Kappner's authoritarianism. See *Family War Stories*, 103–5, 120.

than usual amount of work, but I now have the hang of it, and could always run it.

Sunday, September 18, 1864. Very pleasant morning, but I dont feel tip-top, head & back ache, and I did as little work as possible. Walked out around camp, was glad to receive a letter from home.

Monday, September 19, 1864. Quite a warm day. Cool night, being cool enough to sleep under two blankets in my tent, did not feel very extra but did my duty. Lt Rogers went on picket duty. I should like to go, and I believe it would do me good to get away from the office for a few days.

Tuesday, September 20, 1864. Pleasant, got up and found myself quite sick, and went back to bunk, and staid there most of the day. Got relieved from duty as Acting Adjt, Lt J G Smith[8] being detailed in my place, my head quite dizzy, eyes yellow, very bilious. Our Surgeon gave me some medicine. Orders rec'd that the regiment move tomorrow at 7 A.M. and camp near the picket lines in east part of the City.

Wednesday, September 21, 1864. Pleasant, but I don't feel so, am quite weak, back is out of kilter again. R early, broke camp, and the regiment moved to the East side of City and camped near the picket lines on the Pigeon Roost Road, a fine location, dry ground, a little sandy, plenty of trees and an aristocratic neighborhood, near many fine houses. A Camp was established and a detail set at work throwing up entrenchments, nearly around the same. Think we will like it better here, and no doubt we will get our share of picket duty.

Thursday, September 22, 1864. Continues pleasant, got up, felt some better. We like the new camp quite well, a little dusty being the only objection, water some better, and not a great ways off a spring, quite warm. Musquitos troubled us a good deal. Am quite bilious and have quite a yellow look, did not eat much today.

Friday, September 23, 1864. Cloudy, warm, musquitoes quite ferocious in the night. About midnight we had quite a scare, was awoke by the long roll beating, and heard firing upon the picket lines. Our reg't fell in and marched to position behind the breastworks, ready for a brush, but there was no fight. It proving to be only a skirmish with some guerrillas who attacked the pickets. Today is the day set for the soldiers to vote for

---

8. John G. Smith (born ca. 1843) rose to the rank of first lieutenant of the 68th USCT, Co. D. Previously he had been a private in the 25th Iowa Infantry.

President, & the Commissioners having arrived the polls were opened and our votes were cast, in envelopes, the vote for each state and precinct thereof separately, & on election day, these envelopes to be opened and the votes counted in the proper precinct,[9] and this the first election in which I took part in politics, though at the last presidential election had I been old enough I should no doubt [have] voted for Douglas instead of Lincoln, but since & during my enlistment, I have studied up some of the great issues, the matter has revolved itself over & over again in my mind. That Slavery was certainly wrong, and ought to be stamped out, I was well determined upon, and the Republican party being what the Johnny Rebs called the Abolishionists, I was further determined that it was my party. Again Lincoln was the President in favor of prosecuting the war and restoring the Union. The peace men as the Democratic party called themselves, or the leaders like Seymour,[10] Hendricks,[11] Vallandigham & others, were obstructionists, and doing all in their power to hinder & delay the prosecution of the war, and though Little Mac [is] somewhat of a different sentiment, yet my opinion under the circumstances, the Democratic party were not to be trusted, and I had fully made up my mind to cast my vote for Father Abe and the success of the Republican party, and with some considerable degree of pride I cast it and with an honest wish for their success. The election was very quiet and but a very few cast their vote on the Democratic side.[12] I felt better today.

Saturday, September 24, 1864. Beautiful day. Felt better, expect to be able to go on picket soon. Read the news, saw that the Draft was going on

---

9. Nineteen Northern states passed laws permitting soldiers to vote during the Civil War. For background on this legislation and soldiers' views of the presidential election of 1864, see White, *Emancipation, the Union Army, and the Reelection of Abraham Lincoln*, chap. 1. On the soldier vote in Minnesota, see Walter N. Trenerry, "Votes for Minnesota's Soldiers," *Minnesota History* 36 (March 1959): 167–72.

10. Horatio Seymour (1810–1886), a Democrat, was governor of New York from 1863 to 1864.

11. Thomas A. Hendricks (1819–1885), a Democrat from Indiana, served in the US Senate from 1863 to 1869. He later served as governor of Indiana and as vice president of the United States.

12. Many Democratic soldiers either voted Republican or chose not to vote in the election because they viewed the Democratic Party and platform as disloyal. See White, *Emancipation, the Union Army, and the Reelection of Abraham Lincoln*, chap. 4.

without any trouble in Mo, Ill & Ind. Gen'l A. J. Smith and his force who left here a short time ago have arrived at St Louis, they having marched from Memphis, through Arkansas, and had a fight with Genl Sterling Price & his army and whipped them.[13]

Sunday, September 25, 1864. Quite pleasant day, feel better. Capt Thompson had a visit from some 9th boys, had a pleasant chat, heard preaching in the grove by our Chaplain, quite a turnout. Rec'd St Louis & Chicago papers and had quite a feast looking them over. Learned the glorious news of Sheridans victory, defeating the Rebel Genl Early and his forces.[14] Cavalry pickets driven in tonight by guerrillas, another excitement and the troops all out & in line.

Monday, September 26, 1864. Very pleasant. Do not feel very extra. Rec'd two letters from home and one from Aunty, which tended to cheer me up some. Ans^d them during the day. There is now quite a large amount of travel through the lines. The Johnnys and their friends are laying quite a supply. Work proceeded on the fortifications in front of our camp.

Tuesday, September 27, 1864. Cloudy morning. Saw a beautiful rainbow in the West. Com^d raining at noon and continued for three hours. Recd further news from Sheridans raid, Early's Army nearly annihilated and retreating in great confusion. Glorious. It looks as though we were getting near the end but the rebels have a good deal of tenacity and are not easily disheartened, at least their leaders never seem to show it, though there are many things that seem to indicate that the common soldiery are getting tired of it, one thing there are a good many deserters from their army. Genl Fremont,[15] who was nominated by the Abolitionists, has given notice that he withdraws from the canvas, and advises his supporters to give all their aid & strength to the election of Lincoln. *Sensible*. My breast & back trouble me today.

13. On September 19, Confederate general Sterling Price invaded Missouri but over the ensuing weeks was repulsed by Union forces under generals Thomas Ewing and Andrew J. Smith.

14. During the Shenandoah Valley Campaign, Union general Philip Sheridan (1831–1888) defeated Confederate general Jubal Early (1816–1894) at the Third Battle of Winchester on September 19, and Fisher's Hill on September 21–22.

15. Radical Republicans nominated John C. Fremont (1813–1890) for president at a convention in Cleveland on May 31, 1864. Fremont withdrew from the race in early September since his candidacy would have divided the Republican vote and possibly ushered in a Democratic victory.

Wednesday, September 28, 1864. Rained considerable during the night. It laid the dust nicely, and this A.M. the sun rose clear. Lt Rogers got a pass & went to the City. Capt took his regular turn on the picket lines and while he was gone two Lieuts of the 9th Minn came and I entertained them. A flag of truce came up to our lines today, being sent by Forrest, he desiring an exchange of prisoners, and after some parleying an exchange was effected. More news of the glorious Sheridans dashing victory, several thousand prisoners and considerable artillery taken.

Thursday, September 29, 1864. Rainy, and it kept up nearly all day. Felt better and by request went on duty as officer of the guard. More news from the gallant Sheridan, he drives the enemy 80 miles and as a consequence the war barometer Gold was affected by this prospect of success to our arms, and it fell very suddenly to 175. This is glory enough. Hurrah for the dashing Phil and his brave boys. For a time the story was that a dead cavalry man was a curiosity, but after nearly 3 yrs of war we see a good many. They are certainly doing their share now and deserve the credit, and it is given them. It has not only affected gold, but has increased the prospects of Lincolns election.

Friday, September 30, 1864. Rainy, quite wet and muddy, went on my regular duty, did considerable writing making out Co papers. Heard that Lt Ross[16] and our Adjt were quite sick. Also rec'd a report through the lines that Forrest with his force is now in the vicinity of Nashville.

Saturday, October 1, 1864. Rather wet day, staid in camp all day, worked on returns. Recd news that Gen'l Sterling Price['s] army has attacked Pilot Knob.

Sunday, October 2, 1864. Pleasanter. Not having any special duty to perform, I fixed up and went over to the Camp of 7th Minn and had a good time with the boys. Learned that David Kennedy[17] was either captured or deserted on the Oxford raid. Under the general circumstances the opinion is that he is a deserter, and is reported on the rolls as such. He was always a worthless cuss, enlisted to get a commission and failing in that rendered him lawless and nearly unfit for duty. Had [Heard?] a

---

16. John T. Ross (born ca. 1843) was first lieutenant of the 68th USCT, Co. G.

17. David A. Kennedy (born ca. 1834), a native of New York, was a private in the 7th Minnesota Infantry, Co. B. A perennial skulker, he deserted for the final time at Washington, D.C., on February 9, 1865.

rumor that Petersburg was taken, which created some excitement. Heard preaching in the evening by our Chaplain.

Monday, October 3, 1864. Pleasant, was detailed for Officer of Guard, but was changed at guard mounting for the picket, and was directed to the lines at Pigeon Roost Road, quite near our camp. Reported for duty, and had a good time, quite busy all day, examined a great quantity of goods and a good many persons, found some tobacco not on permits, and some contraband whiskey which was confiscated. Had quite a chat with the sesesh ladies, who lived just outside of lines, and Oh, some of them were such red hot sesesh, yet quite pleasant and talkative to us here, but had they the power would no doubt spit upon us.

Tuesday, October 4, 1864. Rainy during the night, got a few winks of sleep, myself and the other officer keeping watch for the grand rounds as if caught napping by them I might be placed under arrest. They generally come around about 1 P.M. [A.M.], the countersign is given and all is well, and they pass on along the lines. We now have a cavalry outpost picket about a ½ in advance of our lines, on the different roads, as an extra precaution. Learned that the surplus troops leave here, the 7th with them, for Missouri to fight Price. Got relieved at 9 A.M. & went to camp. Found a letter from home, which was quite cheering.

Wednesday, October 5, 1864. Pleasant day. Remained in camp all day, the men out drilling, but I worked on some reports in my tent, and wrote some letters.

Thursday, October 6, 1864. Another pleasant day. Got up & breakfast early, and Lt Rogers & myself got passes and went to the City. Had a pleasant time tramping around, went into the Park and sat down, plenty people there. I had a squirrel come and eat out of my hand, very tame. Bought some new clothes, and we got some provisions for our mess, and before night got back to camp. Had a jacket made out of my soldier coat, to wear on fatigue and picket duty. Was detailed on picket for tomorrow.

Friday, October 7, 1864. Pleasant, got out in good season and reported for picket duty. Had guard mount & then Lt & I took the detail of guards to the Pigeon Roost Picket Station, and we had our hands full all day, & plenty of fun. It was pleasant and there were an unusual no [number] of teams & people passing and repassing. I attended to the men and the examination of goods with the assistance of the Serg't of guard, and Lt in the absence of the Lady Inspector inspected the women. Many of them fairly detested the *Yankee* lady inspectors & preferred to be examined by the Lt, though the men they hated bad enough. Some women submitted without any difficulty and soon were permitted to pass, but occasionally there was one, a saucy, rebel jade, but they were generally handled the roughest, and frequently were required to take off their dresses & skirts, and open their bussems, as contraband goods, especially quinine was carried secretly about their person. Grand rounds came round about midnight. Serg't Wells[18] Co "C" was found off duty and was arrested, creating some stir.

Saturday, October 8, 1864. Pleasant. Did not sleep any during night, though no disturbance on the lines. Was relieved at 9 A.M., made out statement agst Serg't Wells and sent to H'd Qrs. Received a report that a large force of rebs are approaching the City, and everything is being put in readiness to receive them. A detail of 100 men were sent out to White Station to guard the trains, as it is being evacuated, on account of the near approach of the enemy, quite an excitement all around tonight.

Sunday, October 9, 1864. Pleasant, though some foggy. Long roll beat at 3 ½ A.M. and out we jumped, got on our clothes, and many fell in without their shoes. Remained in line of battle until daylight, and no enemy appearing, broke ranks. Authentic report that Chalmers is at Hernando [Mississippi] with 3000 men. Let them come, we are ready. Preaching in the evening.

Monday, October 10, 1864. Pleasant day, not on duty and very little to do. Read the papers, Chalmers reported advancing, and extensive preparations are being made to receive them. Was detailed for picket for tomorrow.

Tuesday, October 11, 1864. Pleasant day, got breakfast and reported, was directed to the State Line road for picket duty. Had a fine time, new people generally, most of the people just outside Pigeon Roost Station I had begun to know by name even, great deal of travel and a large number of permits to examine. After dark before the grand Rounds, I went along the lines, on practice for the boys, they did very well. Laid down in the tent awhile, quite tired but had to keep awake.

18. Yail Wells (born ca. 1822 in Kentucky) was a sergeant in the 68th USCT, Co. C. His name also appears as Yale, Yales, and Yarl in his CMSR and pension records.

Wednesday, October 12, 1864. Continues pleasant. Did not sleep any. Guns were fired along the lines during the night, no doubt first caused by an imaginary foe, and soon got to firing generally. It created quite a scare among the people who lived near the lines. Was relieved from duty about 9 A.M. & went to camp, & took a rest for the balance of the day.

Thursday, October 13, 1864. Pleasant day. Had a good sleep. Got ready to go to City, but did not go. Wrote some letters, but did not receive any. Took it easy reading the papers and looking over skirmish drill tactics, was again detailed for picket tomorrow.

Friday, October 14, 1864. Rather cloudy, but cleared up by 10 A.M. Reported for duty and was directed to relieve the guard at Pigeon Roost Station. Had plenty business, many teams & people passed. The Lady Inspector being absent, I tried my hand as a female inspector, rather new business, I confess, but I did my duty, and I don't believe they carried out many bottles [of] quinine or other unpermitted goods either. Met some lady friends, might call them friends here, but should I accept their hearty invitations to go out and visit them at their homes, no doubt the first thing I would know, I would [be] peeking through the gates of a rebel prison, or standing behind a rebel stockade, but you don't catch me out there, *a leetle too much adventure.*

Saturday, October 15, 1864. Rather cloudy, cleared away about 8 ½ A.M. Was relieved from duty and wended my way to Camp, with at least this kind of picket duty is fun enough, something new every day, new and different kind of customers to deal with, which with the women, their calmness, rage & anxiety, and the examination of them makes it interesting all the time.

Sunday, October 16, 1864. Rather cool, tired and did not get out at roll call. Finally got around, cleaned up, dressed up, got a pass, and went to the City, took in the cemetery, a very pretty place. Saw the graves of many a poor soldier boy, and also the part set apart for the Johnnys. When I returned to camp, found them all excitement over the prospect of a brush with Chalmers, who was west of us in force and not far from the lines. A reliable contraband had come in with the news. Attended meeting by the chaplain.

Monday, October 17, 1864. Quite cool. R at 3 A.M. and long roll beat. Out we jumped, on with our things, and in a great hurry were in line of battle, but proved to be another scare. Was detailed officer of the guard around camp, had in charge nine prisoners whom I kept at work on the works in our front. Gen'l Inspection in the P.M., men looked very well and guns & accoutrements quite well, and the reg't was complemented [sic] on the manual of arms. The enemy being near, the picket lines were ordered closed today.

Tuesday, October 18, 1864. Pleasant, though cooler. Worked on payrolls and had them signed by the Co, already [sic] for the paymaster. Was detailed for picket, to report tomorrow A.M. The picket lines closed again. Rec'd a letter from Aunty, they well [are?] all well.

Wednesday, October 19, 1864. Pleasant, but cooler. R at 3 A.M. Reported for duty and was sent to the Pigeon Roost Station, in charge of 40 men. About noon four men were brought to my tent, under guard, they were endeavoring to pass through the lines. They claimed to be deserters from Hoods Army which was now East of us near Corinth, they had got tired of war and left the army and concluded to come into our lines. They reported the rebel column moving in a northerly direction. I took a minute of their statements, made a report to Gen'l Bucklands Hd Qrs, and sent it with the prisoners under guard to his Adjt Gen'l. Considerable passing and work on the lines all day. The lady inspector was present and I got rid of the job. Rec'd two papers from Aunty which were welcome.

Thursday, October 20, 1864. Pleasant though cool, quite so on the lines. After the grand rounds passed I tried to sleep, but could not. Quite early two wounded Union soldiers were brought through the lines at my post, & they report that the patrol of about 50 to 60 mounted soldiers were ambuscaded and the entire force except themselves either killed or captured, & there was quite an excitement passed along the lines, also in the Camps. Was relieved about 8 A.M. and went to my tent & laid down to rest.

Friday, October 21, 1864. Pleasant but rather cool. Detailed on picket duty again today, and ordered to report at once, and again sent to the old and familiar station on the Pigeon Roost. Lt Talbot was with me. Saw a number of persons whom I had met before, and though had a good many permits to examine, had rather a good time.

Saturday, October 22, 1864. Quite pleasant, was up and on the alert most of the night, went along the lines from picket to picket to see that the boys were wide awake to their duties. The grand rounds passed about

12 M. Countersign given, and all was well. A Mrs Thomas who lived just outside of the lines came in early and brought a handsome boquet which she presented to me, and of course I did not refuse. Was relieved at 8 ½ A.M. and soon was in camp. The paymaster came and we got our pay to Aug 31st/64, men getting $16–per month. After getting mine I went out to picket line and took Lt Pecks place, who was not well, and staid all night, thus making three nights on the lines and no sleep to speak of. Rec'd the glorious news of Sheridans victory over Genl Longstreet, capturing 43 guns and a large number of prisoners.[19] Our Phil is a noble fighter, and is having success after success, his men have such confidence in him that they would go with him anywhere.

Sunday, October 23, 1864. Pleasant, did not have any sleep, and I am now quite weary. A report came in early that the enemy were outside and in line of battle, and created quite a flurry for a time, but the enemy did not appear, only one of the many scares that soldiers have to put up with. It is a continual life [of] excitement, of ups & downs, but we should be *always ready*. Quite early some parties came to the lines & endeavored to pass out. They had passes & permits all right, but upon a strict examination we found some contraband goods, and I took up their permits and sent them under guard with a full report to the Provost Marshals and the fellows didn't swear any, Oh No, but they had to go back just the same. Was relieved at 8 ½ A.M., having quite an eventful trip. Staid in camp all day, took the Co out on dress parade, when our orderly Sergeant and two other soldiers were reprimanded before the regiment for gambling with money. Attended services in the evening by the Chaplain, & then to bed quite early.

Monday, October 24, 1864. Pleasant, had a good sleep, got up quite rested, dressed & fixed up in my best. Got a pass and went to the City after gen'l Inspection by Gen'l Marcy. Bought some things, coat &c and some provisions for our mess, found the six mule team going to camp and sent my things out & I returned by horse car. Was not surprised in finding a detail for me to report for picket duty in the morning. Also found a letter from Mother, in which she stated she was packing a box of things to send me by express.

---

19. Union forces captured forty-three pieces of artillery from the Confederates at the Battle of Cedar Creek on October 19, 1864.

Tuesday, October 25, 1864. Pleasant. Reported for duty, and was sent to my old station with Lt Eckstein.[20] Found a new lady inspector just from the North. She was quite lively, and made it quite so for the *Sesesh* women. Saw a number whom I had met before. It is evident that they expect favor by ackquaintance [sic], but duty is duty. Had a pleasant time. About 8 P.M. Lt Peck came out and relieved me and stated that I was ordered to report at Hd Qrs Dist of Memphis, but what for, he did not say, and I don't know surely. Sent letter to mother and enclosed $10–. Got back to camp and there was handed me Special Order No 259 dated Oct 25/64 directing me to report at Gen'l Buckland's H'd Qrs for duty on a Board of Survey, on ordnance & ordnance stores lost in action by Capt Reavis[21] Co 55th US[CI] at Guntown.

Wednesday, October 26, 1864. Rather rainy morning. Got my things fixed up in shape and started for the City, riding with Maj Densmore in his buggy, and at once reported at the Adj Gen'ls Office, and was there directed to report at Capt Wileys Q.M. Office on front row. Went down there and reported, met the other two members of the Board, and we adjourned until 10 A.M. tomorrow to meet at Hd Qrs 55th US[CI]. Looked around the City for awhile and then returned to Camp. Being now on special duty relieved me from any regtl duty, a new work and a new field, and I must do it well.

Thursday, October 27, 1864. Pleasant, ground drying up fast. Reported at Hd Qrs 55th US[C]I, their camp being in the South part of the City. At 10 A.M. met the balance of the Board, and organized, I was chosen Recorder & then to business, holding a kind of a court. Took the testimony of several witnesses in reference to the Guntown raid, the condition of affairs as to how the ordnance &c were lost. Labored quite diligently until 5 P.M. when we adjourned to meet the next day at 10 A.M. & then ret^d to camp.

Friday, October 28, 1864. Very pleasant, got my breakfast and went over to the Camp 55th US[C]I and reported. Board called together at 10 A.M. and proceeded with the examination, I keeping the minutes of the Board

---

20. John Eckstein (born ca. 1824) was second lieutenant of the 68th USCT, Co. E. Previously he had been a private in the 32nd Iowa Infantry.

21. Arthur T. Reeve (1835–1889) was captain of the 55th USCT, Co. D. Previously he had been a hospital steward with the 7th Kansas Cavalry. He later was appointed major of the 88th USCT.

& taking the evidence. After the case was closed, the matter was decided that the facts were such as to relieve Capt Reavis from the responsibility, and the same were to be accounted for as lost in action at Guntown. The report was made out accordingly and signed by all the members of the Board, and I took the report & papers in charge to be delivered at Hd Qrs. Sent for Frank Leslie's.[22]

Saturday, October 29, 1864. Pleasant, made out muster rolls, and after dinner took the report to Gen'l Buckland's Hd Qrs, and delivered them to the Adj Gen'l. Got a District pass for one day, went down and got some oysters. In the evening went to the Theatre, and about 12 P.M.[23] arrived at camp.

Sunday, October 30, 1864. Pleasant day. Staid in camp all day. Attended divine services by the chaplain. Had Co Inspection and dress parade in the evening, where we had a fine speech by Col Allen[24] Medical Inspector of this Dept. Sent letter to Mother. Detailed for picket tomorrow.

Monday, October 31, 1864. Very pleasant, reported for guard mount and went to the old station. Had a very good time, quite a good many people passed through and many goods. Today the officers of the Reg't elected a Sutler, something very requisite, as the men cannot go out of our camp lines very often, except for duty, and there must be some place within the lines where they can buy their needful commodities. So Spink was elected.

Tuesday, November 1, 1864. Rather cloudy. Rained considerable, no alarm during the night though I was up and stirring around all night, relieved from duty at 9 A.M. Went to camp and to work making out muster rolls. At roll call this evening I received Special Order No 31 from Dept Hd Qrs appointing me as member of a Board of Survey to report upon certain ordnance and ordnance stores lost in action at Guntown by Capt

---

22. *Frank Leslie's Illustrated Newspaper* was a popular weekly newspaper that began publication in 1855.
23. Buswell may have intended A.M., meaning midnight.
24. George T. Allen (1812–1876) had been surgeon of the 14th Illinois Infantry before becoming medical inspector for the Department of Tennessee. As a member of the Illinois state legislature in 1855, Allen was one of five legislators who refused to support Abraham Lincoln in the election for US Senate, thus sending Lyman Trumbull to Washington instead of Lincoln.

Baileys[25] Co 55th USCI, and directed me to report at the 55th Hd Qrs on the 2d inst at 10 A.M. Another job of taking evidence.

Wednesday, November 2, 1864. Foggy, rainy morning. Put on my best and went to Camp 55th and reported, the other members being present and we adjourned the Board until tomorrow at 10 A.M. and at once came back to our camp, and worked hard on muster rolls, and finished them, and other papers.

Thursday, November 3, 1864. Pleasant, but quite muddy. Fixed up and went to 55th Hd Qrs and reported, the Board organized, I being chosen Recorder, and took the evidence in the case, closed it, and took the matter under consideration until tomorrow, then went back to Camp. Com^d boarding with Lt Taisey at $5^{00} per week.

Friday, November 4, 1864. Cleared off fine, quite cool night. Got my breakfast at the new mess, it started in well, then reported at Hd Qrs 55th and after a lengthy discussion on the case, the Board finally agreed that the Capt should be cleared from the responsibility for said ordnance &c and the report was made out and signed, I to take it to Gen'l Buckland^s Hd Qrs, then returned to Camp. The Co had drawn haversacks, knapsacks & canteens for the men, and our new Sutler Spink came and put up his tent.

Saturday, November 5, 1864. Pleasant, got up early, and soon started to the City. Carried and delivered the report at Dist Hd Qrs, then went to the Express Office, but no box, then tramped around for a time and returned to Camp. Wrote a letter to Mother, also received one. Paid Lt Taisey my first weeks board bill of $5^{00}.

Sunday, November 6, 1864. Rather blustry, squally day. Some rainy. Staid in camp all day. Had services in A.M., wrote some letters and read the papers. Quite cool in P.M. Dress parade at 4 P.M., a large crowd was out from the City to witness it, and the regiment did well.

Monday, November 7, 1864. Rather rainy. Staid in camp all day. Quite a heavy thunder shower in P.M., then the sun came out in all his glory, and it was extremely hot. So warm tonight that could not bear to have any clothes on me.

---

25. Cyrus P. Bailey (1833–1902) was captain of the 55th USCT, Co. E. He had previously served in the 52nd Illinois Infantry.

Tuesday, November 8, 1864. Very warm. Showery. Received this A.M. Special Order No 90 signed by Col Comd'g Regt, detailing Maj Holcomb,[26] Lt J. G. Smith, and myself on a Regt^l Court-Martial to try Privates Grover[27] and Philips.[28] Court convened at 10 A.M. and organized. I was chosen advocate and Recorder, we heard the case and found them each guilty, and made report to Regt^l Adjt and adjourned Sine die.[29] Today is election day all over the North. It is Lincoln or McClellan, the votes of the people will decide many great questions—Slavery or Freedom to 5 millions of human beings, honorable war or a dishonorable peace, Union or Disunion possibly. Had quite a chat with the Maj, he is a very fine gentleman. Was detailed for picket tomorrow.

Wednesday, November 9, 1864. Very rainy, blustry, quite disagreeable, quite a number of tents were blown over, which made considerable fun.

Thursday, November 10, 1864. Pleasant, got up, put on my picket suit and reported at guard mount, was directed to my old station, and being a fine day, had a very pleasant time. Saw a good many that I knew, a large amount of goods passed out, some of them going down into Miss and from there no doubt to their friends in the C.S. Army. We notice a good many small articles, needles, pins, thread, these no doubt go into the army, as it is impossible to get them from any source, the blockade being nearly if not quite closed.

26. Oliver H. Holcomb (1833–1887), a native of New York, had previously been a sergeant in the 10th Minnesota Infantry, Co. C.

27. John F. Gordon (born ca. 1841 at Baltimore) enlisted at St. Paul, Minnesota, in 1864. On November 9, he was tried before a regimental court-martial for drunkenness and disobedience of orders for being absent without leave and "shirk[ing] his duty as a soldier." He pleaded guilty and was sentenced to twenty days imprisonment at hard labor while wearing a ball and chain, and the loss of half a month's pay. See Regimental Books of the 68th USCT, Record Group 94 (Records of the Adjutant General's Office), National Archives and Records Administration, Washington, D.C.

28. Anderson Phillips (born ca. 1842 in St. Louis) enlisted in 1864 at Denver, Colorado Territory. On November 9, 1864, he was tried before a regimental court-martial for conduct unbecoming a soldier for stealing two guns from other privates. He pleaded guilty and was sentenced to fifteen days at hard labor while wearing a ball and chain, and the loss of one month's pay. See ibid.

29. A Latin phrase indicating that there is no set date to return to the business of the court.

Friday, November 11, 1864. Very pleasant. No sleep, was relieved from duty at 8 ½ A.M., went to camp, cleaned up, changed my clothes, got a pass and went to the City, and at once to the Express Office, but no box, then returned to Camp. Rec'd some Lynn & Boston papers from Aunty and read them through & through. About 10 P.M. heard heavy firing by gunboats and musketry near the river, which caused quite an excitement, but no orders to march, but learned after that it was on account of the election of Old Abe, he was re-elected by a very large majority. The peace copperheads will now have to keep quiet, the administration and the prosecution of the war is emphatically endorsed.

Saturday, November 12, 1864. Fine morning, everything calm. Got a pass and went to City, remained and went to the Theatre, enjoyed it tip-top, and got back to my bunk about 12 P.M.[30]

Sunday, November 13, 1864. Pleasant day, had company inspection, knapsacks &c, then services by the Chaplain. Rec'd the glorious news that Atlanta was taken by Sherman on the 10th inst. and a great victory.[31]

Monday, November 14, 1864. Rather cloudy. The boys worked on their tents or huts, and got them fixed up quite well, but we dont know how long we stay, liable to move at any time, but we must be comfortable while we stay.

Tuesday, November 15, 1864. Cloudy, worked hard today in Adjts Office. Received two letters from home and Aunty, were quite interesting. Lt Peck's discharge came today, and he bid us good bye and left for the North. Paid Lt Taisey $5.00 for board.

Wednesday, November 16, 1864. Rather cloudy. Assisted the Adjt about his duties, worked on descriptive book, wrote a letter to Aunty. We had hardly got to bunk and lights out when the long roll beat, and out we got lively. Firing was heard along the picket lines, some like an attack. The regiment fell in line of battle and remained so for an hour, and the firing having ceased, the regiment broke ranks and we were soon in our bunks again.

30. Buswell likely meant A.M.
31. It is not entirely clear what Buswell meant here. Atlanta had fallen in early September 1864, and William T. Sherman began his March to the Sea on November 15.

Thursday, November 17, 1864. Dark lowry morning. It rained a good deal in the night. Learned that the firing on the lines was caused by some guerrillas firing upon our pickets. Rec'd Special Order No 281 from Dist Hd Qrs detailing me as a Member of a Board of Survey to meet at Hd Qrs 55th USCI, on the 19th at 10 A.M., to dispose of more ordnance &c lost on the Guntown retreat. News rec'd that Sherman burned Atlanta on the 16th inst and started on his raid to the Sea. Meanwhile Hood at the head of a large army is now threatening the Tennessee lines, and troops are being concentrated at Nashville to contend with him, Gen'l Thomas[32] in command.

Friday, November 18, 1864. Rainy, rained nearly all night. Lt & Capt both on picket, and I in charge of Co in camp. Adjt Root came back to the Regt today, he looks much better. Capt Inness[33] received his dismissal from the Service today for incompetency, drunk might be added, as the first cause or just as you want it.

Saturday, November 19, 1864. Rainy, rather [illegible word] weather. Put on my duds and went to the 55th Hd Qrs and reported. Board all present, but it adjourned until Monday the 21st at 9 A.M., and I at once came back to camp.

Sunday, November 20, 1864. Clouds breaking away, prospect of better weather. Had Co Inspection and services by the Chaplain. Received the first copy of Frank Leslies Ill^d, war pictures principally. Dress parade at 5 P.M. Services in the evening.

Monday, November 21, 1864. Quite a change for the better. Reported at the 55th Hd Qrs but Lt Chittenden[34] a member thereof, being absent, adjourned until the 28th inst and came back to Camp. Got a pass and went

---

32. George H. Thomas (1816–1870), known as "Old Pap" or "the Rock of Chickamauga," commanded the Army of the Cumberland beginning in October 1863. After Sherman captured Atlanta on September 2, 1864, Thomas pursued Hood's army in Tennessee, defeating him at Franklin on November 30, and Nashville on December 15.

33. Alexander Inness (born ca. 1836) was captain of the 68th USCT, Co. G, from June 1864 until his dismissal "for tendering his resignation in the face of the enemy."

34. Basil S. Chittenden (1837–1912) was first lieutenant of the 68th USCT, Co. E. He had previously been a sergeant in the 97th Indiana Infantry.

to the City with the Capt, and we took in Howe's Great Circus. They had a very extensive and fine procession and quite a large show. On our return found quite an excitement in our camp. The Lt Col of our Reg't having been placed in arrest for Cowardice at Tupelo, and a Gen'l Court Martial ordered from Hd Qrs Dist Memphis.[35] Colder towards night. Saw geese flying South.

Tuesday, November 22, 1864. Very cold, ground froze. Kept in my tent most of the A.M. After dinner got a pass and went out to the picket line and helped Lt Sherman,[36] had a No one time. Quite a cold night, was detailed for picket tomorrow. Wrote a letter to Nettie.

Wednesday, November 23, 1864. Quite cool. Reported for duty at guard mount, and with the Capt were directed to relieve picket at the station on Rolla road, a new post to me, found that a good many people passed out at this road. Lt Rogers came out and helped us part of the time. I had to act as Lady Inspector, the lady being sick—and I discharged my duty with reserve and to the best of my ability, and this is Military law.

Thursday, November 24, 1864. Quite pleasant, warmer. Thanksgiving Day. I would like to be at home this day. It seems some times as though I never would get there, there are so many ups and downs in a soldiers experience. Got relieved at 9 A.M. and returned to Camp, and then had to prepare for Genl Inspection which took place at 4 P.M. Orders were rec'd that the lines be closed to all people East of Buntyn's Station, they are permitted to come in but ne'ery can get out. The trial of Lt Col Clendening for cowardice at Tupelo, before the Gen'l Court Martial, commenced today.

35. Lt. Col. James H. Clendening was arrested in October 1864 and was charged with conduct unbecoming an officer and a gentleman, cowardice and misbehavior in the presence of the enemy, embezzlement and misapplication of funds entrusted to him, and fraud to the prejudice of good order and military discipline. His trial commenced on November 25. See Court-Martial Case File LL-3110. In early October, Daniel Densmore noted that Clendening's "rascalities are everyday coming to light." A few days later, Densmore added, "I would rather die than be in his shoes today. His conduct has of late been very mean; and Col Jones is determined that he shall get the worst the law has in store for such villains." Daniel Densmore to brother, October 1, 1864, and Densmore to friends at home, October 5, 1864, Densmore Papers; *Family War Stories*, 84–85, 119–21.

36. James L. Sherman (1839–1900), a native of New York, was first lieutenant of the 68th USCT, Co. G. He had previously served in the 74th Illinois Infantry.

Friday, November 25, 1864. Rather cloudy, looks like a storm. Fixed up in my best, got a pass and went to the City to have some photos taken but when I got there it was too dark. Went in to see Capt Marsh,[37] Picket Officer, and had a pleasant chat. Then went to New Memphis, came back to Camp about 11 P.M. Rec'd two letters, one from home and one from Maggie.

Saturday, November 26, 1864. Cloudy, misty day. Staid in camp all day, wrote three letters, one home, one to Hattie and one to Maggie. The great trial of our Lt Col still continues and is watched by all with a good deal of interest. Lt Rogers went before the high Court as a witness and testified.[38]

Sunday, November 27, 1864. Very cloudy. Company had inspection. So wet no services. Rec'd papers & read them. Sent letter to St Louis for a copy of a group Photo, also to Chicago for Photos. Glorious news from Sherman, he is now reported at Macon, Georgia, with his cavalry at the Capital,[39] and Hood is marching into Tenn. A battle is expected in both places soon.

Monday, November 28, 1864. Cloudy, but cool. Reported at Hd Qrs 55th US[CI]. The Board met and organized. I was chosen Recorder and took considerable testimony and finally concluded the case, made our decision. Signed the report and I took it in charge to be conveyed to Hd Qrs Dist Memphis. The 2d Brig 2d Div 19th A.C. came in today from Duvals Bluff and camped near us.

Tuesday, November 29, 1864. Cloudy but pleasant. Fixed up and went to the City and carried report to Gen'l Bucklands Hd Qrs. Went down to see Williamson & Sparks[40] and had a fine time. Quite a large force came in today, part of the 3d Div 19th A.C., and camped near by. I was detailed for picket for tomorrow.

Wednesday, November 30, 1864. Pleasant day. Went on picket on State Line road. Mrs Parker the lady Inspector. The lines were closed to all

---

37. Albert O. Marsh (1840–1912) was captain of the 59th USCT, Co. F. He had previously served in the 46th Ohio Infantry.

38. At the trial, Rogers testified that Clenending had said to the adjutant, "I don't care a God damn whether it is your duty or not when I tell you to do anything I want you to do it and no words about it either."

39. Macon's city hall served as a temporary state capital in 1864.

40. We are unable to identify Williamson and Sparks.

people living beyond Whites Station. That looks better than it did before. It is bad enough to feed those just outside, but it is not right to feed them anywhere in the Confederacy. Had considerable work as it was, a large force came today.

Thursday, December 1, 1864. Rather cool, had an engagement in the City, but could not get a pass today. Only a certain number of officers can be absent at any one time, and I was behind with my application this time, got a promise for tomorrow. Capt had visitors from the 9th Minn, we had a pleasant chat. Worked on clothing book. A good many troops came in today, among them the 15th Mass Battery. Had dress parade in the evening. Rec'd letter from home, all well.

Friday, December 2, 1864. Rather cloudy, quite smoky, another scare last night. The long roll beat and all the troops about here were out in line. Got my pass and went to the City with Capt, visited some of my friends, had a good time, went to Howe's Circus, very good, got my Photos, quite good, got back to Camp before dark and was detailed for officer [of the] Guard.

Saturday, December 3, 1864. Pleasant day, quite warm, reported for duty as Officer of the guard. Lt Rogers went to the City, more troops came today. Wrote a letter to mother and sent photos. Learned of the news of the great battle at Franklin, Tenn on the 30th ult, Schofield[41] Comd'g against Hoods whole army, of the terrible charges, some 7 of them, by Hood, with a fearful loss to him, and some to Schofield, who having defeated Hood, under cover of night moved his army to Nashville, Hood in the rear.

Sunday, December 4, 1864. Very pleasant, got off duty about 8 A.M., washed and fixed up and had Co Inspection, quite warm for Dec. Lt Weeden[42] & I made a call at Mrs Palmers, with whom we had become acquainted, a nice house and a pleasant place and a couple of fine girls, had a very pleasant call. Dress parade in the evening.

---

41. Maj. Gen. John M. Schofield (1831–1906), an 1853 graduate of the US Military Academy, commanded the Army of the Ohio (Twenty-third Corps) during the Atlanta Campaign and at the battles of Franklin and Nashville.

42. Elnathan S. Weeden (1843–1912) had previously served with the 36th Illinois Infantry and the 5th Veteran Reserve Corps before being mustered in as second lieutenant of the 68th USCT, Co. C.

Monday, December 5, 1864. Pleasant. Was subpoenaed to appear as a witness in the trial of Lt Col Clendening of our Reg't, on trial for Cowardice before a General Court-Martial, and I reported but was soon released after the Judge Advocate[43] had talked with me, I not knowing anything of importance about the case. Was taken with a severe cold. Some fever and considerable back ache. Rec'd letters from Maggie, Aunty and one from Chicago about the Photos.

Tuesday, December 6, 1864. Very warm, pleasant, did not feel well, had a high fever all night, my back is bad, laid in bunk nearly all day. Capt Rogers and Capt Pollion[44] went to the City today to attend the Gen'l Court Martial. Rec'd news that Sherman is now pounding away at the doors of Atlanta,[45] having marched with his gallant army across the Rebel Country again cutting them into,[46] and without encountering any force of consequence. Prospects are certainly better for a speedy termination of the war, especially if Hood is defeated, who is now marching with his army towards Nashville.

Wednesday, December 7, 1864. Rather cloudy, feel better, had a slight Norther as they call it here, and it was quite cold by noon. Rec'd a letter from home and the folks spoke of going to spend thanksgiving with Lucy and her friends, how I would have enjoyed it. I trust ere another year is past this cruel war will be over, and I will be at home. Wrote some letters.

Thursday, December 8, 1864. Rather cloudy, cold, feel quite smart again, was detailed for picket tomorrow. Gen'l Thomas, "Old Pap" as the boys call him, is in command of the forces at Nashville, and now the 7th & 10th boys are there, and a large force is gathering at that point to encounter Hood, Schofields force near Columbia, Tenn. Hood is marching and the next thing there will be another desperate engagement, and many a poor boy to suffer.

Friday, December 9, 1864. Very cold. Quite a storm of sleet & hail falling. Reported for duty & was sent to Pigeon Roost Station. Bad weather

---

43. Wilbur Fiske Henry (1838–1930), captain of the 108th Illinois Infantry, Co. B, served as the judge advocate at this trial.

44. William A. Poillon (1817–1879) was captain of the 68th USCT, Co. E. For more on Poillon, see *Family War Stories*, 77–78, 129–30, 164, 167.

45. Buswell likely meant Savannah, which Sherman captured on December 10.

46. Buswell appears to have accidentally omitted a word after "into"; alternatively, he may have meant "in two."

for picket duty, but yet had quite a good time, not a great deal of travel or business, too cold for these denizens of the South.

Saturday, December 10, 1864. Very pleasant, but still cool. Came off picket at 9 A.M. No disturbance during the night. Went to Camp, got washed up—had breakfast, and about noon had an order to be ready to march at a moments warning and I learn that we go into Ft Pickering for garrison duty, and all are interested in packing up & getting ready. Something new, anything for a change is what soldiers like. Everything had been made quite comfortable here for the winter, but we will get quarters (barracks) in the fort, which will be much better.[47]

Sunday, December 11, 1864. Quite cold. Everything in readiness, the orders given, and the Reg't except the three Co's on left, which included ours, left the Camp and moved down into the City, & thro it to the fort. We to go tomorrow. The quarters there it is said are good. The 120th Ill take our camp, they do not seem to like stopping here.

Monday, December 12, 1864. Rather cool, got up early, ate breakfast at Taiseys for last time, and our Co's broke camp & marched thro the City to the fort, thro the gateway, and were soon enclosed as in a prison, as I learn that it is some like one in here, and we were soon in our quarters, which proved to be very good, new quarters, and we the first occupants, the bunks had not been put in, and a detail of our men was at once made and went at work to put them in. Built tables in officers quarters and made things as comfortable as possible. We ought to enjoy sleeping inside once more, and I believe we will like the change, though it will be close confinement, as the Commander of the Fort, Col Kappner of the 3[d] USC [Heavy] Artillery which reg't now mans the big guns here, is a very strict disciplinarian, we learn. The fort is built on quite high ground on the banks of and overlooking the proud Miss River. From the lookout some 100 ft high I had quite a fine view away up & down the river. The Post Brass Band is a fine one.[48] Its armament is large Da[h]lgren guns,

---

47. The men of the 68th USCT had been building their winter quarters for about a month when they were ordered to move into Fort Pickering (see the November 14, 1864, entry). The orders to move into the fort arrived soon after they had finished, which infuriated Daniel Densmore. See *Family War Stories*, 102–5.

48. The twenty-four-member band, which was fully equipped with German instruments, was "the proud creation of Colonel Kappner." See *Family War Stories*, 117.

principally 64 pounders, and it seems like quite a busy place. I found a boarding house and engaged meals at $1^{00} per day, got the first, our supper. Having thought for some time that I would like a short leave of absence to go North on some business, &c, and our Col stating that he would endorse the application favorably, and the reg't being settled here probably for a time, I made out an application for a leave of 30 days. It was endorsed favorably by the Col, also by Col Kappner Comd'g the Fort, and it was transmitted to the Hd Qrs Dist of Memphis—Brig Genl Buckland Comd'g.

Tuesday, December 13, 1864. Pleasant but quite cold. We slept well and were quite comfortable in our new quarters, being the first time under cover since leaving Benton Barracks, Mo, May 31st last. Was detailed for duty, reported at Hd Qrs and was placed in charge as officer of fatigue duty. There is a great deal of cleaning in and around a fort, a fatigue detail is made every day, and placed in charge of some officer, to see that the grounds are kept in proper shape. I had 75 men in my detail, part of them were grading a road down to the rivers edge. Gen'l Inspection of all the troops in the Fort was held today by Col Wilson,[49] Inspector Gen'l of Gen'l Dana's[50] Staff, he now having command, so I learn, of this Dept. Dress parade in the evening, all seem to like the new quarters better than they expected. The only great objection is the confinement, the rules being that only two officers of the reg't can be absent at a time, and it is certainly quite a prison for the men, as it is difficult for any of them to get out at all. Such duty will do for a change, and soldiers like that, but will soon wish for a more active, freer life.

Wednesday, December 14, 1864. Quite warm day, not being on duty, and needing a table in our room, I got some boards and tools, and made one, and quite a good one too it was called. The detail for guard duty here is very large, 68 of our reg't being on duty today, besides the fatigue. Capt

---

49. Buswell likely meant Brig. Gen. James Harrison Wilson (1837–1925) who had been Ulysses S. Grant's inspector general during the Vicksburg Campaign in 1863, and who was appointed chief of cavalry for the Military Division of the Mississippi in October 1864.

50. Napoleon Jackson Tecumseh Dana (1822–1905), a veteran of the Mexican War who had been colonel of the 1st Minnesota Infantry in 1861, was placed in command of the Department of the Mississippi in December 1864.

Geiger[51] having applied for a leave of absence it was this day returned disapproved, mine will no doubt be served the same way. I have not much expectation, but thought I would try. Wrote a letter to Hattie.

Thursday, December 15, 1864. Rather muggy day, and foggy. Lt Ross came up to see us today. Three Union officers are missing tonight. They went out of the lines to visit some lady friends, as had been the custom by some of the more daring, and it is reported that while enjoying their visit they were surprised, the house being surrounded by Dick Davis' guerrillas, and all three were taken prisoners, many even suspect the ladies getting them into the trap. The report from a reliable contraband is that they were taken out into the timber, first robbed and otherwise maltreated and then were shot to death. I have always been suspicious of these women, who are apparently so friendly, as they frequently pass us while on the picket line, but I think I understand them, this seeming friendship and invitation to visit them was to avoid a strict search being made of their person for contraband, and sought besides to allure us outside the lines and into difficulty. I never trusted them, and notwithstanding the acquaintance & their seeming friendship with me, it ended at the picket line.

Friday, December 16, 1864. Very rainy day, gen'l Inspection at 9 A.M. In the afternoon all troops were out and witnessed the execution of three soldiers inside the Fort, convicted of murder. The usual detail of a corporal's guard—a corporal and eight men did the work, it was quite a solemn scene, and some parts of it I could not bear to look at, the culprits especially at the command to fire. They fell over their coffins on which they were seated, and the work was over, the troops to quarters and their bodies to the soldiers graveyard.[52] Quite an excitement about the missing

---

51. George Geiger (1846–1865) had lied about his age to enlist at Carlisle, Pennsylvania, in 1862 when he was only about 16 years old. In 1864, he became captain of Co. C, 4th Missouri African Descent, later the 68th USCT. He was killed in Blakely, Alabama, on April 9, 1865.

52. On January 15, 1864, five privates from the 1st West Heavy Artillery (later the 3rd US Colored Heavy Artillery)—George Pope, Henry Irving, John Wilks (alias Baker), Manuel Clark, and Alexander Vest—murdered a black civilian named Wiley Griffiths and then "plundered" his home. Pope, who pulled the trigger, was never captured. The other four were court-martialed on February 27 and were convicted and sentenced to be hanged. Irving escaped from prison. See Court-Martial Case Files NN-1707 and NN-1712.

three officers. A cavalry force was organized to make a raid outside the lines, the Comd'g Officers being satisfied of the correctness of the report of the contraband, and orders was given to capture, if possible, and if not to shoot the notorious guerrilla Dick Davis and his men.

Saturday, December 17, 1864. Rainy, misty day. Was detailed on guard and directed to Sally Port No 6. Instructions very particular, as much so as if the enemy were just outside. Quite rainy, not much passing out in consequence, quite [quit?] boarding at hotel and arranged to mess with Capt Holcomb at our quarters. My application for leave of absence returned endorsed by Genl Buckland disapproved, no more leaves to be granted at present, a little too late, this time.

Sunday, December 18, 1864. Rainy, rained most all night, had on my rubber blanket, and then kept under cover as much as possible. Returned to quarters having been relieved at 9 A.M., not feeling very well, found two papers from Aunty. Received news of the great battle at Nashville. Old Pap Thomas was enough and more than enough for Hood, and whipped him & his force soundly, and the enemy are retreating South in not quite as good style as they marched North, a glorious victory, the invasion is ended, Hoods army defeated, Sherman at Savannah, and now only two large armies of Johnnies left, Lee's at Petersburg and Johnstons who is now concentrating to dispute the further advance of Sherman. Two great strongholds, two objective points, are yet in their hands, Richmond & Mobile, both strongly fortified, and though victory for our army seems to be foretold, yet it will require many a hard fought battle, and the loss of many brave boys to reduce these two great strongholds. Fixed up & went to church this evening.

Monday, December 19, 1864. Rained all night, and still continues at intervals and it is wind, wind all around here. Rec'd more news of the great battle at Nashville & Franklin. In the two battles the rebel army cut to pieces and causes much excitement South & North. Johnston who was in command of this wing of the rebel army was removed at the hands of the Confederate government, and Hood placed in command. Johnston was a very cautious man, Hood a rash fighter, and his extreme rashness at Franklin no doubt lost him the great battle afterwards at Nashville. Such a terrible loss there, carried its effect to the latter field. Wrote three letters, one to Lucy, one to Maggie, and one to Alva Dearborn. I hope he is all right, but no doubt I will soon learn of the loss of some of our Co's boys.

Tuesday, December 20, 1864. Rain, rain, and growing colder. Was detailed on duty as officer of the guard at Sally Port No 4. These sally ports are the different entrances to the fort, and are protected by heavy iron gates. All that pass by must either have a pass from Hd Qrs or the countersign, and makes considerable work besides responsibility when there is much passing, and there was a good deal today. Recd two Boston papers from Aunty.

Wednesday, December 21, 1864. Cold and still rainy, very disagreeable weather. Was up most of the night, though with my blanket managed to keep dry until relieved at 1 A.M., when I was taken down with my old back trouble. Went to quarters and to bed, got up after a good nap feeling better. Great excitement this P.M. The cavalry force sent out in search of the notorious guerrilla—Dick Davis. [They] came in and with them as a prisoner, the chief guerrilla Dick Davis. Everyone was anxious to see the blood thirsty devil, and he certainly looked like one, hair long, and all over his face.[53] The history of the capture is that the cavalry soon learned after they were outside of the lines as to his whereabouts, and traced him to a house where he was staying for the night. The cavalry force surrounded the house, and after many shots to & fro between the parties, he was finally obliged to surrender, and with great honor to the Cavalry troop, they successfully brought him in and to the jail in the fort.

Thursday, December 22, 1864. Cleared off cold, ground froze about 8 inches deep. I was detailed on fatigue duty, having 110 men under my charge, part of the men leveling off a bank near the river for the purpose of building a magazine. Fort yet excited over the capture of Dick Davis. A drumhead court martial was convened today, and the notorious guerrilla brought before it for trial, and without much delay he was found guilty of murder and sentenced to be hung,[54] the time being set tomorrow. Had a good look at him. He was not a bad looking man if shaved up, but had gone into this business for the plunder that there was in it. There were many risks, he had to run them, he has had it all his own way for about two years, a terror to this section of country. He had become quite bold, but there is generally an end to such things, and he made his last risk in taking & shooting in cold blood the 3 Union officers, and now he

53. According to one witness at his trial, Davis "has hard eyes, auburn hair, dark complexion and wears whiskers." See Court-Martial Case File LL-2904.
54. The judge advocate argued that one who did what Davis had done should "be considered at war with the entire civilized world."

has to suffer the consequences. His capture brought a great many people to the fort, but extra orders were given to keep all except proper persons out of the works. Considerable warmer towards night, went to bed early.

Friday, December 23, 1864. Pleasant, considerable warmer, feel better today. Orders rec'd for all troops to be present at the hanging of the guerrilla, and well prepared in case of any difficulty arising. Extra precautions were taken, Artillery men placed at each gun along the works and a company of Infantry at each sally port. The gallows had been erected inside the fort, the troops gathered in a square around it. The notorious man was brought out under a heavy guard, he mounted with a firm step the scaffold, a priest went up and commenced with him, which seemed all useless to me as what good could a priest do such a damnable villain and murderer as he is. The cap was drawn down, and at the given signal the drop fell, and his murderous works were forever ended at least in this world. I gazed and looked at him in his death throes with a good grace. Such sights generally sicken me. I prefer not to see them, but this time I had no such sensitive feeling.

Saturday, December 24, 1864. Pleasant morning, was on duty at Sally Port No 6. The guard on duty did not salute Col Kappner the Commander [of the] Fort in a proper manner as he passed, and he stopped and gave me a severe talking to, that I must see that the men had proper instructions &c. Military is more rigid here than in active service, and our men having been on picket most of the time lately, where salutes are not often made, they had got out of practice. This is my first experience in a Fort and I hope the last, as there has got to be a good deal of style with the ordinary duty.

Sunday, December 25, 1864. Pleasant, Christmas Day. Was relieved from duty at 9 A.M., went to quarters, got my breakfast, towards noon it rained quite hard. Capt Cooper[55] of our Reg't, and a nephew of Thurlow Weed,[56] gave a great dinner at the Post Sutlers. I was invited and attended, had a fine time, music & toasts. In the P.M. the officers of our Regt came to our Company head quarters, and Capt and I got plenty of apples and we had an apple feast & enjoyed ourselves hugely, though had

---

55. Edwin B. Cooper (born ca. 1843) was dishonorably discharged from the service in February 1865 "for scandalous and disgraceful conduct."

56. Thurlow Weed (1797–1882) was a powerful Republican politician and newspaperman and a close associate of Secretary of State William H. Seward.

I been at home would have enjoyed the day better. Bells ringing, and great doings down in the City. Christmas is a great day among the blacks.

Monday, December 26, 1864. Pleasant, but quite muddy. Orders received that duty would be lighter on account of the holidays, just as little work and duty as possible, which was generally welcomed, especially if we could have a little more freedom in going out of those prison like walls. Our regiment moved out of quarters into others in the fort that are considered better.

Tuesday, December 27, 1864. Pleasant, detailed as officer of the guard at Sally Port No 4 and there was a great deal of passing, which caused me to stand on my feet most of the time, having to be very particular as the existing orders are very severe. Discharged my duty to the best of my ability like a true soldier, and gave entire satisfaction to the Post Officer of the Day.

Wednesday, December 28, 1864. Pleasant day, was up most of the night looking after my post and guard and was relieved at 9 A.M. Wanted to go to the City and went at once to Post H'd Qrs and applied for a pass, but could not go today. Put down my name, and I will have to wait for my turn. Staid in my quarters most of the day and studied the tactics and regulations.

Thursday, December 29, 1864. Pleasant, got up, got breakfast and went to H'd Qrs to see about the pass, and failed again, but was promised one for tomorrow. Had quite a talk with the Col, he was very friendly and requested that I go into the adjutants office and assist him with his duties. Did not give a direct answer, but took a little time to consider, tho I think I will go. I had a detail of men at work most of the day, putting up bunks in our new quarters.

Friday, December 30, 1864. Pleasant, got up early, went to H'd Qrs, got my pass and went to the City, my first time out of the Fort, and it seemed as if I was a free man. Roamed around the City for a few hours, took dinner at a Restaurant, then returned back to the Fort, came thro the gate and was again in prison as it might be. Having made up my mind to accept the Col's offer, went at once to the Adjt's office and reported for duty, and was assigned work at once on the muster rolls ready for the pay which we expect soon.

Saturday, December 31, 1864. Pleasant, was detailed for guard and notwithstanding my office duty, I reported. Had general inspection at

9 A.M., no guard mount, the guard was divided, and I was directed by Officer of the Day to report with my guard at Sally Port No 6. It was a pleasant day and I enjoyed my duty at this post, and was kept busy most of the time, and frequently something new, new questions arising at such an important post, so many passing back & forth. The last day of the year, and I am fully discharging my duty not only to my country, but to myself, how many more years of such toil and excitement and suspense. May the time be speedy when this service shall terminate and peace once more shall reign upon and over a united Country.

Epilogue

For some unknown reason, Buswell's journal ends on New Year's Eve 1864, although he continued to serve in the 68th US Colored Infantry for another thirteen months. His fellow officers appear to have shared his optimism regarding the end of the war. On January 1, 1865, Daniel Densmore wrote his father, "The Confederacy, we think, is nearly ready to be turned over to the historian. The 1st of June next will probably see it bound in (by) black(s), & with 'board-cover.'" In February, writing from a camp near New Orleans, Densmore added, "Troops are pouring in here tremendously. We are going to start as 'peace commissioners,' taking a bee line (and some of the little burgs by the way) for Richmond and Washington." Densmore was proud that Union general N. J. T. Dana had selected the 68th as "the best colored regiment of his Dept."[1]

The 68th participated in the fighting near Blakely, Alabama, just east of Mobile, from April 1 through 9, 1865. On April 7, Buswell was wounded in an attack by the Confederate gunboats *Nashville* and *Huntsville*. In a battle report issued a few days later, Lt. Col. Daniel Densmore reported that the vessels' fire caused "several injuries by concussion, the most severe of which is that of Lieut. George W. Buswell, Company K, on the 7th; but on the afternoon of the 8th the gunboats were driven away by the 30-pounder or Drew battery." On April 9, the men of the 68th and two other regiments advanced against the Rebels, "passing rapidly" over recently abandoned Confederate rifle pits and "slashing" their way forward. By 5:30 p.m., Union forces had captured the Confederate's works, although the charge cost the 68th seven killed and sixty-one wounded,

---

1. Daniel Densmore to father, January 1, 1865, and Densmore to brother, February 12, 1865, Densmore to friends at home, February 19, 1865, Densmore Papers.

including Col. J. Blackburn Jones and Capt. Oliver H. Holcomb, who were "severely wounded," and Lt. Jacob D. Rogers and Lt. Albert H. Taisey, who were "slightly wounded."[2]

Buswell carried a few things with him from the action near Blakely. His medical record indicates that he was treated for a "contusion left leg & thigh and left side of face from explosion of shell rec'd at Blakely, Ala." By the time he applied for a pension in 1904, his leg must have healed, but he still bore "one scar upon my left cheek under the eye, caused by wound received at Blakely, Ala April 1865." During the fighting Buswell also captured a Confederate sword that he kept in his possession for the next forty-five years.[3]

Buswell remained with the 68th into the postwar period, serving with his regiment at Pineville, Louisiana, in late 1865. On October 13, he was promoted to first lieutenant of Company K, when Lt. Jacob D. Rogers was promoted to captain. A few weeks later, on November 20, he was appointed adjutant of the regiment. (It will be recalled that in September 1864, he had "worked quite hard most of the day assisting the Adjt, and yet I don't get any extra pay, nothing except the bare honor and the experience, but sometime it may count.") For the last few months of his service, Buswell served in detached service as aide-de-camp for US forces in Alexandria, Louisiana. He finally mustered out at Camp Parapet, near New Orleans, on February 5, 1866.[4]

Buswell returned to Minnesota, living in Winona from 1866 to 1868, and Blue Earth from 1868 to 1910. On September 27, 1870, he married Ellen Ruth "Nellie" Chadbourn, an eighteen-year-old native of Maine, whose father, Nathaniel, was a prominent banker. The couple had three children who survived into adulthood—Arthur C. Buswell, born September 26, 1872; Ruth Etta Buswell, born August 4, 1885; and Mary Frances Buswell, born September 1, 1886. They also had twins, born July 1, 1876, who did not survive—Charles H. Buswell died in infancy on September 3, 1876, and George N. Buswell died as a toddler on December 18, 1878.[5]

2. "Report of Lieut. Daniel Densmore, Sixty-eighth U.S. Colored Infantry, of operations April 1–9," in O.R., ser. 1, vol. 49, pt. 1, pp. 297–99; *Family War Stories*, chap. 12.
3. Buswell pension; *Duluth News Tribune*, May 1, 1910.
4. Buswell CMSR, 68th USCT.
5. Buswell pension; *St. Paul Globe*, November 6, 1901. One document in his pension record states that he moved to Blue Earth in February 1869.

In Minnesota, Buswell worked as an attorney. The 1870 census listed him as a twenty-eight-year-old lawyer who owned $1,000 of real estate and $500 of personal estate. (It mistakenly said he had been born in New York.) He served as a clerk in the state legislature from 1875 to 1877 and was active in Republican Party politics, attending the state convention in September 1877 and serving as treasurer of the Blue Earth school board in 1900. In 1897, President William McKinley appointed him postmaster of Blue Earth City. Theodore Roosevelt renominated him in 1902.[6]

When the 1910 US census was taken in Blue Earth on April 15, Buswell was listed as an insurance solicitor living with his wife and two daughters, Ruth (twenty-four) and Mary (twenty-three), both of whom were public school teachers. In late May, just a few weeks after the census was taken, George and Nellie moved to Los Angeles. As he explained in a letter to the Commissioner of Pensions, "though I was wounded in the service, I never made a move for a pension until over 40 years after my discharge & at the time I quit heavy work. By advice of my physician I moved from Minnesota to California in 1910 and now being unable to earn much, I am desirous of receiving the extra $10^{00} per month under the act of June 10th 1918." Shortly before moving, he donated his socket bayonet from his time with the 7th Minnesota Infantry, and the Confederate cavalry sword he had picked up at Blakely, to the Minnesota Historical Society. By 1920, George and Nellie's daughter Mary Welch (who now appears to have been a widow or divorcee) lived with them in Los Angeles. Their other daughter, Mrs. Benjamin F. Woodard, had also relocated to Los Angeles. (Their son, Arthur, remained in Blue Earth.)[7]

During the summer of 1921, Buswell traveled to Portland, Oregon, to visit his ailing younger brother, Frank W. Buswell, and his sister, Mrs. Flora Richardson. On Friday, August 5, he was one of 127 passengers and 80 crew to board the steamship *Alaska*, enroute for San Francisco. The following day, the *Alaska* struck a reef and sank. Among the dead

---

6. Buswell pension; Minneapolis *Star Tribune*, August 24, 1921; *Brainerd Tribune*, October 6, 1877; *St. Paul Globe*, September 5, 1878, January 11, 1881, January 21, 1883, May 6, 1888, August 13, 1897, October 7, 1897, August 12, 1900; *Congressional Record* (January 10, 1898), p. 480; Washington, D.C. *Evening Star*, March 27, 1902.

7. 1910 US census; Buswell pension; 1920 US census; *Los Angeles Times*, August 24, 1921; *San Bernardino County Sun*, May 27, 1910; *Duluth News Tribune*, May 1, 1910. According to records on Ancestry.com, Arthur died in Los Angeles in 1930, Ruth died in 1965, and Mary Frances died in 1966.

and missing were a nineteen-year-old descendant of the Puritan divine Jonathan Edwards named George Edwards, who was on his way to attend the University of California; Minnie Kan, a nineteen-year-old college student at Walla Walla, Washington, who was traveling to visit a married sister in San Francisco; and a Mrs. Charlotte White, who perished with her two-year-old son on their way to join her husband in San Francisco. One survivor recounted, "We had only time to get away in our nightgowns and kimonos, as the boat sank in 25 minutes. Captain [Harvey] Hobey put Miss [Ada] Smith and me into a lifeboat and saw that we were safely off the wreck. That was the last we saw of him as he went down with the ship." In the earliest reports, which appeared in the papers on August 8, Buswell was listed among the missing. The *Los Angeles Times* reported, "Members of the family were vainly striving yesterday to get in communication with him at Eureka, as a man of a similar name is listed among the rescued."[8]

Over the ensuing days, bodies were slowly recovered from the cold waves of the Pacific Ocean, and authorities in San Francisco investigated the crash by examining the hull of the ship. Newspapers reported that charges of negligence would likely be filed against the ship's personnel, while one expert in Washington, D.C., proclaimed that a "baffling phenomenon of ocean current tendencies, just discovered, probably accounts for the loss of the Alaska.... Winds driving parallel to the Pacific ... set up new currents which, unsuspected by navigators, drift inland instead of exactly in wind direction."[9]

Buswell's name appeared among the lists of the missing in the Portland *Morning Oregonian* on August 10 and 11. For days, his family waited in anguish for word of his fate. Finally, on August 22—sixteen days after the wreck—his body washed up onto a beach near Cape Mendocino, about forty miles south of Eureka, California. He was one of at least forty people who perished. Newspapers throughout the United States and in western Canada carried brief notices of his death, remembering the eighty-year-old veteran as "a Los Angeles capitalist" who had "established a wide reputation" as a lawyer "in the Northwest."[10] The brief obituaries said little about his contributions during the Civil War era. Fortunately,

---

8. Portland *Morning Oregonian*, August 8, 11, 1921; *Los Angeles Times*, August 8, 9, 24, 1921.

9. Portland *Morning Oregonian*, August 11, 1921.

10. Portland *Morning Oregonian*, August 10, 11, 1921; Minneapolis *Star Tribune*, August 24, 1921.

his diaries, photographs, and other records have been carefully preserved at the Huntington Library in San Marino, California, while his bayonet and the Confederate sword he captured remain in the collections of the Minnesota Historical Society. These documents, images, and relics recall the experiences of a young man who was transformed by what Abraham Lincoln called the "mighty scourge of war."

ACKNOWLEDGMENTS

We thank Paul N. Beck of Wisconsin Lutheran College, David Craigmile of the Lac Qui Parle Historical Society, Ruth Ann Buck of the Sibley County Historical Society, Kayla Stielow and Jenny McElroy of the Minnesota Historical Society, and Stewart Bennett of Mississippi Final Stands for answering questions by email. We thank Keith Wilson and the anonymous readers for the University of Virginia Press for giving this manuscript a careful read and helpful critique. We also thank Gary Clayton Anderson and Paul N. Beck for reading and commenting on the introductions to chapter 1–4, and Thomas E. Parson for reading the introduction to chapter 6. We thank Julia Swanson and Fordham University Press for the use of the maps in this book. At Christopher Newport University we thank Lynn Shollen and Brent Cusher, chairs of the Department of Leadership and American Studies; Provosts David Doughty and Quentin Kidd; Jay Paul, director of the Honors Program; and especially Nathan and Elizabeth Busch, co-directors of the Center for American Studies, for their financial support that made this project possible. Finally, we thank Nadine Zimmerli, Clayton Butler, and Ellen Satrom of the University of Virginia Press for patiently shepherding this project to completion.

INDEX

African Americans, 120, 124, 128, 142, 144, 145, 147, 162, 163–64, 173, 177, 238, 241. *See also* contrabands; Fort Pillow; Godfrey, Gusa; slavery; US Colored Troops

Army of the Potomac, 11, 50n5, 56, 130, 149–50, 158. *See also* Grant, Ulysses S.; McClellan, George B.; Richmond, Virginia

Baker, James H. (colonel, 10th Minnesota), 78, 157
Banks, Nathaniel P., 155
Bartlett, Alfred (private, 7th Minnesota), 142, 154, 182, 190
Beever, Frederick John Holt (Sibley's staff), 91–92, 98
Benton Barracks, 127, 132, 141, 233
Big Mound, xxi, 70–71, 86–88
Birch Coulee, battle of, xxi–xxii, 3–5, 17
black soldiers. *See* US Colored Troops
boards of survey. *See* trials
Brices Cross Roads (Guntown Raid), xxiv–xxv, 167–69, 172n11, 176–77, 180, 182–84, 190–91, 194–95, 222–24, 227
Brown, Joseph R., 4, 15–17
Buckland, Ralph P., 172, 175, 196, 205, 208, 220, 222–23, 224, 229, 233, 235
burials, Indian, 79, 80, 81–82, 105
Buswell, George W.: desire to fight Confederates (instead of Native Americans), xvii, xxii–xxiii, 6–7, 39, 41, 68, 95, 97, 101, 107–8, 157; employs black servant, 162; fears imprisonment, 186, 219; portrays a Native American, 156; studies military tactics, xxiii, 49, 59, 65–66, 73, 127, 132–36, 144, 149, 152, 155, 157, 158–59, 238; thoughts on military strategy, 171; views of African

Americans, 30, 144, 145, 162–63, 167–68, 173, 177, 207; views of Confederate soldiers, 109–10, 144, 147, 158, 188, 215; views of Native Americans, 12, 18, 19, 22, 27–30, 46–47, 64, 67, 73, 81, 90, 100; views of slavery, xxiv–xxv, 144, 145, 147, 149, 162–63, 214, 225

Cairo, Illinois, 121, 125, 146, 168, 170
Camp Release, 5, 29n55, 33, 34n68, 73, 78
captives: Indian, xxii, 5–6, 10n22, 30, 34, 35, 38, 40–41, 45, 59, 69, 90, 93–94; white and "half-breed," xxi, 4, 5, 16, 22, 24, 28, 29–30, 33, 35, 40, 64, 84–85
Chalmers, James R., 153, 171, 187, 194, 218, 219
chiefs. *See* Little Crow; White Lodge
Clendening, James H. (lieutenant colonel, 68th USCT), 151, 160, 180, 185–86, 189, 199n11, 228–29, 231
conscription, 131, 214–15
contrabands (black refugees from slavery), 200, 219, 234–35
courts-martial. *See* trials
courts of inquiry. *See* trials
Crooks, William (colonel, 6th Minnesota), 24–25, 34, 75–76, 77, 91
Curtis, John W. (captain, 7th Minnesota), 9, 54, 59, 61, 77, 158

Dana, Napoleon Jackson Tecumseh, 233, 241
Davis, Dick, xxv, 175, 234–35, 236
Davis, Jefferson, 127, 195n6, 209
Dead Buffalo Lake, xxi, 70–71, 89
Dearborn, Alva E. (private, 7th Minnesota), 51, 52, 61, 106, 107, 142, 143, 146, 151, 154, 182, 190, 201, 235
Democrats, xxv, 105–6, 115–19, 144, 147, 151, 153, 197, 207–9, 211, 214–15, 226

249

Densmore, Daniel (lieutenant and major, 68th USCT), with Buswell, 180, 198–99, 222; Buswell's views of, 160, 225; views of black soldiers, xxiii–xxiv, 127, 241; views of Confederates, 171n10, 241; views of other officers, 152n48, 160n58, 199n11, 212n7, 228n35, 232n47

Douglas, Stephen A., xxv, 207, 209, 211, 214

draft. *See* conscription

Duley, Laura, 64–65, 94n41

Duley, William J., 47, 64, 75

Eastman, Ermon D. (orderly sergeant, 7th Minnesota), 9, 34, 72, 77, 203

Emancipation Proclamation, 195, 200

executions, xxi–xxii, xxv–xxvi, 6, 15n30, 21n41, 30n57, 45–47, 64, 175, 234–36

Forrest, Nathan Bedford, 175n16; at Fort Pillow, 153–54, 171; in Kentucky, 157; in Mississippi, xxiv–xxv, 21n44, 154, 167–70, 172n11, 176, 178, 184–88, 190, 193–94, 204–5; at Murfreesboro, 23n49; at Nashville, 216; raid on Memphis, 194, 204–5, 208, 216. *See also* Brices Cross Roads; Tupelo, battle of

Fort Abercrombie, 79, 80, 81, 82, 86, 96–97, 156

Fort Donelson, 50, 122–23, 125, 129

Fort Pickering, 175, 212, 232–33, 234, 235, 236–39

Fort Pillow, 153–54, 171

Fort Randall, 68, 72

Fort Ridgely, 3–5, 12–19, 33, 39n78, 40, 42, 70–71, 75, 98

Fort Snelling, xvii, 9–10, 18, 32, 42, 66n29, 95, 98, 99, 100–101, 132

Foster, Charles W., 133, 135

Fremont, John C., 151, 215

"friendly Indians," 3, 5–6, 29, 48, 69–71, 105

Gamble, Hamilton R., 138

Gettysburg, battle of, 85, 93, 129, 130

Godfrey, Gusa (Joseph), 30–31

Grant, Hiram P. (captain, 6th Minnesota), 4, 16, 17n37, 86, 93

Grant, Ulysses S.: Buswell has confidence in, 50, 129–30, 148–49, 157–58, 159, 170, 209; Buswell sees, 136–37; early career, 120, 170; movements in the East, 170, 178, 209; movements in the West, 50, 74, 85, 122, 123, 129–30, 184, 193, 198; promoted to lieutenant general, 50n5, 146, 150

Gratiot St. Prison, xxiii, 110, 126–27, 129, 133, 135, 138, 140, 141

Greeley, Horace, 195

Grierson, Benjamin, 182, 183

guerrillas: attack Union soldiers, 125, 173, 175, 179, 183, 213, 215, 226–27, 234; captured/imprisoned by Union soldiers, 126–27, 129, 191, 234–37; hide near rivers, 120–22, 170–71; in Illinois, 116–17; Nathan Bedford Forrest considered, 153, 157, 171, 175n16. *See also* Davis, Dick; Morgan, John Hunt

"half-breeds," 24, 29, 30, 82, 84, 85, 93, 96

Harrison, Samuel H. (corporal, 7th Minnesota), 20, 60, 142–43, 144, 145

Hayes, James W. and Laura A., 38, 39, 76, 81, 106, 108, 130, 142, 153, 154

Hendricks, Thomas A., 214

Holcomb, Oliver H. (major, 68th USCT), 225, 235, 242

Hood, John Bell, 196, 220, 227, 229, 230–31, 235

Hopson family, 38, 40, 42, 50, 76, 107, 111, 130, 138, 142, 153–54

Hurlbut, Stephen A., 194, 204, 208

Illinois regiments: 7th Illinois Cavalry, 148; 13th Illinois Cavalry, 116, 144, 152, 156; 14th Illinois Infantry, 223; 15th Illinois Infantry, 159n58, 160; 83rd Illinois Infantry, 122; 113th Illinois Infantry, 116, 118; 120th Illinois Infantry, 232

Iowa regiments: 1st Iowa Infantry, 142; 8th Iowa Infantry, 149; 9th Iowa Cavalry, 144, 154; 11th Iowa Infantry,

INDEX

149; 12th Iowa Infantry, 149; 15th Iowa Infantry, 149
Irving Block Prison, 197, 208

Jefferson Barracks, 120
Johnston, Joseph E., 196, 235
Jones, J. Blackburn (colonel, 68th USCT), 160–61, 173, 175, 179, 182, 186, 196, 199–200, 209–11, 228n35, 233, 238, 242

Kansas regiment: 9th Kansas Cavalry, 184
Kappner, Ignatz (colonel, 3rd US Colored Heavy Artillery), 212, 232–33, 237

Lee, Robert E., 85, 159, 170, 178, 235
Lee, Stephen D., 167, 169
Light, Oliver P. (chaplain, 7th Minnesota), 21, 39, 66, 73, 76, 78, 140
Lincoln, Abraham: calls for troops, xvii, 148; and civil liberties, 147n38; and the election of 1864, xxv, 173, 207, 211, 213–14, 215, 216, 225, 226; and emancipation, 144, 145, 195, 200; in Illinois, 119, 223n24; and Indian affairs, xix–xx, 6, 38n77, 69; and military affairs, 50n5, 146, 150n45, 211; and Reconstruction, 138n19
Little Crow, xxi, 3, 5, 15n30, 16, 29, 33, 48, 58, 64, 69–70, 82, 84, 90–91, 93, 100. *See also* Wakeman, Thomas
Lower Sioux Agency (Redwood Agency), xxi, 3–5, 11, 16, 26, 30, 38

Marcy, Randolph B., 96, 153, 221
Marsh, John S. (captain, 5th Minnesota), 26
Marshall, William R. (lieutenant colonel, 7th Minnesota), 5, 21–22, 35–36, 60, 65–66, 73, 87–88, 99–101
Massachusetts regiments: 15th Massachusetts Battery, 230; 19th Massachusetts Infantry, 56n18, 145
McClellan, George B., xvii, 96n42, 141, 207, 209, 211, 214, 225

McDonald, A. C. (chaplain, 68th USCT), 160, 176, 178, 196, 211, 215, 217, 219, 221, 223, 226, 227
McPhail, Samuel (colonel, 1st Minnesota Cavalry), 5, 17, 78, 87–88
Memphis, Tenn., 119, 166–69, 171–73, 176, 179, 181, 191–95, 196–97, 198, 200, 201, 204–13, 215, 216–19, 221–24, 226–33, 238. *See also* Fort Pickering; smuggling
Metcalf family, 49–51, 107, 108
Miller, Stephen (colonel, 7th Minnesota), 20–21, 32, 44, 61, 74, 77, 101
Minnesota Historical Society, 243, 245
Minnesota regiments: 1st Minnesota Cavalry (Mounted Rangers), 1, 5, 17, 25, 35–37, 38, 70, 77, 78, 79–80, 83, 84, 86–92, 94, 97, 125; 1st Minnesota Infantry, 21, 23n49, 77n14, 84n26, 86n20, 87n31, 233n50; 2nd Minnesota Battery, 134; 3rd Minnesota Infantry, 5, 23, 25, 27–28, 33, 34–35, 36, 38, 39, 48; 3rd Minnesota Light Artillery, 78; 5th Minnesota Infantry, 26; 6th Minnesota Infantry, 4, 10–12, 15–16, 21n46, 25, 32n60, 34–35, 36, 40, 42, 44n88, 63, 75–77, 89, 92n39, 101; 7th Minnesota Infantry, xvii, xx, xxiii, 5, 8–48, 53–68, 72–101, 105, 108–9, 112, 119, 131–32, 133, 135, 137, 139–43, 151, 154, 158–59, 173, 179, 180–83, 185, 186, 190, 199–203, 205, 216–17, 231, 235, 243; 8th Minnesota Infantry, 21n42, 156, 160, 172n13, 182; 9th Minnesota Infantry, 21n45, 40, 76, 77, 97, 101, 109, 172, 176–77, 182, 188, 194, 201, 205, 215, 216, 230; 10th Minnesota Infantry, 7n7, 34n66, 37–38, 39, 42, 68, 73, 74, 76, 78, 81, 86, 89–90, 96n42, 98, 101, 107nn7–8, 108, 109, 115, 118, 119, 130, 131, 140, 142, 152, 153, 154, 157, 173, 178, 182–83, 201, 225n26, 231; Renville Rangers, 38, 40
Missouri regiments: 7th Missouri Infantry, 145; 11th Missouri Infantry, 149; 12th Missouri Cavalry, 152; 15th Missouri Infantry, 150; 18th Missouri Infantry, 147. *See also* US Colored Troops

Morgan, John Hunt, 171, 175n16, 178
music, 7, 11, 120, 137, 140, 205, 237; by African Americans, 120, 210; dances, 45, 49, 62, 107, 111, 118; by Indians, 67, 72; minstrel show, 75; singing by the troops, 75, 76, 92, 113, 148, 150, 154, 165, 192, 210

Nashville, Tennessee, 106, 120, 122–25, 149, 167, 216, 227, 230–31, 235

oath of allegiance, 124, 125, 129, 138n19, 140, 174

Petersburg, Virginia, 209, 217, 235
Pile, William A., 127, 132, 135, 141–43, 146, 148, 153–54, 155–56, 157–60, 162–64
Polk, James K., 124
Pope, James R. (private, 10th Minnesota), 37, 107, 130, 157
Pope, John, 48, 69, 99
Price, Sterling, 147, 171n8, 215, 216, 217
prisoners: military, 112, 119, 225n27, 234n52; political, 117–19, 126–27, 147, 174
prisoners of war: Confederate, xxiii, 105, 109–10, 113, 119, 126–27, 129, 133, 135, 139–40, 141, 152, 184, 188, 190, 197, 204, 208, 216, 220, 221, 236; Union, 23, 25n51, 56n18, 125, 143n32, 157, 171, 175n16, 176–77, 179, 194, 205, 208, 216, 234. *See also* captives

Ramsey, Alexander, 3, 6, 78, 98–99
Redwood Agency. *See* Lower Sioux Agency
refugees. *See* captives; contrabands
Rice, Archibald A. (lieutenant, 7th Minnesota), 9, 56, 77, 199
Richmond, Virginia, 68, 101, 150, 158, 170, 235, 241
Rogers, Jacob D. (lieutenant, 68th USCT), 156, 158–60, 162–63, 165, 172, 177, 179, 195–96, 200, 208, 213, 216, 217–18, 228–31, 242
Root, Enoch (adjutant, 68th USCT), 160, 173, 180, 196, 209–10, 216, 227, 229n38, 238
Rosecrans, William Starke, 135–37, 141, 144, 145, 148, 159

Sanitary Fair, 127–28, 154, 161–64
scalping, xxii, 67–68, 72, 89, 92
Schofield, John M., 230, 231
Schofield Barracks, 105, 109, 112, 114, 126, 128, 131, 132, 133–34, 139, 145
Seymour, Horatio, 214
Sheardown, Samuel B. (surgeon, 10th Minnesota), 7, 83, 131
Sheridan, Philip, 215–16, 221
Sherman, William T., xxiv–xxv, 167, 169–70, 193, 196, 205, 226–27, 229, 231, 235
Sibley, Henry H.: before the Civil War, xviii, 30n57, 75n11; and the 1862 US-Dakota War, 3–6, 16–19, 27n53, 28, 29, 33, 48; and the 1863 expedition into the Dakota Territory, 69–72, 75–78, 80, 86–87, 90n35, 91, 97, 99, 101, 105
slavery: abolition of, 139n19, 149, 195n6, 200; Buswell's views of, xxiv–xxv, 144, 145, 147, 149, 162–63, 207, 214, 225; and Confederate policy, xxiii, xxvi, 144; in Minnesota, 30n57; in Missouri, 126–27, 147, 163n62; and the slave trade, 166, 169. *See also* African Americans; contrabands; Emancipation Proclamation; Lincoln, Abraham
smallpox, 76, 131
Smith, Andrew Jackson, xxv, 155, 169–70, 176–78, 180–82, 185–87, 190, 193–94, 198, 201, 204, 215
Smith, Lucius B. (surgeon, 7th Minnesota), 21, 60, 66
smuggling, xxvi, 174, 217–22, 225, 228, 229–30, 234
Springfield, Illinois, 109, 115, 119
Standing Buffalo, 70, 71, 84
Starr, Ebenezer L. (private, 10th Minnesota), 37–38, 63, 107, 152, 153–54, 157, 190
Stevens, Albert H. (lieutenant, 7th Minnesota), 9, 55, 57, 59, 77, 95, 96, 130, 137, 201

St. Louis, Missouri, 105–6, 109–15, 118n23, 119–20, 125–65, 170, 173, 215, 229
Stony Lake, battle of, xxi, 71–72, 90
Sturgis, Samuel D., xxiv, 167, 172, 176–77, 180, 183, 185, 190

Taisey, Albert H. (lieutenant, 68th USCT), 172, 224, 226, 232, 242
Talbot, Edward R. R. (lieutenant, 68th USCT), 172–73, 175, 220
Thomas, George H., 227, 231, 235
Thomas, Lorenzo, 146, 150, 158
Thompson, James G. (captain, 68th USCT), 194–96, 198, 215, 216, 227, 228, 230
trials: by court-martial, 39, 84n26, 94n40, 139, 175, 225, 228–29, 231, 234n52, 236; by court of inquiry or board of survey, 177, 222–25, 227, 229; of Dakotas, 6, 16n34, 21n42, 25n50, 30, 33n62, 41n83, 93–94
trophies (from battle), xxii, 28, 89, 92, 242, 243, 245
Tupelo, battle of, xxv, 21n44, 51n12, 167–69, 185–90, 193, 228

Upper Sioux Agency (Yellow Medicine Agency), 3–5, 12n26, 16, 28, 29n55, 39n78, 63, 69
US Colored Troops, 132–33, 141, 144, 153, 171; 3rd US Colored Heavy Artillery, 212, 232, 234; 55th US Colored Infantry, xxiv, 167–68, 177, 222, 224, 227, 229; 59th US Colored Infantry, xxiv, 167–68, 177, 181–82, 183–84, 229n37; 61st US Colored Infantry, 172, 201n13; 62nd US Colored Infantry (1st Missouri African Descent), 146n35, 151; 65th US Colored Infantry (2nd Missouri African Descent), 143, 144, 145, 146, 147–48, 149n43; 67th US Colored Infantry (3rd Missouri African Descent), 142n28, 143, 144, 145, 148; 68th US Colored Infantry (4th Missouri African Descent), 148, 151–52, 155–65, 169–76, 178–80, 181, 183–91, 195–206, 208–13, 217–21, 223, 224–29, 231–33, 236–39, 241–42

Vallandigham, Clement L., 147, 209, 214
Vicksburg, 74, 85, 93, 114, 129–30, 173n14, 233n49

Wakeman, Thomas (also known as Wowinape), 94, 95. See also Little Crow
Weiser, Josiah S. (surgeon, 1st Minnesota Cavalry), 70, 71, 83, 86
Western Sanitary Commission, 118, 127, 153, 161. See also Sanitary Fair
Whipple, Henry B., xix–xx, 38, 99
White Lodge (chief), 94
Wilkin, Alexander (colonel, 9th Minnesota Infantry), 77, 177, 188
Winnebago Agency, 42, 48, 49, 67
Winnebago Indians, 41, 48, 51, 59, 63, 66–68, 72, 73
Winona, Minnesota, xvii, 7–9, 46, 50n6, 51–52, 58, 61, 100, 101, 107–8, 113, 242
Wisconsin regiment: 35th Wisconsin Infantry, 156
women: Confederate, 139–40, 174, 184, 217–18, 219, 222, 234; Confederate sympathizing, 118; inspection of, 174, 217–18, 219, 220, 222, 228, 229, 234; and the Sanitary Fair, 153–54, 156, 163; Unionist in the South, 155–56, 157, 162, 164, 221, 230. See also captives
Wood Lake, xxi, 5, 26–28, 48, 78, 94n40

Yellow Medicine Agency. See Upper Sioux Agency

Zollicoffer, Felix, 123

RECENT BOOKS IN THE SERIES
A Nation Divided: Studies in the Civil War Era

Reconstruction beyond 150: Reassessing the New Birth of Freedom
ORVILLE VERNON BURTON AND J. BRENT MORRIS, EDITORS

Dueling Cultures, Damnable Legacies: Southern Violence and White Supremacy in the Civil War Era
JAMES HILL WELBORN III

The Civil War Political Tradition: Ten Portraits of Those Who Formed It
PAUL D. ESCOTT

The Weaker Sex in War: Gender and Nationalism in Civil War Virginia
KRISTEN BRILL

Young America: The Transformation of Nationalism before the Civil War
MARK POWER SMITH

Black Suffrage: Lincoln's Last Goal
PAUL D. ESCOTT

The Cacophony of Politics: Northern Democrats and the American Civil War
J. MATTHEW GALLMAN

My Work among the Freedmen: The Civil War and Reconstruction Letters of Harriet M. Buss
EDITED BY JONATHAN W. WHITE AND LYDIA J. DAVIS

Colossal Ambitions: Confederate Planning for a Post–Civil War World
ADRIAN BRETTLE

Newest Born of Nations: European Nationalist Movements and the Making of the Confederacy
ANN L. TUCKER

The Worst Passions of Human Nature: White Supremacy in the Civil War North
PAUL D. ESCOTT

Preserving the White Man's Republic: Jacksonian Democracy, Race, and the Transformation of American Conservatism
JOSHUA A. LYNN

American Abolitionism: Its Direct Political Impact from Colonial Times into Reconstruction
STANLEY HARROLD